Gardening, Naturally

A chemical-free handbook for the Prairies

SARA WILLIAMS
& HUGH SKINNER

COTEAU BOOKS

www.coteaubooks.com

Edited by Roberta Coulter
Designed by Tania Craan
Typeset by Susan Buck and Tania Craan
Printed and bound in Canada by Friesens

Library and Archives Canada Cataloguing in Publication

Williams, Sara, 1941-
       Gardening, naturally : a chemical-free handbook for
the Prairies / Sara Williams & Hugh Skinner.

Includes index.
ISBN 978-1-55050-449-1

       1. Organic gardening--Prairie Provinces--Handbooks,
manuals, etc. I. Skinner, Hugh, 1951- II. Title.

SB453.5.W55 2011   635'.048409712   C2011-900060-1

10 9 8 7 6 5 4 3 2 1

2517 Victoria Avenue
Regina, Saskatchewan
Canada   S4P 0T2
www.coteaubooks.com

Available in Canada from:
Publishers Group Canada
2440 Viking Way
Richmond, BC, Canada   V6V 1N2

Coteau Books gratefully acknowledges the financial support of its publishing program by: the Saskatchewan Arts Board, the Canada Council for the Arts, the Government of Canada through the Canada Book Fund, the Government of Saskatchewan through the Creative Economy Entrepreneurial Fund, the Association for the Export of Canadian Books and the City of Regina Arts Commission.

To the memory of Helen Skinner (1915-2009)
She practiced organic gardening until cabbage worms began
to eat her cabbages or thrips damaged her gladioli.

– Hugh Skinner

To Bobbi, friend and mentor
and
To the memory of Brian Baldwin (1964-2009)

– Sara Williams

Table of contents

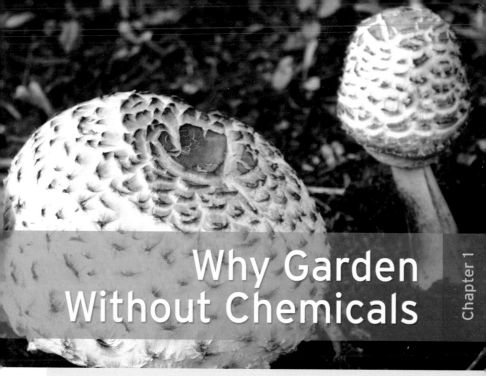

Why Garden Without Chemicals

Healthy gardens are complex communities of many different organisms. The plants that we cultivate grow in interaction with a host of fungi, bacteria, insects, birds and mammals. Some of these organisms consume the plants we grow; others cause diseases. But many are essential for the successful growth of the plants we desire.

Many organisms, including earthworms, nematodes, bacteria and fungi, are required to break down and recycle the nutrients in organic matter. Without these decomposers, dead organic material would not become available to other plants as nutrients for the renewal of life. Likewise, bees and other insects are necessary for pollination of many flowers. Without them, plants would not produce seeds and fruit, which make up much of our diet. Their service to plants, and to humans, is invaluable.

The giant meadow mushroom is one of the many organisms that lend beauty to our landscapes while decomposing and recycling nutrients for our garden plants.

Going pesticide-free allows us to re-establish a balance, encouraging natural predators and parasites that keep harmful insects within bounds.

Many insects and animals are herbivores; they eat plants to satisfy their needs for energy and nutrients. Many of these insects and animals multiply very rapidly. Think of aphids, which over a few days appear to grow to a population of thousands. With all these plant eaters about, how is it that the earth is overwhelmingly green? Why don't the herbivores simply consume all of the plant material? The answer is that in nature there are other organisms that keep herbivores in check. Other insects, birds and animals eat them; bacteria and fungi infect them and cause disease; and plants themselves develop chemical defences that make them unpalatable to the herbivores.

Why then are we so determined to use chemical pesticides? Part of the answer lies in successful marketing by the companies that produce them. As well, the 1950s suburban dream of a perfect lawn and landscape to present to one's neighbours is still powerful. But as a colleague once exclaimed, you should not be judged by the appearance of your lawn. We would hasten to add that your lawn is not your living room. Accept some imperfections.

When we use chemical insecticides to control insects, they affect more than the target insect. In some instances, they kill the animals, birds and other insects that prey on the target insect. If the predators are not killed outright, the chemicals may be concentrated in them and passed up the food chain, where they can cause disease or affect reproduction.

Our pristine lakes provide beauty, recreation, water for irrigation and drinking, and an aquatic environment for fish, birds and other species.

Using chemical pesticides creates dependence. Like an addictive drug, the more we use them, the more we need to use them. Why? First, insects and disease organisms are continually mutating and are capable of building resistance to many of these chemicals. Second, when we use insecticides to kill insect pests, we also kill their natural predators, giving the herbivores free reign to eat our crops. Similarly, when we use pesticides to control disease, beneficial organisms that keep the disease-causing organisms, called pathogens, in check are also killed. Many disease organisms are opportunistic and will colonize the leaves or roots of a plant when other bacteria or fungi aren't present. As a result, we have to keep looking for new and stronger ways to control insects and diseases.

Chemical-free public parks and gardens reduce health risks. We must weigh these risks against a greener lawn or a tree without tiny bumps on the leaves.

It's not just our gardens we have to worry about. The herbicides, insecticides and fungicides that we apply to our gardens can have impacts far from where they are applied. For instance, the herbicide 2,4-D has low soil absorption. Consequently, much of it ends up in surface water and groundwater. Its impact is not limited to plants. It is highly toxic to fish, and even moderate exposure severely impairs reproduction in honeybees.

When we grow a garden, we do find it necessary to control certain herbivores and disease-causing organisms to be successful. But these controls

Excess nitrogen and phosphate fertilizer often ends up in our lakes and rivers, causing oxygen depletion and the growth of harmful bacteria and blue-green algae.

need not be chemical pesticides. Our aim should be to cause as little disruption as possible to the balance that naturally keeps these harmful organisms under control.

The cost of fertilizers

Chemical fertilizers produce lush growth, but this lush growth is not without costs. We apply chemical fertilizers to our lawns and gardens to produce an abundance of "healthy" growth, but within a few weeks, we haul a great deal of it to landfills in the form of grass clippings, leaves and branches. Then, when it breaks down in the landfill, natural gas and ammonia are released into the atmosphere instead of being returned to the soil to sustain future crops and landscapes.

Chemical pesticides often enter the food web, ending up in the food we consume.

If an excess of nitrogen or phosphate is applied to the land, it may run off and fertilize plants in the water. As these plants die, the decomposing bacteria use up the oxygen in the water and make it inhospitable to fish and other organisms. Phosphate is particularly harmful as it stimulates the growth of blue-green algae and bacteria. In addition to the downstream costs of pollution, there are environmental costs in the production of fertilizers, most of which are made with natural gas.

Health concerns

Pesticides are poisons. Their toxicity to humans varies, but all are designed to interfere with the metabolic processes of the target organism. Canada's Pest Management Regulatory Agency depends on information provided by the companies registering the products. This data must demonstrate that the active ingredients, if used as directed, pose a minimum risk to the applicator or other humans. However, this information is based mainly on the acute toxicity –

Many vegetables such as Swiss chard are easy to grow without the use of chemical pesticides, lending beauty to our gardens and sustenance to our diets.

the ability to kill – of the active ingredient under closely controlled conditions. While the exposure parameters provide for wide margins of safety under these conditions, they do not concern themselves with "inert" ingredients – solvents, surfactants, diluents, carriers, catalysts, synergists, intensifiers, etc. – in the formulations.

Nor do they concern themselves with the breakdown products of the pesticide, or the synergistic effects of exposure to multiple pesticides. They do not concern themselves with accidental exposures to significantly greater concentrations than the label specifies. They do not concern themselves with long-term effects, which are much more difficult to test for and to evaluate.

Pesticides are important to the production of crops in our industrial agricultural system. In a risk-benefit analysis, we may decide that the risks are worth the benefits of an abundant supply of food. However, what we do in our yards and gardens requires an even more stringent analysis. The risks involved in the use of these chemicals include an increased incidence of cancer, adverse neurological effects, birth defects, reductions of fecundity and fertility and immune system disorders in ourselves. An extensive literature review in 2004 by the Ontario College of Family Physicians entitled *Systematic Review of Pesticide Human Health Effects* found increased risk of all of these disease conditions with exposure to pesticides. We must weigh these risks against a greener lawn, a tree without little bumps on the leaves or more perfect flowers or fruit.

Are "inert" ingredients really inert?

The dictionary definition of "inert" is inactive, slow or lifeless, but in pesticide terminology, inert means any pesticide ingredient other than the active ingredients. Inert ingredients may be solvents, surfactants, diluents, carriers, catalysts, synergists, intensifiers, etc., which makes these ingredients anything but inert according to the dictionary definition. A solvent could be water or it could be an organic liquid that dissolves the active ingredient. A surfactant reduces the surface tension of the product and allows it to penetrate more easily, as does soap or detergent. Diluents and carriers may be relatively inert, but catalysts, synergists and intensifiers speed up or intensify reactions. These ingredients could change the ultimate effects of the chemical. Recent Environmental Protection Agency policy in the United States allows the term "other" to be substituted for the term "inert" on pesticide labels.

Chapter 2

Getting Started

As horticultural students in the 1970s and 1980s, we were taught that almost every garden problem had a similar solution: "Spray with malathion (or diazinon or carbaryl or 2,4-D...)." Only one of our professors mentioned the value of timing, barriers or crop rotation. Mulching was considered a bit weird. Organic matter was never added to the horticultural field plots. Degrees in hand, we took our studies to heart and passed our learning on to the general public.

In the last two decades, we've progressed from pushing an arsenal of broad-spectrum chemicals to offering a compendium of tools and cultural methods based on the life cycles and characteristics of individual pests and diseases. With research and collective observation, our knowledge base has come a long way. In the process, we've also dealt with folklore, traditional practices and urban (and rural!) legends. Some of these are effective, others are not, and some are downright toxic.

Often found near water and lovely to look at, dragonflies are voracious predators of other insects.

7

This book is a distillation of what we've found. Your grandmother was well aware of the value of plant collars, the working end of a hoe and hand-picking insects.

'Hazeldean', a heritage shrub rose, is highly resistant to black spot.

None of that has changed. But at the opposite end of the spectrum are the newly introduced biological controls, many of which were originally developed for commercial vegetable and fruit growers and have only recently been made available to home gardeners.

Regardless of our own health and environmental concerns about pesticides, or municipal bylaws on pesticide use that are imposed on us, like it or not, we can't move from one philosophy of gardening to another without using at least some of the tools and methods included in these chapters. You may have questions, you may be skeptical, but finding that you like these new methods may be as easy as Dr. Seuss suggested so many years ago: "Try them, try them, and you may!"

As in implementing any innovative concept, each of us will find our own comfort zone among these many solutions that do not rely on chemical pesticides. Some of us will embrace the biological controls; others will stick to row covers. We don't all have to do *everything* recommended here to make pesticide-free gardening work, but the more we do, the more effective our control.

One of our objectives in managing pests in our gardens should be to gain a level of control with the least harm to the environment and the least risk to people and pets. We can usually do this by growing a diversity of healthy plants. If weeds, insects or diseases develop to the point at which they are causing unacceptable damage, there are strategies that allow us to control them without the use of the harmful chemicals that have been the staple of pest control for the past fifty years. Some of these methods have been used for centuries and make use of minerals and salts. Others employ the natural enemies of pests and attack them with predators, parasites and diseases.

These solutions are generally accepted to be less harmful than chemical pesticides, but they are not all harmless. If you use pest control products, you must read and follow label directions and use them in a prudent manner. Even those that have very low toxicity may sensitize people who have allergic tendencies, so we should avoid breathing them or getting them on our skin. And finally, be aware that homemade remedies are not necessarily safe remedies.

Initially, converting to organic landscape management may require more attention and effort than the traditional use of chemicals, but as we protect and re-establish beneficial organisms and learn to work with nature, we should have good results with less work than when we were annihilating pests with powerful poisons. We will also enjoy more butterflies, dragonflies, frogs and birds in our yards.

Fundamental strategies for chemical-free gardening

Some gardening practices offer multiple benefits, discouraging both harmful insects and diseases. Among these are: growing healthy plants, optimal placement and spacing, rotation, diversity, selecting resistant plants, sanitation and mulching.

Keep plants healthy

Healthy plants are less vulnerable. Begin with healthy nursery stock. Don't be the bleeding heart that adopts and pays for a sick plant. Unhealthy-looking plants may be merely dried out or neglected, or they may be harbouring clematis wilt or be infected with a devastating and contagious disease like Cytospora canker. Plant virus-free stock, especially of fruit and hosta.

Over-fertilizing with nitrogen induces lush foliage vulnerable to disease and insects and delays fruit production.

If you are planting from seed, use seeds that have been hot-water treated. Many commercial seeds, especially vegetables, are routinely hot-water treated to kill disease organisms. This will be indicated on the packet. (Commercial seeds may also have been treated with a fungicide. Fungicide-treated seeds are a pinkish-red, green or blue colour and will be labelled as such.)

Optimize the health of your plants so they can outgrow weeds or better resist insects and diseases. Provide adequate water and fertility, but be careful not to over-fertilize. Too much nitrogen can force lush growth that is more prone to infection by fungal and bacterial diseases and is more attractive to some insects. Applications of compost or other organic fertilizer keep plants supplied with slow-release nutrients when they most need them. Water deeply but not frequently to promote deeper root growth.

Plant the right plant in the right place

Plants growing under favourable conditions are better able to resist disease. Plants that are adapted to shade will grow best under those conditions, while those that prefer full sun will be healthier in sunny locations. Many trees, shrubs and perennials grow naturally in forests, where they are protected from extreme sun and wind by the nearby trees. These plants are more likely to

Barberries do best in full sun and well-drained soil and need little fertilizer.

thrive in a shady mixed border with other plants than in a lawn in full sun. Some plants are more tolerant of wet soils, while others prefer good drainage and tolerate drought. Group plants with like water requirements together to allow optimal conditions for all. If you have soil conditions that aren't easily changed (like high salinity), choose plants that are tolerant of those conditions. Generally, your best strategy is to provide good air circulation and soil drainage, except of course if you are planting bog plants.

Provide optimal spacing

The optimal space between plants will vary, depending on the plant and the insect pest or disease that you wish to discourage. Closer spacing may raise humidity and decrease air circulation, resulting in foliar diseases. But in the case of cabbage, cauliflower, broccoli and Brussels sprouts, closer spacing produces a cooler, shadier environment that is not to the liking of flea beetles, one of their major pests, and may inhibit them. Generally, though, more distant spacing may make it a little more difficult for insects to find their plant of choice and will increase air movement and decrease humidity, thus discouraging disease.

Rotate your crops

Crop rotation is a regular schedule of planting in which different annual vegetables are planted in different parts of the garden each year. Put more simply, the rule of thumb is: Don't plant the same veggies in the same spot two years in a row. Although its major application is in the vegetable garden, rotation can also be useful with annual bedding plants, especially if you have favourites that are planted year after year. For more information, see Chapter 8, Vegetables.

Pumpkins flourish in full sun with lots of space. Group them with cucumbers, squash, watermelons and melons in your rotation.

Diversify

Remember the old adage, "Don't put all your eggs in one basket"? If you grow only one type of tree, have an acre of glads, are devoted to petunias or cultivate an enormous potato plot of the same variety, when insects or diseases strike, they will generally strike hard. Given favourable environmental conditions and a seemingly endless supply of the food they thrive on, insect populations can explode and diseases spread rapidly. Diversify, diversify, diversify!

In many decades of gardening, we have never needed to use an insecticide or fungicide in our home gardens. Why? Our plant populations are extremely diversified. Diversity encourages a wide range of beneficial insects and birds. Insects have to search for their desired food while avoiding their predators. A balance is achieved, plants are healthy and the gardener is happy.

Choose resistant varieties

'Pamjat Serdsta' clematis is both hardy and resistant to clematis wilt.

Choosing insect- and disease-resistant and tolerant varieties is an easy way to avoid problems. "Resistant" means a particular variety will not be infected by a particular disease. For example, 'Thunderchild' flowering crabapple is resistant to fireblight; 'Dropmore' linden is resistant to leaf gall mite; 'Marshall's Delight' monarda is resistant to powdery mildew. "Tolerant" indicates that a plant will show few symptoms and continue growing even when infected, and is a much better choice than a cultivar that is susceptible to a particular insect or disease. Read catalogues and seed packets carefully. Cultivars recommended by prairie universities and research stations are often disease-tolerant or they would have failed the trials in which they were tested. By selecting these varieties, you're halfway home.

Keep in mind that new strains of a disease pathogen may develop in the future, making a particular cultivar no longer resistant. As well, if a plant is under a great deal of environmental stress, resistance may break down.

Don't import pests or diseases

Whether they come as gifts from friends or neighbours, or are purchased from nurseries, garden centres or big-box stores, new plants may not come alone. Before planting, check them carefully for signs of insects, larvae or eggs. Slugs often find their way into your garden in this way. The scarlet lily beetle travelled from Ontario to the prairies in nursery stock, as did the emerald ash borers now threatening North Dakota. Hosta virus X has been spread mainly through sale of infected plants by wholesalers and retailers. Be observant and take the time to look before you plant.

Control weeds, even outside the garden

The need to control weeds within our gardens is obvious, but it is also important to do so on the fringes. Remove or mow weeds or nearby grassy areas that act as alternate hosts or overwintering sites for insect pests and diseases. To discourage them, mow or remove the weeds from these areas using the methods described in Chapter 4, Controlling Weeds Without Chemicals.

Perennial coneflowers provide pollen and nectar for many of the "good" insects that are predators of those that consume our garden plants.

Mulch

Although mulch is used primarily for water conservation and weed control, it is also useful for reducing insect and disease problems. The rough surface of materials such as post peelings deters slugs. As a dense barrier on the soil surface, mulch prevents many soil-borne disease organisms from being splashed or blown onto susceptible plants.

Mulch also provides a good home for beneficial predator insects such as lady beetles, especially as a hibernation site. It is a better environment for beneficial insects than bare cultivated soil. Mulch is a far better option than purchasing commercial predators that might "fly away home" almost instantly once you've released them.

Clean up

Once harvest of the vegetable garden is complete and annual flower beds have been laid low by fall frosts, remove spent plants. Some insects and many disease organisms survive over winter on the previous season's plant debris. If no disease organisms or harmful insects have been present and if your compost pile is "hot" enough, this material can be composted. If the compost heats to 57°C (160°F), disease organisms and insects will be killed. Otherwise, debris should be buried at least 30 cm (12 in.) deep, burnt or sent to a municipal compost facility.

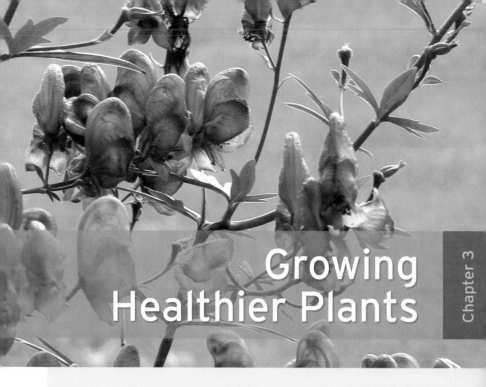

Growing Healthier Plants

Plants, like people, are healthier and less vulnerable to disease and other problems if their basic needs are met. From a plant's perspective, these include enough light and space in which to develop, good soil, adequate nutrition and water and mulch.

Light and space

Different plants require different intensities and durations of light, and it is in your best interest as well as your plants' to put them where they'll thrive. These needs are based on their evolution and adaptation to their native habitats. In less than full sun, a rose or delphinium will languish and be prone to disease, while most ferns and hostas wilt and become sun-scorched if planted in full sun. Some plants will grow well in either sun or shade but will flower less in shade.

Monkshood is one of those rare, tall, true blue perennials. It thrives in full sun to partial shade in moist fertile soil.

Generally, shade plants have large, smooth, thin leaves. The leaves of sun plants tend to be thicker. Sun plants may also have tiny hairs on their leaves that to the naked eye give the foliage a silvery appearance. These increase the shade and protect the leaf against desiccation by slowing air movement.

Plants also need sufficient space in which to develop. When crowded together, they must compete for light, water and nutrients. Plants that require sun are often shaded out. This weakens them and makes them more vulnerable to insect and disease problems. Close spacing also means that insects and disease organisms have a bountiful feast without having to go far to find the next plant. Lack of air circulation encourages the development of many diseases.

Before you plant, it is absolutely essential that you consider the mature height and width of your plants as well as their sun or shade requirements. With young plants, this is often a compromise. We know that the cute little spruce tree we've just planted will eventually grow to 18 m (60 ft). That will take awhile, and in the meanwhile, we place other plants around it. But eventually, these plants will become overcrowded, and some will have to be removed (perhaps along with the spruce, which will probably dwarf your home and take up much of the yard). Most gardeners move plants around as their gardens mature, but this is not always possible, so a little forward planning is essential, especially with trees and shrubs.

Soil

Improve sandy soils with the addition of organic matter.

Soil is sometimes a hard sell. Because it is natural and all around us, even third-generation urbanites feel it should be free. Soil seldom provides the instant gratification of a colourful hanging basket, a massive, well-placed rock or a new interlocking brick patio. While most of us willingly spend hundreds of dollars on plants, we are reluctant to spend a similar amount to improve our soil. Nor will we happily expend the time and labour required to dig and amend our soil to ensure the good growth of plants. Yet soil is the key to healthy, vigorous plant growth, and healthy, vigorous plant growth is the best way to protect against harmful insect pests and diseases.

If you've recently purchased a new home, you're probably anxious to begin landscaping. But before planting, check out your soil. New homes in new developments may or may not include topsoil: the topsoil may have been sold, buried or moved in the process of grading, developing infrastructure (roads, sewers, etc.) or building the house itself. Even if your home is in a mature neighbourhood, it's worth the time and effort to evaluate and improve your soil. This is also a good idea if you've been gardening in the same soil for a long time and the fruits of your labour have become less than satisfactory. You can try to determine the characteristics of your soil yourself or let local soil-testing labs do it for you.

Texture

Many problems related to growing plants centre around soil "texture". Texture is the relative proportion of sand, silt and clay particles in a given soil. Sand particles are the largest, easily seen with the naked eye. To see a silt particle we need a microscope. Clay particles are so tiny they can be seen only with an electron microscope.

Soil texture is a big factor in determining the size, shape and number of air spaces or "porosity" in our soil. Soil porosity in turn determines water movement, retention and aeration. Soil texture is also an important factor in how well the soil retains nutrients for plants to use as they grow.

Loam is a term that is often misused. It has nothing to do with organic matter, but refers to a soil with an equal proportion of sand, silt and clay particles – the ideal texture for gardening. Loam soils are easily worked and well-aerated, with good moisture and nutrient retention. Happy is the gardener with a loam soil, but many of us have soils that are either sandy or clay-like.

Sandy soils drain easily, warm up quickly in the spring and are easily worked. The down side? They dry out quickly and need to be watered frequently. Nutrients are easily leached from them, and when exposed to wind and rain they are very vulnerable to erosion. To improve a sandy soil and increase productivity, add organic matter in the form of compost, well-rotted animal manure, peat moss, leaf mould, mushroom compost or sawdust. These will improve the soil's aeration and water- and nutrient-holding ability as well as its aggregation (its ability to hold together) and crumb-like structure.

Clay soils hold water and nutrients extremely well. But these soils are often slow to drain after rain or irrigation, warm up slowly in the spring and may be subject to alternate expansion and contraction in spring and fall due to freezing and thawing cycles. Expansion

Amend clay soils with generous quantities of organic matter in combination with equal volumes of coarse sand.

and contraction of clay soils can cause root damage as well as the "heaving" of plants out of the soil. Clay soils may also crust on the surface, blocking airflow. They often crack and are usually difficult to work – either impossibly gummy or hard as cement.

Like sandy soils, clay soils can be improved by amending them with generous quantities of organic matter in combination with an equal quantity of *coarse-textured* sand. Be warned: mixing fine sand with clay can result in a product not unlike concrete! Coarse-textured sand has an irregular, jagged shape and a particle diameter greater than 0.5 mm. To make a significant change, large quantities of coarse sand and organic matter, well mixed together, will be needed. It's wise to experiment with a smaller area to determine the optimum quantities required for your particular clay soil. Thoroughly incorporate the mixture of organic matter and sand into the existing soil.

Organic matter

Your next step is to figure out how much, if any, organic matter the soil contains. A rough estimate is possible by looking at the colour of your soil. This is straightforward. Regardless of texture, the darker the colour, the more organic matter is present – and the more the better. Black soils are high in organic matter; grey soils are low. Organic matter helps retain moisture and nutrients; improves the tilth, or workability, of the soil; and pro-

Compost recycles raw organic matter into an excellent soil amendment and slow-release fertilizer.

vides an ideal home for beneficial micro-organisms. Most soils benefit from the regular annual additions of some form of organic matter. For permanent mulched plantings or lawns, incorporate these prior to planting. For annual flower beds or vegetable gardens, add every few years.

Salinity

Salts are naturally present in our soils, and in small amounts do no harm. It's when the percentage of salt increases that plant growth is adversely affected. Soils containing enough salt to retard plant growth or kill plants are called "saline." Such soils are often found in low-lying areas with poor drainage. They occur in areas where water collects, bringing in the salt either as surface runoff or groundwater. As the water evaporates, the salts left behind build up over time. When these soils dry out, a white crust is visible. In the same way that our skin will dry out when we swim in the ocean, plant tissue will dry out in saline soils.

Applying too much fertilizer or irrigating with water with a high salt content also contributes to the accumulation of salts in soil. Chemical fertilizers are, after all, salts, and should be used in moderation if at all. If using well water, check its salinity before applying it to your garden. Avoid adding manures with a high salt content.

If you have areas of saline soil, there is no magic cure or chemical that will make them better. It is difficult to remedy soils that are

Using salt-tolerant plants such as sea buckthorn is the simplest way to deal with saline soils in larger landscapes where it can sucker.

naturally high in salt. But there are practices that lessen the effect of high salinity on your plants. Avoid frequent light waterings. Instead, irrigate deeply but infrequently. The object is to dissolve the salts and then leach them down into the soil profile, beyond the reach of plant roots. Leaching out salts by improving drainage is possible, but often difficult and expensive. It may involve the use of drain tiles. Its expense means it is not always an option. You should also incorporate organic soil amendments that are low in salt such as peat moss, compost or grass clippings. These materials act in the opposite manner of salts, helping to increase the soil's moisture-holding ability. In effect, by increasing the amount of water held by the soil, they are diluting the salt concentration within the soil.

pH

The pH of a soil is a measure of its acidity or alkalinity. pH is largely determined by the rock from which it originated. Readings of pH are given on a scale from 0 to 14. A pH of 0 is the most acidic; 7 is neutral; and 14 is the most alkaline, or basic. The pH scale is logarithmic: a pH of 6 is ten times more acidic than that of 7, and a pH of 5 is 100 times more acidic than that of 7.

Nutrients in the soil are held on the surfaces of organic matter and clay mineral particles, which is why organic matter and clay content are important. Nutrients are released from these surfaces into the soil water. At a neutral pH (7), the majority of nutrients are available in the soil water and are readily absorbed and used by most plants. A pH of 6.5 to 7.5 is generally ideal for horticultural purposes. As the soil pH moves further away from neutral in either direction, nutrients are held more tightly onto organic matter and clay surfaces, becoming less available to plants. When this happens, plants show signs of nutrient deficiencies, including stunted growth or yellow leaves.

Most soils in the prairies are neutral to weakly alkaline (pH 6.5 to 8), while those in British Columbia and from Ontario eastward tend to be weakly acidic (pH 5 to 6.5). While many plants can tolerate a fairly wide pH range, others are more sensitive. Blueberries, azaleas and rhododendrons prefer an acid soil, baby's breath a more alkaline soil.

It is very difficult to change the pH of a soil permanently. The first step is a soil test. If your soil is weakly acidic (seldom if ever an issue in the southern and central prairies), the addition of dolomitic limestone will raise its pH. Dolomitic limestone is rich in calcium carbonate (like an antacid). If your soil is weakly alkaline and you're determined to grow blueberries or other acid-loving plants, try using elemental sulphur, peat moss or organic matter such as compost or well-rotted manure to lower its pH.

Amending your soil

Although the materials may be the same, amending the soil is different from mulching. When amending, you do not want the added material to sit as a distinct layer on or within the soil, resulting in layers of different textures within your garden soil. This would impede the capillary action of water in the soil, slowing its movement from one layer to another. It would also discourage root penetration and encourage shallowly rooted plants, which are more vulnerable to heat, cold and drought. Your goal at this point is to incorporate the organic matter thoroughly into the existing soil, forming a gradient that gradually decreases in organic matter as you go deeper.

To do this, cultivate your existing soil to a *minimum* depth of about 20 cm (8 in.). Deeper is better. This can be done by hand digging (said to build character) or tilling. Loosening the existing soil makes it much easier to incorporate later additions of topsoil or amendments thoroughly.

Once you've tilled your existing soil, you're ready to add topsoil, soil amendments

Compost begins as a combination of "yellow" and "green" matter.

or a combination of these. For lawns, you'll need a minimum of 15 cm (6 in.) of fertile topsoil; for flower beds or mixed borders of perennials and shrubs, 30 to 45 cm (12 to 18 in.). If this seems like a lot, visualize the diameter of the root balls of most shrubs, or even perennials such as peonies or delphiniums. Add a 10 cm (4 in.) layer of topsoil and/or amendments to the existing soil, rototill thoroughly to avoid leaving layers, add more of the topsoil or amendment, till again, and continue in this fashion until the desired depth of good soil has been obtained.

Soil amendments to choose from

Compost recycles organic material from the landscape that would otherwise be lost forever to landfills and garbage dumps. The end product is an excellent soil conditioner and slow-release fertilizer. You can make your own compost or purchase it commercially or from municipal composting facilities.

Purchasing topsoil

If your existing soil is infertile but predominantly loam soil amendments will help. If the texture is poor or verging on unworkable, you are well advised to purchase topsoil. Ask friends, neighbours and co-workers about reputable topsoil dealers with proven customer satisfaction. If in doubt, make an on-site visit and ask if you can take a small amount (half an ice cream pail) home so you can examine it and identify problems before making your purchase.

First, check for salt content. Excess salt is often indicated by white powder or crystals on the dry soil. A high salt content stunts plant growth. This might not be apparent on a load of moist topsoil, but generally shows up on the soil once it is dry.

The darker the soil, the more organic content it contains. Next, determine the soil's texture by hand texturing. Rub a small amount of the moistened soil between your thumb and forefinger. If it's sticky, it's predominantly clay. If it feels gritty and you can feel individual particles, it's predominantly sand.

Finally, to determine its quality, place some of the soil in a pot and sow seeds. Choose a seed that has a high germination percentage and quick germination rate such as lawn grass seed or lettuce. Water it and place it in bright indirect light. If the seeds germinate and grow as expected, the soil is fine. If the seedlings are stunted or fail to germinate, the soil may have a high salt content, or residual herbicides may be present. If a multitude of weed seedlings emerge, it's an indication of weed seed contamination. Weeds can introduce new problems to your yard, especially perennial weeds such as thistle or quack grass.

Manures vary in their nutrient content. Manure quality depends on the type of animal, the age and storage conditions of the manure, the animals' diet and the amount of bedding in the manure – the more bedding, the fewer nutrients but the more organic matter. The sex or sexual capacity of the animal has nothing to do with quality – steer manure is neither better nor worse than cow, bull or heifer manure. Manure's nitrogen level decreases with its age and its exposure to wind and rain or snowmelt. While you would think that fresh manure

Compost

Compost is living material on its way to becoming humus – the dark, crumbly, sweet-smelling stuff that is the result of decomposition. Compost recycles organic materials from your kitchen and landscape by fast-forwarding normal biological processes. It does this by providing optimum conditions of oxygen and moisture for the raw materials. This results in an excellent soil amending slow-release fertilizer.

The soil micro-organisms that do the work for you require water, oxygen and a balance of nitrogen and carbon. The nitrogen is supplied by "greens" such as grass clippings, kitchen waste and fresh garden refuse. The carbon comes from "yellows" – dry grass, leaves and straw. These materials, plus the soil you add to the compost, usually contain enough micro-organisms to make it work.

Do not compost the following: meat and bones; weeds that have gone to seed; cat, dog, pig and human feces; or diseased or insect-infested garden material.

There are various ways of composting; the "bin" is the one most urban gardeners opt for, while the "pile" is more used in rural areas. Many plans are available. The minimum effective size is 1 m^3 (1 yd^3), but larger is generally better. Smaller piles are prone to moisture and heat loss.

The contents of the pile or bin are placed in layers, 10 to 20 cm (4-8 in.) deep, alternating between the carbon (yellow) and the nitrogen (green) with a few centimetres of soil in between. Add enough water to keep the compost moist but not soggy. Turn the pile often enough so that oxygen is present. This also prevents odour.

To be effective, compost should heat to 70°C (160°F), hot enough to kill most weed seeds and decompose the raw material. On the prairies, it may take a full growing season to get useable compost, but this depends on moisture, temperature, the materials used and their size (the smaller the particles, the faster they decompose).

would be more effective, fresh manure contains high levels of ammonia and salts that will desiccate or "burn" plants, as well as millions of viable weed seeds. Composting allows the ammonia to volatilize into the air and the salts to be washed out by rain, and may heat weed seeds to the point where they are no longer viable. As it ages, manure contains fewer nutrients but becomes a better soil conditioner, and this "well-rotted" manure is what you want to buy. How can you determine if manure is well-rotted? It is said

Although well-rotted manure has fewer nutrients, it also has fewer viable weed seeds.

that if you can stick your arm into a pile of manure up to your elbow and feel good about the experience, chances are pretty good that the manure is well-rotted. Commercially available dried manures are easier to spread than bulk manures and contain fewer weed seeds, but are more costly. Neither well-rotted nor dry manure should have an offensive odour.

Animal by-products include blood meal, bone meal and hoof and horn meal. They contain a higher level of nutrients (including micronutrients) but less organic matter than manures. Blood meal and hoof and horn meal have forms of nitrogen that are quickly released. Bone meal contains a form of phosphorous that is more slowly released.

Peat moss, derived from the leaves and stems of sphagnum moss, is capable of holding ten times its weight in water, a characteristic retained even when it is processed and baled. Although low in nutrients (3 percent nitrogen, but little else), it improves the soil's ability to hold nutrients and water, as well as its aeration. With a pH varying from 3.0 to 4.5, it is ideal for acid-loving plants such as blueberries and azaleas, or for reducing the pH of alkaline soils. For easier application, moisten slightly prior to use. Coarse peat moss has been sifted or screened the least and is useful as a mulch.

Peat moss improves the water- and nutrient-holding capacity of sandy soils and the workability of clay soils.

It is stringy and chunky rather than powdery and may contain bits of sticks. You may have to order it, and it may be slightly more costly than the powdery type, but it is a much more effective and longer lasting soil amendment or mulch.

Leaf mould consists of decayed leaves. Gather your own in the fall, mow (for faster decomposition) and immediately incorporate into beds and borders or add to the compost pile for later use.

Mushroom compost is the mixture of animal manure and straw that remains following the mushroom harvest. An excellent soil conditioner, it has few nutrients and may contain salts.

Sawdust, wood shavings and bark chips may be added to sandy soils to increase their water- and nutrient-holding capacity. These materials can also be added to clay soils to improve aeration. They contain about 6 percent calcium and smaller amounts of nitrogen, phosphorus, potassium and

In praise of peat moss

Peat moss improves soil aeration, increases its ability to hold nutrients and water and adds organic matter to the soil. It's an ideal amendment for areas intended for lawns, flower beds and vegetable gardens. It's used in the media intended for pots, baskets and containers as well as seeding mixes. Existing lawns can be "top-dressed" with a mixture of coarse sand and peat moss, especially following aeration. Peat moss is low in nutrient value, containing only about 3 percent nitrogen, but excellent as organic matter. Its pH is between 3.0 and 4.5, making it useful for acid-loving plants such as azaleas and blueberries.

Considering all of its good characteristics, it's disturbing to read articles in gardening magazines and the popular press about the imminent demise of Canadian peat bogs because of high demand by gardeners. There is often an attempt to shame us into using alternate, sometimes inferior, amendments in an effort to be "green." But there is no reason to feel guilty about buying a bale of peat moss. First, it takes a lot more energy to process and bring tropical coconut hulls to Canada than it does to harvest our northern bogs. Second, it is the peat bogs of Europe that are the concern, not Canada's, and it's not our demand for gardening products that is depleting them. Peat has been harvested and processed for thousands of years in Europe, mainly for use as a fuel. In Ireland, peat continues to be used as a fuel, primarily to run electric power plants.

There are more than 113 million hectares (279 million acres) of peat bogs in Canada. Less than 0.02 percent of this area is currently being used to harvest horticultural peat moss. What's more, peat bogs are sustainable. Strict guidelines have been developed by the industry in consultation with researchers, conservation and environmental organizations and Environment Canada. Peat is accumulating nearly sixty times faster than it is being harvested, and Canadian bogs are being restored to the wetlands they once were within five to twenty years. With responsible management policies, they are indeed sustainable.

magnesium (less than 0.15 percent). They are high in carbon and therefore decompose slowly, tying up nitrogen in the short term. To compensate, add nitrogen such as blood meal, alfalfa pellets or compost to the soil at the rate of 1 kg (2.2 lb) per 45 kg (99.2 lb) of wood amendment.

Coarse sand is added to predominantly clay soil, mixed with an equal volume of organic matter. Remember to look at the sand particles under a magnifying glass and avoid using fine sand with small, round particles.

Commercial soil amendments appear on the market with alarming regularity, but there are few if any "miracle" soil cures. Neither perlite nor vermiculite is recommended for outdoor use. They become ineffective within a season or two and may make existing soil texture problems worse.

Fertility

To grow and thrive, plants need nutrients. These become the building blocks, the energy sources and the regulators for their growth. The air itself is the source of carbon dioxide and oxygen, two key building blocks of the sugars that form the structure of the plant, but we normally think of fertility as the mineral nutrients that plants extract from the soil. These nutrients are taken up from the soil dissolved in water. The major nutrients that plants need are nitrogen, phosphate and potassium (the N, P and K on fertilizer packages). Nitrogen (N) aids green vegetative growth; phosphorus (P) supports roots, flowers, fruit and seeds; potassium (K) makes plants more resistant to diseases, insects and other trauma. There are many other nutrients, called micronutrients, that are essential for plant growth but in smaller quantities.

A plant does not distinguish between sources of nutrients. It can use nitrogen or phosphate from chemical fertilizer as well as from organic sources. In the light of this, what are the advantages and disadvantages of using organic nutrients as compared to mineral nutrients?

Mineral nutrients are relatively concentrated and easy to apply. They are easily purchased and the analysis (amount of each nutrient present) is known. When they are applied, they are soluble and generally readily available to the plants. However, it is easy to apply too much, which can burn or desiccate plants, elevate salts in the soil to toxic levels and be leached into the groundwater. Nor do chemical fertilizers contribute to the structure and tilth (the workability) of the soil.

By contrast, organic fertilizers are bulky and their nutrients are not immediately available. The nutrients must be broken down to mineral form by soil micro-organisms before plants can use them. The precise analysis is usually not known. However, they improve the water- and nutrient-holding capacity of the soil by adding organic matter. They also provide an environment that increases the level of micro-organisms in the soil and thus helps to control certain plant diseases. Even a small addition of composted manure significantly improves the tilth of the soil.

Organic fertilizers

Organic fertilizers are derived from natural sources. Compared to inorganic fertilizers, they are generally less concentrated and held in a non-leachable form that is released slowly into the soil. They require the activity of soil micro-organisms to release nutrients so that they are available for uptake by plants. This activity generally does not take place until temperatures are greater than 10°C (50°F) and sufficient soil moisture is available. Cold, dry conditions delay the release of nutrients from organic sources.

Organic fertilizers are often more costly per unit of nutrients (and more bulky) than inorganic fertilizers, but they have advantages not found in inorganic products. They stimulate microbial activity in the soil, improve soil structure, increase the water- and nutrient-holding capacity and porosity of the soil, and are generally renewable.

Among the more readily available organic fertilizers are:

Bone meal is a slow-release organic fertilizer high in phosphorus.

Bone meal (2–4% N, 15–27% P, 0% K), a product of slaughterhouses, is steam processed and can be expensive. One of its disadvantages is that the phosphorus is more readily available to plants in soils that have a pH below 7.0, not always the case in the prairies. Nutrients are generally released within one to four months. Apply and till in 4.5 kg per 10 m² (10 lb/100 ft²).

Blood meal/dried blood (10–14% N, 1–2% P, less than 1% K) is a dried and powdered by-product from slaughterhouses. It is generally used as a top dressing and watered in. Broken down to ammonia by soil bacteria, nutrients are released for one to four months. Avoid over applying it (especially when conditions are warm and moist) or applying it to seedlings because it may "burn." Do not use on peas, beans and other legumes as it may interfere with their own ability to fix nitrogen. Apply and till in 2.25 to 4.5 kg per 10 m² (5–10 lb/100 ft²) Note: For the last decade, regulations and protocol in slaughterhouses have been very stringent so that BSE (mad cow disease) does not get into the food chain or organic fertilizer products.

Alfalfa pellets/meal (3% N, 1% P, 2% K) are readily available in garden centres and feed stores. They contain triacontanol, a plant growth regulator (stimulant). They can be applied as a top dressing and watered in, or as a "tea", using 0.5 kg of alfalfa pellets per 20 litres of water (1 lb/gal). They should not be used near roots or seedlings. Nutrients are released for one to four months. Apply and till in 1 to 2.25 kg per 10 m² (2–5 lb/100 ft²), or 20 kg per 30 m (50 lb/100 ft) of row.

Corn gluten meal (9–10% N, 0% P, 0% K) is a by-product of the milling process used for cornmeal and corn syrup. A good source of nitrogen, it is also a pre-emergent herbicide and should not be applied to seeds or seedlings. Nutrients are released in one to four months. Apply 10 to 20 kg per 100 m² (20–40 lb/1,000 ft²).

Although alfalfa pellets have only small amounts of nutrients they release triacontanol, a growth stimulant.

Water

Water and plants

Plants cannot live without water. Photosynthesis, chemical reactions and cooling all depend on it, and nutrients dissolved in soil water enter the plant through the roots and are carried through the plant by water. On a hot, dry, windy day, the amount of water lost to transpiration can be quite high, requiring large replacement amounts of soil moisture to prevent wilting. The reality of gardening on the prairies (where the average annual precipitation is 300 to 500 mm (12–20 in.) is that some irrigation will be needed to supplement natural rainfall.

Dry stream beds can channel excess rain water away from plantings that might otherwise become waterlogged.

Sometimes, however, too much water is the problem. Few plants tolerate seasonally or permanently waterlogged soils. This is because air moves very slowly through the soil if the air spaces are filled with water. Plant roots cannot get the oxygen they need, and they begin to die. Drainage will likely be a problem if your lot is in a low area of a development with other lots draining towards yours, or if your soil is predominantly clay.

If you find yourself in either of these situations, and water sits for a while in spring or after a heavy rain, there are solutions. You can build "dry stream

How to water

Too little water, too much water – both are detrimental to plant growth. When irrigating, always water deeply and thoroughly, to the depth of the root system and a little beyond to encourage deep root growth. Roots will only grow where soil is moist. They will not extend into dry soil. Frequent shallow watering confines roots to the upper level of the soil, leaving plants shallow-rooted and prone to rapid drying out between waterings.

Aggressive, shallow-rooted plants or those with extensive, deeper, fibrous root systems such as lawns, ground covers and herbaceous weeds, can be particularly competitive, robbing valuable soil moisture, especially from newly planted trees.

To schedule watering effectively, you should know the water needs of your plants, the infiltration rate of the soil in which they are growing and the microclimate in which they are situated. Water to the depth of the entire root ball, allowing the soil to dry out partially prior to the next watering. Plants are generally more tolerant of moderate drought than prolonged saturation. Saturation limits oxygen availability to the roots, effectively suffocating them. Seedlings and small or newly planted plants will need to be watered more often but for shorter durations than will larger, deeper-rooted plants. As plants become larger, irrigation can be less frequent but deeper. Water before signs of moisture stress are evident.

You can tell when to water by the feel of your soil. If the soil is too dry to form a ball when a handful is firmly squeezed, you are waiting too long to water. If it is moist enough to form a ball but is somewhat crumbly, it's time to irrigate. If it forms a durable ball and is slick, there is no need to irrigate yet. Ultimately, water scheduling will be based on your cumulative experience with your plants and soil.

The best time to water is early morning, when it's calm and cool and the relative humidity is high. Little water is lost to evaporation and plant foliage dries quickly, reducing the risk of foliage diseases such as powdery mildew.

beds" that act as drainage channels, carrying excess water away from your landscape. These can lead to a back lane or across a front sidewalk into storm sewers. On larger properties they can be channelled into holding ponds that can be used for irrigation during dry periods. Check with your municipal authorities for guidance and information about drainage bylaws.

A second solution is to plant flowers, bulbs and small shrubs on raised berms so their root systems are not sitting in seasonally standing water. A berm is a mounded planting bed up to about 60 cm (2 ft) in height and 2 to 3 m (6–9 ft) in width, with sides that slope gently down to the original grade. Besides keeping plants out of waterlogged soil, berms create a more interesting backyard topography on the flat prairies. When developing a berm, add generous amounts of organic matter so it doesn't dry out in the prairie wind. Berms that are gently curved to fit the space they occupy are more pleasing than rigidly geometric ones. In vegetable gardens, drainage problems can be avoided through the use of traditional raised beds.

Water and soil

Water, whether from rainfall or irrigation, percolates into the soil from the surface, filling the pore spaces between the solid soil particles. It forms a "wetting front" if the groundwater levels are low, gradually moving downward and displacing the air until the soil has reached the saturation point. Below the wetting front, the soil remains dry. Once the soil is wet to a particular depth, the water in the pore space is either used by plants or evaporates from the soil surface into the atmosphere. Water that has moved below the rooting zone of plants is unavailable and lost to their use.

Soil texture makes a difference here too. Soils that are predominantly clay hold more water than sandy soils. Clay soils are able to absorb and hold a great deal of water, but have a very slow infiltration rate. If water is applied faster than it can be absorbed, runoff or puddling occurs. Sandy soils absorb water quickly but have a low water-holding capacity. The same volume of water moves further and more rapidly in sandy soils as compared to clay soils. If water is applied as drip irrigation, the wetting pattern is usually deeper but not as wide in a sandy soil as compared to a heavier clay soil.

Other factors also make a difference. The greater the organic-matter content of a soil, regardless of texture, the more water it is able to hold. Soil compaction impedes water movement and infiltration downward, as does the layering of soils of different textures. Deeper soils hold more water than shallow soils. Saline soils decrease the amount of water available to plants.

Mulch is a permanent layer of organic matter, laid on the soil surface to conserve moisture and control weeds.

Mulch

Derived from the Middle English word *molsh* or the German *molsch*, meaning soft or rotten (referring to decaying organic matter), mulch is a permanent layer of organic material, 10 cm (4 in.) deep, laid over the soil surface between plants. In contrast with more traditional gardening methods that take pride in regular tillage and "black dirt". mulching imitates nature: leaves fall naturally onto the soil surface to form a layer of organic matter, eventually decaying and returning nutrients to the soil.

Some of the benefits of mulching are obvious: water conservation, weed control and soil improvement. Many are interrelated: Mulches lower soil temperatures, thereby reducing evaporation. A 5 cm (2 in.) layer of pine needles reduces soil evaporation by 65 percent compared to an unmulched area. The softer soil, as Ruth Stout recognized more than half a century ago, increases water percolation and decreases runoff. Because the mulch layer protects the soil from the effects of wind, evaporation is further reduced. The rough texture of the mulch often acts as a snow trap, resulting in additional soil moisture through spring snowmelt.

"My way is unscientific, but it has produced fine vegetables for eleven years. I simply spread mulch where I want the compost to be eventually. It rots and becomes rich dirt, with the valuable by-products of keeping down weeds, keeping the earth soft, holding moisture and eliminating plowing and spading, hoeing and cultivating." – Ruth Stout, 1955

Ruth Stout began mulching in Connecticut in the 1930s, and her book, *How to Have a Green Thumb without an Aching Back: A New Method of Mulch Gardening*, was published in 1955. With the introduction of chemical pesticides and fertilizers following the Second World War, many considered her a madwoman intent on flying in the face of progress. She continued to garden well into her nineties, presumably without an aching back, and she is today considered a pioneer in sustainable agriculture.

The mulch layer controls weeds by excluding the light, which many seeds require for germination. Although annual weed seeds may remain viable for thirty years or longer, if kept in the dark under the mulch, they do not germinate. Mulch also provides a physical barrier, preventing the emergence of weed seeds from below as well as the establishment of those that might blow onto its surface.

One of the advantages of mulch over tillage for weed control is that it does not injure the roots of trees and shrubs. Roots injured through hoeing or tilling respond with new growth, often suckering – sending up new shoots, usually where they are not wanted. Even trees notorious for suckering, such as poplars, are generally better behaved when mulched.

Applying a mulch layer

Mulches can be applied at any time during the growing season. Once in place, they are not incorporated into the soil, but are regarded as a permanent feature of the landscape - topped up as needed but not turned under.

Before applying the mulch layer, ensure that the area is weed free, especially of perennial broadleaf weeds (such as dandelions and thistles) and grasses (such as quack grass and brome). Mulch works many miracles, but suppressing brome grass is not one of them. Next, water the bed or border to a depth of 30 to 45 cm (12-18 in.) and, if you are concerned about a possible short-term nitrogen deficiency, apply a light layer of screened manure or compost to the soil surface prior to mulching.

The depth and evenness of the mulch layer is crucial. Too shallow and it simply doesn't work. It is better to mulch a smaller area well than to spread the mulch too thinly over a larger area. Too deep, however, and mulch can inhibit the gas exchange between the soil atmosphere and the air above, resulting in oxygen depletion to the roots of sensitive trees, like linden and lilac, in heavier soils. Mulch should be applied in a layer approximately 10 cm (4 in.) thick. When applying mulches around low herbaceous or woody plants, take care not to smother them. Keep the mulch layer about 20 cm (8 in.) away from the trunks of trees to avoid possible rot.

Water again after applying the mulch. Deep but less frequent watering is the key to irrigating mulched borders.

The permanent mulch layer will need renewing every three or four years. How often depends on the depth of the layer, climatic factors such as moisture and temperature and the durability of the material. Mulches last longer in the drier prairies than in more humid Ontario. Once weeds begin to appear, kill or remove them before applying additional mulch over the original layer.

As the mulch layer decays, it releases nutrients, adds organic material to the soil and improves soil aggregation. A mulched soil is less vulnerable to wind and water erosion, crusting and cracking. The mulch acts as a cushion, reducing soil compaction, especially of heavier clay soils, as we work in our beds and borders. It also cushions falling fruit, reducing bruising.

A subtle and perhaps underrated function of mulch is temperature modification. By cooling the soil temperature during the hot days of summer, it encourages healthier root growth. Mulches reduce alternating freezing and thawing of soil during spring and fall. Hard freezing is postponed into the fall, allowing trees and shrubs to withdraw water from the soil over a slightly longer period. (On the negative side, mulches may delay the onset of dormancy, making woody plants more vulnerable to winter injury.)

By absorbing water, the mulch layer prevents rain and mud splash on flowers and soft fruit such as strawberries, thus reducing soil-borne diseases spread by rain and soil splash. A sawdust mulch of 10 cm (4 in.) discourages flies from laying their eggs; eggs already laid are less likely to survive. Mulch also seems to encourage beneficial insects. We have found more lady beetles per square foot of mulch than we ever dreamed possible.

Mulches also serve a design function. They add colour and texture to our landscape while unifying planting beds, an important function especially when the beds are new and the plants themselves still small. In a subtle way, they announce that a border should be walked around, not through. They make beds more accessible in inclement weather. Used around individual specimen trees in a lawn, they protect the trunks from overzealous lawn mower or string-trimmer operators. From a design point of view, it is more pleasing to use coarser mulches (post peelings) around trees and shrubs, and finer mulches (chopped post peelings, grass clippings topped with coarse peat moss or flax shives) in flower beds.

Landscape fabric and plastic sheeting

Landscape fabrics are unnecessary and interfere with the soil improvement function of mulches. Plastic sheeting between the mulch and the soil is not only unnecessary but harmful to plant growth. It interferes with the gas exchange between the soil and the atmosphere, prevents rainwater from reaching plants and is a barrier to the release of nutrients and organic matter into the soil. Neither one should be used in home gardens.

Mulch options

Some of the best mulches are by-products and so may be free except for the hauling. Availability varies from region to region. Cocoa-bean hulls were once unique to Smith Falls, Ontario, and wild-rice hulls to La Ronge, Saskatchewan, but straw, grass clippings and post peelings are fairly universal.

Characteristics of a good mulch include ready availability, low or no cost, resistance to wind and ease of application. They should be free of weeds, insects and disease.

Grass clippings – The universal mulch! Readily available, free and easy to apply. Use as soon as they're raked or bagged. If lawns are mowed when 7.5 to 10 cm (3–4 in.) in height, no grass seed should be introduced with the clippings. If you find the appearance of grass clippings unattractive, top-dress them with a thin layer of coarse sphagnum peat moss. Obviously, if a broadleaf weed killer has been used on the lawn, you should not use the clippings as a mulch on your flower beds.

Coarse sphagnum peat moss – Attractive, lightweight and weed- and insect-free, this is an excellent material to use as a thin top dressing over grass clippings in flower beds. Coarser grades are preferred but may be more difficult to find. For easier application, first moisten the peat moss. Once in place, if allowed to completely dry out, it may initially resist rewetting.

Post peelings – A by-product of the fence-post industry, post peelings are easily applied with a long-tined, curved manure fork. They are suitable for tree and shrub borders, and if slightly chopped or shredded, they work equally well on perennial borders. They look and smell nice, are slow to break down, allow free water percolation and resist compaction and blowing.

Slightly chopped or shredded post peelings work well as a mulch on perennial beds and borders.

Crushed rock and gravel

The use of crushed rock and gravel is not beneficial to either plants or soil and should be discouraged. Costly in terms of the energy required to mine, crush and transport, they absorb heat, reflect light, raise temperatures and create an atmosphere inhospitable to most plants. They do nothing to improve the soil, and removing weeds from a gravel bed is hard on the knuckles.

Decorative bark – Reddish brown and more chunky in appearance than post peelings, its characteristics are similar. Specifically produced for the landscape industry, it can be expensive if used over large areas. Because of its light weight, it is more vulnerable to wind displacement.

Chipper debris – This may be free for the hauling from municipal pruning crews, private companies or utility companies. Texture, colour and composition vary with the species being pruned and will include leaves in summer. It is coarse textured, allows free water percolation and does not blow or scatter. It is useful on tree and shrub borders. If the companies providing the chippings also drill out stumps, the chippings may include soil. This is a problem because windblown seeds can become established on the surface of your mulch.

Sawdust and wood shavings – Free and readily available from sawmills, retail lumber stores and local high school and community college shop teachers, these products are used to mulch bush fruit (strawberries, raspberries, currants, haskaps and sour cherries), trees, shrubs, vegetables and bulbs. Coarse sawdust from lumber mills is preferred to fine sawdust that may cake and repel water. These wood products decompose relatively quickly, so nitrogen depletion is sometimes a problem. Spread compost, alfalfa pellts or screened manure over the soil surface prior to application to be on the safe side.

Evergreen needles and cones – While there is a pervasive and perverse tendency in our landscapes to grow lawns under evergreens, the natural forest floor is carpeted with cones and needles, retaining moisture, supplying nutrients and discouraging the growth of a competitive understorey. Why not emulate nature? Allow your evergreens to develop without humiliation, with their lower branches intact and a natural mulch of their own cones and needles. It's attractive, free, does not compact, allows free water percolation and decomposes slowly.

Straw – Weed-free wheat, rye, oat and barley straw is readily available, inexpensive and useful with coarse-textured plantings where appearance is not important: orchards, bush fruit, shelter belts, newly planted trees and cool-season vegetables. Straw conserves moisture, suppresses weed growth, allows good water percolation and cools the soil.

Flax shives or straw – A by-product of flax straw used in the production of specialty paper, shives forms a dense cover, fine enough for herbaceous plants but also useful on tree/shrub borders. Like the linen cloth used to wrap Egyptian mummies, it is extremely long lasting. If shives are unavailable, use chopped flax straw.

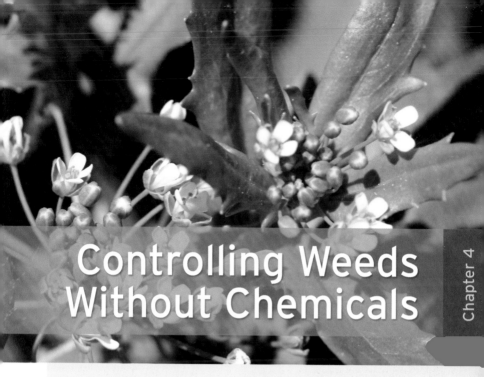

Controlling Weeds Without Chemicals

Weeds can withstand adversity, and they positively thrive where conditions are favourable – in our landscapes and gardens! Generally speaking, weeds lack culinary or aesthetic value, but perhaps it is true that weeds are simply plants growing where they are not wanted. Dandelions have many culinary uses and are quite attractive; bluegrass is a valuable plant in the lawn but a weed in the vegetable garden.

The vast majority of our prairie weeds hail from Europe and Asia, and some (like dandelions) were deliberately introduced as food or medicinal plants by early settlers. Despite their potential usefulness under the right circumstances however, weeds compete with desirable plants for space, sunlight, nutrients and water. They also harbour many insects and diseases, often providing overwintering sites. And some weeds have allelopathic characteristics: they produce growth regulators that inhibit the germination and growth of the very plants you are trying to nourish. All of these are good reasons to keep your yard and garden weed-free.

The white flowers of stinkweed produce a prodigious amount of seeds.

There are a number of ways to control weeds without using chemicals. While there is no magic one-step/no-effort formula, your grandmother had it right in one sense: A hoe will do the job while saving you the cost of a summer membership in the local gym. She also knew that weeds are easier to control when young and should always be dealt with before they go to seed, or you'll have more weeds. But there are other ways to control weeds besides the working end of a hoe. Weed-control methods generally can be divided into two categories – cultural methods, and less toxic alternatives.

Cultural methods of weed control relate to how we take care of our landscape. They usually employ mechanical means (a hoe, tiller or cultivator) or some form of mulch.

If you do some of your weeding on your knees, a Japanese hand hoe is indispensible and will last for years.

Less toxic alternatives include commercial products, most of which have been introduced and registered in the last decade, such as corn gluten and horticultural vinegar. These products are less toxic but achieve levels of control similar to chemical pesticides. Biological controls focus on the natural enemies of weeds. These are insects and diseases that have been doing their job for centuries, but have only recently been registered for use and made available commercially.

Cultural methods

Growing conditions

Provide good growing conditions (light, water, spacing, fertility, soil) so your plantings are able to compete effectively with weeds that invade the area.

Weed thoroughly

Hoe, pull or dig and destroy weeds to prevent them from seeding (remember, they are prolific, and you don't want more weeds) and to deplete the nutrients from the roots of perennial weeds. You may need to pull larger weeds or those growing close to valuable plant specimens. Hoeing, cultivating and tilling are effective but must be done in a timely manner. Annual weeds are usually easier to kill if their roots are exposed, and it's easiest to control weeds by hoeing

Solarization

Solarization was developed in Israel for the control of weeds on commercial vegetable farms in the 1970s. It has also been used extensively in California and Texas. Clear polyethylene film is laid over moist, fallow soil, and left in place for four to eight weeks during the heat of the summer. Because summer temperatures in Texas, California and Israel are considerably higher than those in western Canada, weed seeds and seedlings in these areas will probably be killed to a greater depth than we can hope to achieve on the prairies. In our climate it is probably more beneficial to use heavy black plastic to exclude light for an extended period of time to kill existing vegetation. This will not be as effective at killing weed seeds in the soil, but experience has shown that often we do not reach temperatures high enough to accomplish this.

This method can be used to kill existing lawn grass for new flower or vegetable beds or to kill areas that you want to reseed. First mow the grass as short as possible to ensure that the plastic is in as close contact to the soil as possible for maximum heating. Water the area to a depth of 10 to 15 cm (4-6 in.) and apply the plastic. Check the crowns and the roots of the grass under the plastic after four weeks. If the roots are black rather than white, you've done it! If they still appear healthy, leave the plastic for a few more weeks and check again. If the roots are dead, you can rototill and reseed or prepare the area for planting.

when they're small. There are a variety of hoes that are effective for cutting off small weeds. Hoeing techniques also vary, but if you keep the hoe nearly parallel to the ground, effort is less, and you move a minimum of soil. The idea is to shallowly cultivate soil, not to chop weeds. Till in the fall and early spring. In vegetable gardens, a small rototiller works well for the edges and between rows, but it's still a down-on-your-knees job to weed within the rows. If you can obtain a Japanese hand hoe, it is a wonderful and durable tool.

Control perennial weeds

Before planting beds or borders with trees, shrubs or perennials, control perennial weeds such as Canada thistle, quack grass and dandelions by digging, cultivating or "solarizing". Perennial weeds may require several cultivations to deplete the roots of their food supplies, leaving them vulnerable to winterkill. Ideally, pull them when they are at about the four-leaf stage for maximum effectiveness.

Mulch

Annual weed seeds may remain viable for up to thirty years, but most annual weeds will not germinate without light. Mulches are effective at controlling germination if they are thick and dense enough (10 cm/4 in.) to exclude light. Some vegetable gardeners mulch the area between the rows with commercially available biodegradable mulches, some of which are available in rolls that can be cut to length and are either recycled paper products or films made from starch.

Mulching permanent planting beds will prevent germination of perennial weed seeds and make seedlings that do germinate easier to pull.

Made from recycled paper products or starch films, biodegradable mulches are ideal for vegetable gardens.

Mow

Some annual weeds may be controlled by mowing just before they flower and set seed. Frequency of mowing will depend on the type of weeds.

Torching - CAUTION!

When playing with fire, caution is in order. During dry weather, torching tall weeds at the edge of a yard might have disastrous results if the fire were to burn out of control. Torching weeds near valuable plant specimens might control more than the gardener had bargained for. Check with your local municipality regarding burning bans and bylaws.

Control weeds adjacent to your planting beds to keep them from spreading to your garden. Before they develop seeds, mow weeds on the edges of planting beds and rough areas around lawns to prevent the seeds from ending up in the garden or lawn.

Keep clean

Clean equipment and footwear before entering a garden area. Use clean soil and planting stock to avoid bringing weeds into your landscape.

Scorch and scald

If you have weeds coming up between the blocks of a concrete block driveway, germinating in a gravel path or growing in an open cultivated area, the top growth can be killed by burning them with a torch. Some garden supply stores sell torches that are designed for this purpose. They don't control the roots of established perennial weeds like dandelions, sow thistle or quack grass, but can rid a pathway of annual weeds or seedlings. You could also douse them with boiling water.

Less toxic alternatives

Corn gluten meal

Corn gluten meal controls dandelion, lamb's quarters, portulaca, redroot pigweed and plantain. It is now becoming widely available in a number of formulations. It doesn't have any effect on established annual or perennial weeds, but if spread in early spring (about two weeks before weed seeds begin to germinate) it will significantly reduce weed seedling establishment. A word of caution: corn gluten inhibits germination of all seeds, so if you use it for weed control in a vegetable garden or other area where you grow plants from seed, wait until the seedlings are well established before application.

Corn gluten meal has no effect on established plants but will significantly reduce seedling germination.

Horticultural vinegar

Horticultural vinegar has a much higher concentration of acetic acid than household vinegar (20 percent instead of 5 percent). It "burns off" or desiccates foliage when sprayed. We've found it to be effective against small seedling weeds, but it only burns the tops of perennial weeds with established roots, so needs to be sprayed repeatedly to be effective on these.

Fiesta™

Fiesta™ is a chelated iron product that has recently been patented and introduced as a herbicide. It has a very low toxicity to mammals and controls a variety of broadleaf weeds in grass, including dandelions, white clover, black medic, Canada thistle, common chickweed and narrow-leaved plantain. Its action is quick, and reports claim that levels of control are comparable to multi-part chemical herbicides (such as 2,4-D, mecoprop and dicamba). It should not be applied to a lawn more than twice in a season.

Biological control measures

In their native growing areas, most of the plants that are significant weed problems are kept in check by a variety of insects and diseases that limit their spread and numbers. Researchers who study biological control return to the areas where these weeds are native to find these insects and diseases.

Sarritor® is a fungal disease registered for the control of dandelions.

Insects that consume weeds, such as the beetles that attack leafy spurge and the weevils that attack the seed heads of Canada thistle, are under investigation. Thus far, neither of these has proven practical for weed control in the home garden, and no products have yet been registered, but there has been some success.

Sarritor® is a new product registered for the control of dandelions. See Chapter 7, Lawns for more information.

Controlling common perennial weeds

Canada thistle

Canada thistle (*Cirsium arvense*) is an aggressive, long-lived perennial that grows from deep running rootstocks. It is an occasional problem in established lawns. The leaves form a rosette before bolting into a flowering stem that rises up to 1 m (3 ft) in height bearing rose-purple thistle-like flowers. The leaves are lance-shaped and deeply incised with sharp prickles at the tips of incisions.

SOLUTIONS:

Cultural methods:

- Mow and hand-pull thistles from established lawns and planting beds to prevent their spread and to deplete food reserves in the roots. It may take up to two years of careful control by cultivation to eliminate roots.

Less toxic alternatives:

- Recent research is looking at infecting Canada thistle with a disease, *Pseudomonas syringae* pv. *tagetis*, as a control method.

Although called Canada thistle, this is actually a weed introduced from Eurasia.

Creeping bellflower

Creeping bellflower (*Campanula rapunculoides*) is a particularly difficult perennial weed to control, especially in lawns. The purple, bell-shaped flowers are indeed attractive and can initially suck innocent gardeners into thinking it's not too bad a plant. But beware! The roots are thick and creeping, allowing it to spread by both rhizomes and seeds (3,000 to 15,000 per plant annually.)

Stems are 60 to 100 cm (2–3 ft) tall. The leaves are alternate; lower leaves are heart-shaped and coarsely

Canada thistle is easily recognized by its rose-purple flowers.

Don't be lured into what can become a permanent relationship by the purple flowers. Creeping bellflower is one of the most difficult weeds to eradicate.

toothed, while the upper leaves are lance-shaped and sessile. The flowers develop in one-sided inflorescences along the stem.

SOLUTIONS

Cultural methods:

- Dig out as much of the creeping bellflower as possible.
- Cultivation must be deep and repeated as small pieces of root will quickly regrow.
- Mow or pull the plants before they go to seed.
- A healthy lawn will suppress growth of the bellflower but if it's

established you might be best to tolerate some bellflower foliage in a mowed lawn.

Less toxic alternatives:

- Horticultural vinegar may burn off the top growth.

Dandelion

Dandelion (*Taraxacum officinale*) is a deep-rooted, stemless perennial. It is native to Europe, where it is still grown as a vegetable and medicinal plant. The 1914 edition of *The Standard Cyclopedia of Horticulture* by L. H. Bailey gives instructions on how to grow dandelions, not how to get rid of them! Dandelions are still grown for both culinary and medicinal purposes in many parts of the world. The leaves can be eaten as salad greens in the spring and the flowers used to make dandelion wine; the roots can be dug in fall and dried for use as a coffee substitute.

Remember when we used to tie dandelions in chains and celebrate them?

It's no trick to identify the yellow flowers of a dandelion. The seeds are scattered by the wind. It proliferates by seed or from root pieces in moist soil.

SOLUTIONS:

Cultural methods:

- To kill dandelions, cultivation must be deep and repeated. Dandelions will regrow from root pieces left in the soil. You must re-move at least 10 to 15 cm (4-6 in.) of root to gain significant control.
- Specialized tools and hose-end at-tachments are available to remove dandelions from lawns or perma-nent plantings. Refill any dislodged soil and reseed if in lawn.

Less toxic alternatives:

- Corn gluten meal prevents germination of new seedlings.
- Horticultural vinegar destroys dandelion seedlings and the top growth of established plants.
- Tops can be burned off using a torch on non-flammable surfaces, or by pouring boiling water on them.

Ox-eyed daisy

Ox-eyed daisy (*Leucanthemum vulgare,* syn. *Chrysanthemum leucanthemum*) is a perennial that produces single, white, daisy-like flowers from a basal mat of coarsely divided dark green leaves. Plants produce one to several stems. They spread by stolons and seeds, and are adapted to moist or dry sites. Avoid "wildflower" mixes that contain it.

SOLUTIONS:

Cultural methods:

- Dig out the plants, being sure that all root pieces are removed. Refill the depression that is left and reseed.

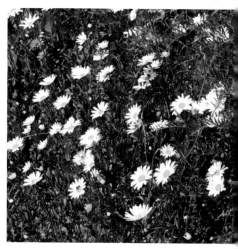

Ox-eyed daisy is particularly harmful in pastures. If consumed by cows, their milk has an off taste.

Perennial sow thistle

Perennial sow thistle (*Sonchus arven-sis*) is a shallow-rooted, spreading perennial. It is seldom a problem in established lawns but can spread quickly in gardens. It grows from a branched, fleshy rhizome which can spread rapidly if top growth is al-lowed to flourish. It is difficult to remove by digging because the much-branched root system is very brittle. Most of the rhizomes grow near the surface of the soil, although roots and rhizomes can penetrate to a depth of about 2 m (6 ft).

Sow thistle has yellow daisy-like flowers. Their leaves are lighter green and less prickly than those of Canada thistle.

Plants develops rosettes of saw-toothed leaves. The hollow flowering stems bolt up to 150 cm (5 ft). If cut, they bleed white sap. The stem branches at the top give rise to a number of yellow, daisy-like flowers. The seed has a tuft of white hairs that propels it on the wind like a parachute.

SOLUTIONS:

Cultural methods:

- Control through repeated cultivation prior to seeding or planting permanent beds.
- Cultivate vegetable gardens and unmulched annual beds every year.
- Dig or pull in mulched beds.
- Remove or mow sow thistles near lawns and permanent planting beds to prevent seeding.

Less toxic alternatives:

- Horticultural vinegar will destroy the top growth.
- On non-flammable surfaces, tops can be burned off with a torch. Boiling water can also be used.

Quack grass

Quack grass (*Elytrigia repens*, syn. *Agropyron repens, Elymus repens*) is a coarse perennial grass that grows from creeping rhizomes. It is aggressive and will cover an area up to 3 m (10 ft) in diameter in a year if left uncontrolled. It grows rapidly if conditions are good and will persist under very harsh conditions. The straw-coloured rhizomes have sharp points and can penetrate tubers and roots of desirable plants.

Quack grass is a particularly harmful weed because it is allelopathic – the rhizomes produce chemicals that reduce the growth of other plants, particularly trees and shrubs. It spreads by seed as well as by rhizomes.

SOLUTIONS:

Cultural methods:

- Solarize using a heavyweight black material such as a pond

Quack grass is an aggressive perennial weed with rhizomes sharp enough to penetrate potato tubers.

The tender shoots of lamb's quarters can be eaten like spinach. The common name comes from the likeness of the leaf to the quarter of a lamb.

liner, which will take from one week to two months depending on temperature.

- Cultivate repeatedly during dry periods to desiccate the rhizomes and deplete their food reserves.
- To eliminate it from small areas, dig the rhizomes and send them to the landfill.
- In an existing lawn, dig them, replace the soil and reseed.

Less-toxic alternatives:

- Spray with horticultural vinegar.
- On non-flammable surfaces, burn off with a torch. Boiling water may also be used.

Controlling common annual weeds

Lamb's quarters

Lamb's quarters (*Chenopodium album*) are fast-growing annual weeds that germinate in warm soil during the summer. The young leaves are triangular with wavy margins and are covered with silvery mealy particles. Plants will grow quickly to up to 1 m (3 ft) in height. Clusters of tiny flowers are produced in leaf axils and at the tops of stems.

SOLUTIONS:

Cultural methods:

- The leaves of lamb's quarters can be harvested and used in a similar fashion to spinach.
- Young seedlings are easily controlled by cultivation, hoeing and pulling.

Less toxic alternatives:

- Spray young plants with horticultural vinegar.

Portulaca

Portulaca (*Portulaca oleracea*) is a succulent, prostrate annual that forms a mat up to 50 cm (20 in.) across. Stems are reddish and fleshy. The tiny alternate leaves are thick and 0.5 to 2.5 cm (0.25–1 in.) long. Small yellow flowers are borne singly in leaf axils and give rise to pointed capsules with many tiny seeds.

Stems can form roots if broken off, easily re-establishing, particularly if the soil is moist. Cultivation at an early stage will kill the tiny seedlings. Germination occurs after a rain in warm weather. Get down low to the ground. If portulaca is germinating in a garden, the surface of the ground will have a purple cast.

Portulaca can be harvested and used for thickening soup or cooked as a mucilaginous porridge.

SOLUTIONS:

Cultural methods:

· Portulaca can be effectively controlled by cultivation only when plants are in the two-leaf stage or earlier.

Redroot pigweed

Redroot pigweed (*Amaranthus retroflexus*) and prostrate pigweed (*Amaranthus blitoides*) are annual weed that germinate once the soil

If portulaca is germinating, the surface of the soil will have a purple cast; that is the best time to control it with a hoe.

One of the most common annual weeds in gardens, its name comes from its red root and popularity among swine.

warms up in early summer. One plant can produce thousands of seeds. Seedlings have dark red stems. Plants grow quickly in warm moist soil, producing clusters of small greenish flowers. Redroot pigweed grows 30 to 50 cm (12–20 in.) in height. Prostrate pigweed, as its name implies, grows flat along the ground and can reach a diameter of up to 60 cm (2 ft).

SOLUTIONS:

Cultural methods:
- Small seedlings of pigweed are easily controlled by cultivation.
- Hoe or pull plants close to desirable plants.

Less toxic alternatives:
- Spray with horticultural vinegar.

Shepherd's purse

An introduced weed from southern Europe, shepherd's purse (*Capsella bursa-pastoris*) arrived in North America prior to 1672 and has traditionally had a variety of medicinal and culinary uses.

It is a rosette-forming annual or winter annual. The branched flowering stems rise to 15 to 50 cm (6–20 in.) with many tiny four-petalled flowers. It can grow as a winter annual, but will also germinate through the summer. Seed pods are an inverted triangle.

SOLUTIONS:

Cultural methods:
- Cultivate to destroy seedlings.
- Hoe or pull seedlings close to

trees, shrubs or perennials before the seeds are dispersed.

"The peppery pods add flavour to soups and salads. The young leaves, when boiled, are palatable and taste like cabbage." Robert Shosteck, 1974

Stinkweed

Stinkweed (*Thlaspi arvense*) grows as an annual or winter annual. The round to oblong leaves are smooth, with prominent veins on the underside. The leaves have a distinctive sharp odour when crushed, hence the common

The foliage of stinkweed has an unpleasant odour when crushed, which gives it its common name.

name. The petiole, or leaf stem, is about as long as the blade and may have one or two shallow indentations. The plant develops into a rosette. If it germinates in the fall it will overwinter in this rosette stage. Numerous small white flowers develop in spring or early summer on stems that are 20 to 50 cm (8–18 in.) high.

Stinkweed produces prodigious quantities of seed. If allowed to go to seed, the area can have a thick carpet of seedlings the following year. Seeds may remain viable in the soil for many years, germinating under favourable conditions when they are exposed to light. Stinkweed generally grows where nitrogen levels in the soil are high. It is very competitive for nutrients and moisture if allowed to grow thickly.

SOLUTIONS:

Cultural methods:

- Cultivate the soil to kill small seedlings. If the plants start to bolt, mow the tops before tilling or cultivating.
- Late fall cultivation controls seedlings and helps to prevent stinkweed from getting ahead of you in the first few warm days of spring. Rosettes that have survived winter are difficult to kill and can survive if only one small root remains attached to the soil.
- Pull if close to desired plants.

Chapter 5

Controlling Insects Without Chemicals

"Cultural" controls refer to the ways in which we care for our gardens and landscapes without the use of chemicals or biological controls. They are simple, sometimes labour-intensive, sometimes old-fashioned, and often innovative gardening methods. Gardeners have always squashed bugs and exposed insects to their predators by cultivating between rows of vegetables, whether in Egypt or in Edam (and probably in Eden). Row covers and pantyhose are more recent introductions.

Preserve the natural enemies of insect pests

You cannot – and should not – keep your yard entirely insect free. Most insects are beneficial. Avoid pesticide use and grow a diversity of plants (especially flowers for nectar and pollen) to encourage these insect predators and parasites to stay in the garden.

Lady beetles can consume up to 25 aphids per day. They also prey on scale insects, spider mites and mealy bugs.

Most insects have natural enemies that keep them under control in nature. By avoiding the use of chemical pesticides (which are generally broad-spectrum) and using methods that are targeted specifically to the pest, you can preserve many of their natural enemies. Some natural predators and parasites include lady beetles, carabid beetles, tachinid flies, minute pirate bugs, parasitic wasps, hover flies, lacewings, nematodes and a variety of spiders.

Hand-pick

Minor infestations of soft-bodied insects like aphids or sawfly larvae can be controlled by squashing. You can also hand-pick them, dropping them into a pail of water with a little bit of oil or soap on the surface. Colorado potato beetles, slugs and caterpillars are also easily hand-picked. Once they have been drowned, simply dispose of them.

Prune out insect nests or galls

Gall-forming insects such as eastern spruce adelgid and nest-dwelling insects like the eastern tent caterpillar can be controlled, especially if infestations are minor, by pruning the galls or nests out of the tree or shrub and destroying them.

You need to catch them at the right time. Gall-forming insects only remain in the protective galls for part of their life cycle. Eastern tent caterpillars leave the nest to feed during the day; destroy the nest in the late evening to catch them at home.

Forest tent caterpillar egg clusters are easily removed in early spring before they hatch.

Remove eggs

Some insects lay their eggs in distinctive clusters. Some are geometric with a beautiful symmetry. If you can find and identify them, destroy the egg clusters to prevent an infestation later in the year or the following season. Forest tent caterpillars lay eggs on small branches in distinctive bands that can be easily scraped off.

Cultivate off-season

Remove plants and cultivate vegetable gardens and annual flower beds in early spring prior to planting and in late fall after harvest. This exposes over-wintering insects, their eggs and larvae, leaving them vulnerable to cold temperatures and birds. This practice can go a long way towards reducing insect pest populations.

Spray with water

Aphids, spider mites and other small insects and mites can be discouraged and dislodged by a strong stream of cold water aimed at the plants on which they are feeding. You may have to repeat this treatment every two to three days for as long as they keep coming back, but it will reduce their numbers and limit damage. Be sure to spray both sides of the leaves to remove a higher proportion of the offending insects.

Use transplants rather than direct seeding

If certain vegetables have a history of being chomped on or totally con-sumed by insects, try using bedding plants or transplants instead of seeding them directly into the soil. Insects may eat the same amount, but larger, more vigorous plants can tolerate the damage because a smaller percentage of their total leaf area is lost.

Transplants can tolerate insect damage that would destroy smaller seedlings.

Remove fallen leaves from around infested plants

Clean up the garden in the fall. Some insects overwinter in the leaf litter in the garden or under trees or shrubs. These include bad guys such as the im-ported currant worm, as well as good guys like lady beetles. However, if you have insect problems, clean the litter from the garden in the fall and destroy the above-ground parts of infested herbaceous plants. If you've had insect problems on a particular vegetable or flower, destroy the foliage by burning or burying or sending it to the landfill rather than composting.

Yellow sticky traps attract whiteflies, aphids and fungus gnats, while blue ones attract thrips.

Use sticky traps

Designed to immobilize the adult flies prior to egg laying, sticky traps can attract and capture insects. Yellow sticky traps attract whiteflies, aphids and fungus gnats. Blue sticky traps attract thrips. Tree bands painted with Tanglefoot® can be used to capture wingless female cankerworms. Red traps resembling apples are used to attract apple maggot flies. These can be home- made or purchased, and should be set out by the last week in June. Although most are not lovely to look at, place them where they are visible on the edge of the canopy. The sticky substance must be reapplied as needed. The downside of most traps is that they will catch beneficial as well as harmful insects.

Tanglefoot® traps female cankerworms as they climb up the trunks of trees. Unfortunately, both traps and tree bands also catch beneficial insects.

Use barriers to protect vegetables and fruit

Commercial row covers exclude insects that eat vegetables, lay their eggs on them or transmit disease, as well as providing a certain amount of frost protection and enhanced germination. Snagged pantyhose also have a remarkable afterlife as barriers in our vegetable gardens. They can be especially useful in protecting cobs of corn from the European corn borer. They can also be used on cabbage, cauliflower and broccoli to exclude flea beetles from feeding or white butterflies from egg laying. The flexible nature of pantyhose allows for expansion as vegetables develop.

Row covers exclude insects that eat vegetables or lay their eggs on them. Ensure that the fabric is in firm contact with the soil.

Homemade or purchased commercially, plant collars are placed around individual transplants, such as young tomatoes, peppers, cabbage and cauliflower, to protect against cutworm damage. The collar should be wide enough to contain the plant but not crush it, and tall enough so it can be inserted about 5 cm (2 in.) into the soil and leave 7 cm (3 in.) above the soil. Use juice cans, coffee cans, milk cartons, large Styrofoam cups and other household objects, with their tops and bottoms removed.

Circular mats placed around the stem of transplants prevent flies from laying eggs at their base; they are especially useful in controlling onion maggots.

Place tarps under fruiting bushes to prevent larvae that develop in fruit from entering the soil to pupate. This interrupts the life cycle of the pest. The infested fruit can be destroyed. Mats are particularly useful for preventing flies from laying their eggs at the base of members of the onion family. At the same time, they discourage weeds and conserve moisture. Mats are made of paper or rubber carpet underlay about 20 cm (8 in.) square, with a diagonal cut made from an edge to the centre so that they can be laid flat on the soil around the stems of susceptible plants. Commercially available mulch rolls, made from fabric, recycled paper or other products, can be cut to size as required. Some are more permanent, others biodegradable.

Aluminum foil mulches

Aluminum foil placed shiny side up on the soil surface around vegetables of high value that are susceptible to aphids and leafhoppers may act as a repellent. The glare is said to disorient the insects. They may also discourage thrips. The downside? Not aesthetically pleasing!

Less toxic alternatives

When we're looking for methods to control insects in the garden, we should look for controls that are the least harmful to people and the environment. Our choices should be products that have low toxicity to people and mammals, and we should target the pest insect while preserving beneficial insects where possible. Less toxic alternatives include substances like soaps or oils, which suffocate insects, and diatomaceous earth, which dehydrates them. Some of the controls offered here, like borax, sugar and iron, are indeed chemicals. Others are biological and use living organisms that are the natural enemies of these pests. As with all pesticide products, follow label instructions carefully.

Pure soaps

Use with caution, as even mild household soap may damage plants. Test it by applying the solution to a small part of the plant. Combine one to two teaspoons of mild liquid dishwashing soap (such as Dove or Ivory), pure soap (such as Ivory or Dr. Bonner's) or castile soap with 1 l (1 qt) of water. Do not use extra-strength, grease-cutting or antibacterial soap.

Insecticidal soaps

Insecticidal soaps are potassium fatty-acid soaps formulated for the control of insects. They disrupt the cell membranes of insects and quickly cause death. Soaps are most effective against small soft-bodied insects such as aphids, leafhoppers, whiteflies, thrips and spider mites. They can also be used to control caterpillars, but normally do not harm larger beneficial flying insects such as bees and syrphid flies. To be effective, the soap needs to contact the offending insect. Insecticidal soaps lose their effectiveness when they dry out, so it is best to spray in early morning or evening, or during cloudy weather. They have little residual activity.

Natural, but safe?

PYRETHRINS Once grown extensively in East Africa and exported as a cash crop, pyrethrins are natural insecticides produced by certain *Chrysanthemum* species (*C. cinerariaefolium, C. cineum*). A broad-spectrum insecticide, they kill beneficial as well as harmful insects. They contain poisons that rapidly penetrate the nervous systems of insects. However, a "knockdown dose" does not necessarily kill insects, and insects can break down pyrethrins into non-toxic chemicals. To enhance their potency, synergists are commonly added to pyrethrins. Piperonyl butoxide, which is derived from sesame seeds but has been shown to affect hormone-related organs, is the most common of these synergists. There are presently no formulas sold in Canada that do not include piperonyl butoxide. It is prohibited for organic production.

Pyrethrins are natural but are by no means safe. They are a common cause of insecticide poisonings. Symptoms of poisoning include headaches, dizziness and difficulty breathing. In addition, they can trigger life-threatening allergic responses. Pyrethrins are extremely toxic to aquatic life, are toxic to bees and are slightly toxic to birds. Some cats are particularly sensitive to pyrethrins. If you are using these products, you should avoid inhaling them.

Safer's Trounce®, a pyrethrin-soap product, is registered for control of chinch bugs. It is available as a concentrate or a hose-end product. It is not approved for organic production and should be avoided.

GARLIC Commonly used as a mosquito repellent and to kill aphids and imported cabbage worm, garlic is the basis of many homemade remedies. A broad-based insecticide, it is effective but does not discriminate between the "good guys" and the "bad guys," killing lady beetles along with aphids.

NEEM OIL Neem oil is pressed from the seeds of the neem tree (*Azadirachta indica*), which is native to Southeast Asia, where it has a variety of uses. It is considered a broad-spectrum pesticide with toxicity to fish. It is brown in colour, with a bitter taste and a garlicky, sulphurous smell. Its active ingredient, azadirachtin, interrupts the moulting cycle of insects, causing their death. It also acts as an antifeedant or repellent.

It is sold in Canada only as a leaf shine, but is sometimes recommended as a natural product for insect and disease control. However, because of human health concerns, neem is *not* registered as a pesticide by the Pest Management Regulatory Agency of Health Canada. Lack of registration also means that its biochemical composition and concentration will be variable. *It is illegal to buy, sell, or use neem oil as a pesticide in Canada.*

Insecticidal soaps have low toxicity to mammals, but they may be irritating to eyes or skin. Wear rubber gloves and goggles when spraying. They are toxic to certain plants, so you should test-spray a small area and wait twenty-four to forty-eight hours to assess the damage before spraying the entire plant. To minimize the risk of plant damage, avoid spraying during drought conditions or when the plant is under stress.

Insecticidal soaps damage cell membranes of soft-bodied insects such as aphids, leafhoppers, whiteflies, thrips and spider mites.

Diatomaceous earth

Diatomaceous earth is a finely ground powder made from the fossilized remains of diatoms, which are microscopic shelled algae. The powder consists of sharp grains of silica that will cut the exoskeleton of insects, causing them to dehydrate and die within a few hours or days. It isn't selective and will kill beneficial insects along with pests. The efficacy of diatomaceous earth is diminished if it gets wet, which limits its usefulness outdoors. It has a very low toxicity to mammals, but you should wear a mask to protect your lungs when you apply it.

Diatomaceous earth works by dehydration, but is not selective and kills beneficial insects along with pests.

Horticultural oils

Horticultural oils have long been used for the control of certain plant pests. Traditionally, they were used only when the plants were dormant to avoid damage to leaves, but more refined superior oils can be used during the growing season. The term "dormant oil" now refers only to the application timing.

Traditional oils are derived from petroleum. Oils that are high in paraffin and low in naphthalene are more toxic to insects and less toxic to plants. Vegetable oil products are now on the market. The most effective insecticidal vegetable oils are based on cottonseed oil or soybean oil.

Oils kill insects by blocking their airways and smothering them or by interfering with normal metabolism. For effective control, the insects must be covered with oil. The oils evaporate rapidly and pose little risk to humans or other mammals if used according to directions.

Biological control methods

Biological control measures make use of living organisms to control harmful insects. They are registered only after extensive testing to ensure both their efficacy as a control agent and their safety to people and beneficial organisms. Your grandmother was probably well aware of lady beetles; Bt (*Bacillus thuringiensis*) not so much. But both involve the same principles.

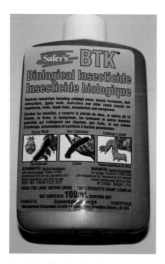

Bacillus thuringiensis

Bacillus thuringiensis, or Bt, is a spore-forming bacteria isolated from silkworms in Japan in 1902. They are mass-produced through fermentation for commercial use. Different strains are used to control different insect pests, ranging from caterpillars to mosquito larvae. Bt is now a patented, commercially available biocontrol for many pests. It works within a few hours by paralyzing the gut of the pest insect. Feeding and movement stop, and death follows within a few days. It only works on the larvae of insects with an alkaline

Bacillus thuringiensis kurstaki is a bacteria that causes the larvae of butterflies and moths such as the cabbage butterfly moth to stop feeding.

Different Bts for different insects

RACE OF BT	CLASS OF INSECT
Bacillus thuringiensis kurstaki (BtK)	Lepidoptera - butterflies and moths
Bacillus thuringiensis Israelensis (BtI)	Diptera - mosquitoes and black flies
Bacillus thuringiensis tenebrionis (BtT)	Coleptera - beetles*
Bacillus thuringiensis san diego (BtS)	Coleptera - beetles*

* These products are not registered in Canada at the time of publication.

gut such as Lepidoptera (butterflies and moths), Diptera (flies) and some beetles. It does not affect bees, wasps or ants. Insects enclosed within folded or rolled leaves or webs cannot be controlled with Bt.

Bt formulations are considered to be non-toxic to mammals and birds, although you should avoid inhaling them or getting them in open cuts or in your eyes. Different formulations are specific to specific types of insects so they are less likely to harm predator insects than chemical insecticides. Bt is not known to cause injury to plants.

When using Bt, you should spray it on the undersides of leaves as well as the topsides. Many caterpillars feed from the undersides of leaves and Bt is broken down by sunlight.

Nematodes

Steinernema and *Heterorhabditis* nematodes control a range of ground-dwelling and wood-boring insects, such as white grubs and lilac (ash) borers. *Steinernema carpocapsae* can seek out and destroy caterpillars. These nematode species have symbiotic bacteria in their gut. Once the nematode is within the harmful insect, it defecates these bacteria, which then kill the host within a few days.

Beneficial nematodes are sold partially desiccated and combined with a clay gel that mixes easily with water to form a suspension. They should be kept in the refrigerator until they are used. The entire package should be mixed with water and applied with a sprayer or watering can. These nematodes are very prone to drying out, so applications should not be made at midday. Apply them as a soil drench in the evening, irrigating with at least 1 cm (0.5 in.) of water. They must be kept moist for a week and are generally inactive at temperatures below 12°C (53.6°F).

Thousands of tiny *Heterorhabditis* nematodes have parasitized this larva.

Commercial nematode suspensions should be refrigerated until applied as a soil drench.

Predator insects

These are the "beneficial insects" that prey on those that eat our plants. All of these predator insects are part of the natural environment. Prior to the widespread use of broad-spectrum chemical insecticides introduced after World War II, these were the "good guys" that kept the harmful insects under control. Some of these predators are native, others introduced. Purposefully introduced predators are carefully monitored for possible negative effects prior to their introduction.

Lady beetles

Lady beetles are yellow, orange or red beetles with distinctive patterns of black spots. Larvae resemble small alligators and are orange with blue and black markings. Both larvae and adults are voracious feeders on aphids and other small insects and will each eat twenty-five or more aphids per day. Lady beetles can be purchased for release in the greenhouse or garden. They can be quite effective for aphid

It's more effective to encourage native lady beetles by not using broad-spectrum insecticides than it is to purchase introduced species that often fly away.

control in the greenhouse, but outdoors they often fly away. It is usually more effective to encourage native lady beetle populations by not using broad-spectrum insecticides.

Green lacewings

Green lacewings (family *Chrysopidae*) are a slender green insect up to 15 mm (0.6 in.) in length with four lacy wings.

The larvae are long, segmented, alligator-like and are often called "aphid lions." Both larvae and adults are voracious predators of aphids. They will also feed on thrips, mealy bugs and whiteflies. They are available from insectaries in California and are shipped as eggs or larvae, so are more likely to be effective in the garden than lady beetles that are shipped as adults.

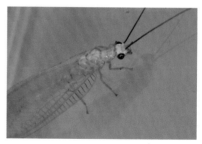

Its delicate appearance to the contrary, green lacewings are voracious predators of aphids.

Minute pirate bugs

Minute pirate bugs (*Orius tristicolor, O. insidiosus*) are tiny predators that are approximately 2 mm (0.1 in.) in length when mature. They are black with white wing patches and eat thrips, whiteflies, aphids, mites, small caterpillars and insect eggs. They will feed on nectar and pollen when insects are scarce but cannot survive on plants alone. Their feeding habits mean that it is easier to keep them in the garden than many other predator insects.

Plants that attract them include angelica, Canada anemone, goldenrod, penstemon, shrubby potentilla and coneflower.

Although tiny, minute pirate bugs prey on thrips, whiteflies, aphids, mites, small caterpillars and insect eggs.

Big-eyed bugs

Big-eyed bugs (*Geocoris* species) are tiny, 3 mm (0.1 in.), black or grey true bugs with proportionately large eyes. They feed on mites, small caterpillars, lygus bugs, thrips, whiteflies and insect eggs.

Big-eyed bugs feed on mites, small caterpillars, lygus bugs, thrips, whiteflies and insect eggs.

Carabid beetles

Carabid beetles are ground beetles that are predators of many pest species, such as slugs and cutworms.

Like lady beetles, they are at home under a mulch. The species *Pterostichus vulgaris* has been studied as a control for the strawberry root weevil.

Happy under a mulch, carabid beetles are ground beetles that consume many pest species including slugs and cutworms.

Hover fly

Hover fly larvae (*Syrphidae*) prey on aphids and thrips.

Parasitic insects

These insects lay their eggs within the bodies or eggs of harmful insects. The eggs hatch into larvae that consume the host. Not what bedtime stories are all about, but nevertheless effective. They are usually used indoors and in greenhouses, and little is known about how they perform in the garden, with the exception of

Birds

Many species of birds are natural controls for insect pests. Examples include swallows, which feed on mosquitoes, flies and moths; woodpeckers, which eat wood-boring insects; and chickadees and nuthatches, which eat insects from under the bark of trees. If bylaws permit, a few chickens go a long way in controlling insects.

Peristenus digoneutis, which is being studied for outdoor control of lygus bugs in strawberries, and tachinid flies, some of which are native.

Peristenus digoneutis

Peristenus digoneutis is a braconid wasp that is parasitic on the lygus bugs that are so damaging to our fruit crops. It has been established in southern Ontario and Quebec and the northeastern United States to control this pest.

A braconid wasp parasitizing a caterpillar.

Encarsia formosa

Encarsia formosa is a small, 0.6 mm (0.02 in.) long parasitic wasp that is commercially available for control of whitefly in greenhouses. Whiteflies must be present for the wasp to survive. It consumes nymphs and lays one egg in each nymph. Very little is known of how *Encarsia* will act outdoors.

Amblyseius cucumeris

Amblyseius cucumeris are predatory mites that are 0.5 mm (0.02 in.) in length. They are effective against thrips and mites in greenhouses. They are not effective outdoors because they require temperatures between 19° and 27°C (66–80° F) and relative humidity between 65 and 72 percent to do their job.

Braconid wasps lay their eggs within the larvae of other insects. The small white projections on this hornworm are the cocoons formed by the wasp larvae.

Tachinid flies

Tachinid flies are large flies, 5 to 15 mm (0.2 to 0.6 in.) in length that mimic bees in their colouring and flight. They are parasites on the larvae of moths, sawflies and beetles. Most tachinids lay eggs directly on the bodies of their hosts. The larvae hatch and burrow into the host and feed internally. Some tachinids lay their eggs on foliage that is then eaten by host insects. The larvae hatch in the host's gut and burrow through the gut wall.

Adult tachinids are large, bright orange and black flies that parasitize the larvae of moths, sawflies and beetles.

Beauveria bassiana

Beauveria bassiana is a fungus that causes a disease called white muscardine. When spores come in contact with the cuticle of an insect, they germinate and penetrate the insect's body. There they produce toxins and rob the insect of nutrients until it dies. Once the insect dies, the fungus grows back out through the cuticle and covers the now dead insect with a white mould that releases numerous spores into the environment.

It is slow-acting and needs a moist environment, but will kill leaf-feeding insects such as whiteflies, aphids, thrips, mealy bugs, leafhoppers and

A European corn borer larva infected with the fungus *Beauvaeria bassiana*, causing white muscardine disease within 7–10 days.

weevils. Products with *Beauveria* as the active ingredient that are registered in Canada include BotaniGuard®, Mycotrol® and Naturalis®.

Spinosad

Discovered in a soil sample in the Caribbean in the 1980s, *Saccharopolyspora spinosa,* the basis of spinosad, is a soil-dwelling actinomycete species (a filamentous bacteria). A broad-spectrum larvicide, it works by disrupting the insect's nervous system, causing loss of muscle control. Insects stop feeding and die fairly quickly. It is highly toxic to bees, so avoid spraying when plants are in flower. It should be applied at the peak of egg laying.

Spinosad is registered for control of insects in turf, outdoor ornamentals, fruits and vegetables. It controls thrips, eastern tent caterpillar, imported cabbage worm, diamondback moth, European corn borer and the Colorado potato beetle. Entrust® 80W and GF-120 NF Naturalyte® are two formulations registered for use in Canada; organic commercial orchardists are using them to control apple maggots.

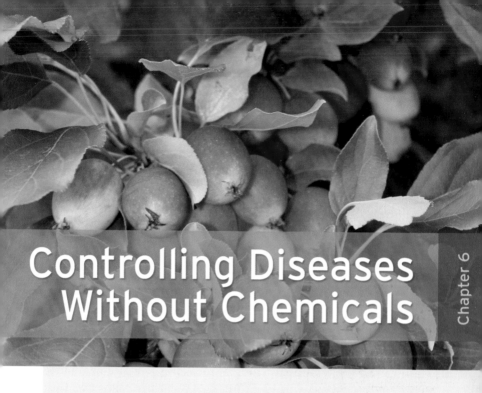

Controlling Diseases Without Chemicals

For a plant to develop a disease, three factors are required: 1) a disease organism; 2) a susceptible host; and 3) conditions that favour the disease organism. Many disease organisms exist in our landscapes, but generally in small populations. They may go virtually unnoticed. Most are dependent on environmental conditions to flourish. But when these conditions are favourable and susceptible host plants plentiful, look out!

We can't control the weather, but we can avoid monoculture, improve air circulation, use resistant varieties and give our plants optimum growing conditions.

Cultural methods

Protect plants from winter injury

Many trees, shrubs and fruit trees are most susceptible to winter injury when they are just getting established. Winter injury causes damage to tissues that can open these woody plants to infection.

Many apples, such as 'Dolgo' crabapple, have been selected for resistance to fireblight.

Sunscald generally shows up on the south or west side of the trunk, but light reflected by glass or siding can also be damaging.

Trunk protectors prevent both sunscald and rodent and deer damage to young trees.

Mulching the soil reduces the depth to which frost penetrates and moderates the cycles of freezing and thawing. It keeps the soil frozen a little longer in the spring and slows growth at a time when plants might be injured by hard frost. As well, watering trees and shrubs well in late fall prevents desiccation over the winter.

Tree trunks can be damaged by rapid temperature changes in late winter, when the bark warms in the strengthening sun, activating the metabolism, but then freezes rapidly as night falls. This can result in a condition known as sunscald, where the bark is damaged or the trunk is split with frost cracks. Wrap the trunk of the tree with burlap or with white plastic tree wraps that shade it from the sun. Fruit trees are sometimes protected by painting the trunks of young trees with white latex paint (diluted with an equal amount of water). The white plastic or paint reflects light rather than absorbing the sun's heat.

Shade barriers can be used to protect evergreens – particularly cedars – from late winter sun. Strong sun in late winter can desiccate needles at a time when the soil is frozen and roots are unable to draw replacement water from the soil. Put stakes on the south and west sides of the tree and staple burlap to the stakes to provide shade for the tree.

Prune to promote strong structure

Pruning trees and shrubs can improve their structure and vigour. Trees with good structure are less prone to breakage due to wind and weather. Proper pruning eliminates broken branches or stubs that provide entry points for disease. If crowns of trees are opened up, air circulation and

Cut your losses!

Many plant diseases, such as late blight of tomatoes, have no cure. Once infection occurs, the plant will simply die. If you have identified an incurable disease, your best action is to get rid of the plant as quickly as possible to avoid spreading the disease to neighbouring plants. The kindest course for both garden and gardener is a quick removal.

light penetration are increased. This can limit the development of fungal diseases on the leaves or needles.

Diseases such as fireblight and black knot can be controlled by pruning diseased wood at least 30 cm (12 in.) below the point of infection. When removing diseased branches, prune in dry weather and disinfect tools between each cut by dipping them in a 5 percent bleach solution or in 70 percent isopropyl alcohol. Diseased branches should be removed from the site and burned or buried.

Irrigate carefully

Use drip instead of overhead irrigation to avoid wetting plant foliage, which may encourage the growth of fungal diseases. Splashing water can also spread spores and bacteria. Avoid these situations by using trickle irrigation, other low-flow emitters or rubber soaker hoses placed just below soil level. If you do use overhead irrigation, water early in the day so the plants dry before night.

Perforated hoses, placed just below soil level, conserve water while reducing the spread of spores and bacteria by water splash.

When deer browse on trees and shrubs, as well as damaging their structure, they leave wounds that may provide entry for disease.

Protect plants from damage

Diseases are often spread by insects feeding on leaves or invading the bark of trees. Leaf-feeding insects such as aphids and leafhoppers may carry bacterial and viral diseases. Controlling these insect "vectors" will help to control the spread of these diseases.

Rodents and deer also feed on the leaves or bark of trees. They can leave wounds that provide entry to disease, or they can spread disease from tree to tree.

Avoid working in the wet

Avoid working with plants when they are wet due to either irrigation or natural precipitation. A film of water provides the germination habitat required for the spores of many fungal species. You and your boots, gloves and tools can inadvertently carry disease organisms from one plant to another. Hold off weeding, picking, pruning or supporting plants until they are dry.

Harvest carefully

Harvest fruit and vegetables as they ripen. Don't wait until they are overripe. Handle them carefully to avoid inflicting any wounds or injuries that might act as entry points for disease organisms. This is especially important for root crops, where a problem that began with a fork going through a potato tuber ends up with a disease that shows up in storage months later.

Less toxic alternatives

Yes, these are indeed "chemicals." Some have been used for a very long time. Although they are considered less toxic compared to modern chemical pesticides, gardeners should nonetheless take precautions when using them, following label directions.

Copper-based fungicides

Copper-based fungicides such as fixed copper (50 percent copper oxychloride), Bordeaux mixture (copper sulphate and hydrated lime) and copper hydroxide have been used for centuries for the control of certain fungal diseases, bacterial diseases and mites. They should be applied to dry foliage to the point of runoff. Fixed copper fungicide is easier to prepare and use than Bordeaux mixture, but Bordeaux mixture is more persistent, particularly during cold, rainy periods.

These compounds are accepted for organic production, but they are poisons that must be handled with appropriate precautions. They must be kept out of reach of children. Applicators should wear goggles or a face shield, chemical-resistant gloves and protective clothing. Care must be taken to avoid contaminating aquatic habitats when spraying, cleaning equipment and disposing of waste. Avoid contaminating food and feed.

Sulphur, lime sulphur

Microscopic sulphur (finely ground sulphur) and lime sulphur have long been used to control fungal diseases, bacteria and mites. Both are corrosive, so take appropriate precautions when handling them. Keep out of reach of children, avoid contact with skin and eyes, and avoid breathing spray mist or dust. Avoid contaminating aquatic habitats.

Lime sulphur is often used with dormant oil as a "clean-up" spray to suppress fungal and bacterial diseases and insects on dormant fruit trees. It can also be applied to the foliage, but it may cause injury or defoliation so it should be tested on small areas before overall spraying. Spray to the point of runoff. Do not spray when the foliage is wet.

Making Bordeaux mixture

Use 1 g copper sulphate ($CuSO_4$) to 0.5–1.0 g fresh hydrated lime ($Ca(OH)_2$) per 1 l (1 qt) water. Dissolve the copper sulphate in half the water and the hydrated lime in the other half. Mix the two solutions together by pouring through a cheesecloth or similar cloth to strain out any undissolved lime. Keep the mixture agitated in the sprayer. Once the mixture is prepared, it should be used the same day.

Microscopic sulphur should be mixed with sufficient water for thorough coverage of the foliage. Do not apply when temperatures are above 25°C (77° F) or if humidity is high, or if these conditions are expected during the three days following application. Do not use within thirty days following an oil-spray application.

Sodium bicarbonate, potassium bicarbonate

Baking soda (sodium bicarbonate $NaHCO_3$) has long been employed as a home remedy for fungal diseases, especially powdery mildew, but it can injure plants. Potassium bicarbonate ($KHCO_3$), also used in baking, is now being used to control some fungal diseases. These chemicals are considered harmless to mammals and to the environment if used appropriately. Commercial fungicides incorporate potassium bicarbonate, sodium bicarbonate and other ingredients that act as spreaders and stickers to enhance control and lengthen the application intervals.

Chelated iron

If lime-induced chlorosis is present, apply chelates according to label directions. Foliar applications are less expensive and more effective than soil

Lime-induced chlorosis, a foliar disorder, is caused by a high pH soil that makes iron unavailable. The leaf blade is yellow while the veins remain green.

> ## Disinfect your tools
>
> Rubbing alcohol and bleach are useful for disinfecting tools, especially between cuts when pruning. Rubbing alcohol (70 percent isopropyl alcohol) is particularly useful when pruning plants that are disease-infected. Bleach is generally diluted with water to a 5 percent solution by adding 250 ml bleach to 5 l of water (1 c/gal). Tools can be dipped or wiped with this solution to destroy disease organisms and prevent them from being spread. It can also be used to disinfect seeds or lily bulbs that are being scaled for use in propagation, as well as lily or gladiola bulbs that are suspected of harbouring insects or disease organisms.

applications in the short term. Soil applications are more likely to have a carry-over effect into the next season.

Biological control methods

Trichoderma

Trichoderma harzianum Rifai strain *KRL-AG2* (RootShield® Biological Fungicide) is a fungus that suppresses disease organisms that attack the roots of plants. It is registered only for use in greenhouses on tomatoes, cucumbers and ornamentals. Trials have shown that *Trichoderma* has low toxicity to humans and other mammals and there is little risk from exposure. Because it is registered for use in greenhouses, there is little concern of release into the environment.

Bacillus subtilis

Bacillus subtilis (Serenade® MAX, Serenade® ASO, Rhapsody® ASO, Serenade® Garden Concentrate and Serenade® Garden Ready) is a bacteria that is registered for the control of a variety of fungal and bacterial diseases, including downy mildew, powdery mildew, white mould, grey mould and sclerotinia rot.

Streptomyces griseoviridis

Streptomyces griseoviridis (Mycostop® Biofungicide) is registered for control of damping off, root and stem rot and *Fusarium* wilt in greenhouses. Mycostop® can be mixed dry with seed as a seed treatment. It may also be mixed with planting media or with water to form a suspension for dipping cuttings. It can be applied as a soil drench or sprayed on leaves, flowers and fruit for suppression of grey mould.

Pseudomonas fluorescens

Pseudomonas fluorescens A506 (Blightban©A506), *Pantoea agglomerans* strain C9-1 (Blightban C9-1, Bloomtime™) and *Bacillus subtilis* strain QST 713 (Serenade®) are bacteria strains that will colonize flowering shoots and reduce the incidence of fireblight infection.

Agrobacterium radiobacter

Agrobacterium radiobacter (Dygall™) is a bacterial control agent that prevents infection by crown gall (*Agrobacterium tumefaciens*). It will not control existing infections. It is usually used as a dip when plants are being transplanted.

Lawns

Lawns give us play areas for children and pets, provide a place for us to socialize and are the foreground of our gardens. Most of us can't imagine our landscapes without a sward of mowed green grass.

But our love of lawns is a big part of our environmental problem. Yes, a healthy lawn takes in carbon dioxide from the air and gives back oxygen. Its roots hold the soil, prevent erosion, and absorb and slow the runoff of rainwater. In a traditional landscape, however, lawns consume large amounts of chemical fertilizer and pesticides. These chemicals are tracked into our homes on the feet of people and pets, and pollute our streams and groundwater. Mowing uses energy (either human, electrical or gas), produces pollution from gas-powered mowers and trimmers, and generates large amounts of organic waste in the form of grass clippings, which are often gathered and sent to landfill sites rather than being composted or used as mulch.

The benefits of changing lawn-care practices from traditional to more environmentally sensitive methods are very significant.

Lawns set off other features in the landscape and provide a place to play and to socialize.

Chapter 7

Some additional effort is required, especially at first, but it is possible to have attractive lawns that are healthy and make a positive contribution to the environment.

The most important factor in growing such a lawn is building healthy soil. With the addition of compost and manure, you encourage organisms that help control diseases and harmful insects. The cost may be higher for the first few years, but as the level of organic matter in the soil increases, a reserve of nutrients will be available to plants as they need them, and you can reduce the amount that you apply each year.

As you consider switching to organic lawn care, you may decide to plant less grass, substituting trees, shrubs and ground covers in lawn areas that are not actually used as lawn, thereby saving on maintenance and mowing. Planting attractive flowers and shrubs to create focal points takes attention away from grass that is less than perfect at certain times of the year. If parts of your lawn are in deep shade, use shade-loving ground covers to avoid thin grass that is difficult to maintain. Likewise, areas that are droughty can be replaced with beds of drought-tolerant perennials and shrubs.

White clover: friend or foe?

Until the late 1940s, white clover (*Trifolium repens*) was an important component of quality grass seed mixtures. With the introduction of chemical weed killers, it became a weed because there was no chemical that would preserve grass and clover and kill other weeds. Its reputation as a weed was sealed by publicity from companies selling weed-control chemicals.

If clover is incorporated as 5 percent of a lawn mixture, it will provide about half of the nitrogen needed for optimum health of the lawn. Clover lawns can often be grown with no additional fertilizer by returning the clippings to the lawn. They will remain green during drought conditions and will resist pests and diseases more successfully.

To achieve a 5 percent cover of clover, seed about 30 g of clover seed per 100 m² (1 oz/1,000 ft²). If you are using corn gluten meal to control weed germination, remember to skip a treatment before you seed the clover.

You may also decide to plant a lawn that incorporates species other than grasses. Before the widespread use of chemicals to control lawn weeds, white Dutch clover was often added to lawn grass seed mixtures. The clover remains green during extended periods of drought, while at the same time fixing nitrogen that can be utilized by the grass. Another alternative to a traditional lawn is a wildflower meadow of hardy species that thrive under local conditions and attract butterflies, bees and birds to your yard. Plant wildflowers, ground covers and native grasses on slopes that are difficult to mow or on the edges of large properties.

Maintaining a healthy lawn

Healthy soil is the key to a healthy lawn. Good levels of nutrients promote vigorous growth that crowds out weeds. The percentage of the three major nutrients – nitrogen (N), phosphate (P), and potassium (K) – is indicated by the numbers listed on fertilizer packages. Nitrogen promotes top growth, phosphate promotes root growth and potassium promotes growth that is more resistant to injury and cold temperatures. In addition, grass plants extract other nutrients from the soil such as calcium, iron and magnesium. A soil test is important to evaluate the existing nutrient levels in the soil and to determine additional nutrients needed for optimum growing conditions.

Compost tea – brew a tonic for your grass

Applied frequently to your lawn, especially in the first two years after converting to organic management, compost tea will help to restore a healthy balance of micro-organisms that will control many fungal diseases.

To make compost tea, place a jute bag or an old pair of pantyhose filled with finished compost in a pail of water and leave it to brew for about thirty-six hours. Avoid using manures and don't add extra nutrients, but do add air. Using an aquarium pump, bubble air through the water while the tea is brewing to maintain good aeration. This will promote the growth of aerobic bacteria and fungi and discourage harmful anaerobic bacteria. This method should prevent growth of E. coli, but in the interest of safety you should avoid applying it to food crops. Good compost tea should have a sweet, earthy smell. If it has an offensive odour it has probably become anaerobic and should be discarded.

Compost tea should be applied once it is ready because the numbers of beneficial organisms will soon begin to decline. Apply approximately 1 l per 100 m^2 (1 qt/1,000 ft^2) with a watering can, hose-end sprayer or siphon.

Planting a new organic lawn

Developing an organic lawn is much like planting a conventional lawn, but there is more emphasis on preparation, thus making it easier to maintain without using chemicals. The key steps are:

1. Evaluate the drainage patterns to ensure that water drains away from buildings and won't pool on your lawn. Rough grade the area to provide a smooth drainage surface.

2. Ensure that the area is free of perennial weeds. Dig out the roots of quack grass, dandelions, sow thistle and other perennial weeds, or "solarise" the area in the heat of the summer. (See Chapter 4, page 37.)

3. Evaluate the quality and depth of the existing topsoil. Dig down to 30 cm (1 ft). What is the soil texture? A soil test should indicate the existing level of available nutrients and what nutrients you need to add. It will also tell you the pH, and if it is necessary to add amendments to modify it. (See Chapter 3, Growing Healthier Plants.)

4. Is there adequate topsoil to establish deep-rooted grass plants? Fifteen to twenty centimetres (6–8 in.) of fertile, well-worked topsoil allows the grass to form deep roots. An adequate depth of good soil saves maintenance expense and water in the long run and gives you a much better lawn. If you need to purchase topsoil, it should be of good texture, be free of weed roots, have a pH of 6.0 to 7.5, and be free of chemical residues. Add compost or manure along with bone meal to provide nutrients.

5. Once the topsoil and amendments are in place, work it to establish a fine seedbed. Then rake it with a wide landscape rake and pack it level and firm. When you are finished, footsteps should leave prints that are no more than 1 cm (0.5 in.) deep.

6. Select a grass mixture that is adapted to your area and to the microclimate of your yard. Sod provides quick cover, but seed is often preferable when planting an organic lawn. It allows you to choose a seed mixture that is suited to the variety of conditions in your yard.

7. Use a high quality blend of Canada No. 1 certified seed. If the creeping red fescue and perennial rye grass seeds are endophyte-enhanced (a type of fungus that grows within the roots), they will be resistant to chinch bugs and sod webworms. A seed mixture with Kentucky bluegrass, creeping red fescue and perennial rye grass will be more suited to shaded and drought-prone areas and will resist insect pests better than a lawn composed of only Kentucky bluegrass.

8. Water frequently until the grass is established. Once the grass is established, move to a regular maintenance program.

The nutrient needs of an organic lawn are met in a variety of ways. If you use corn gluten meal to control seedling weeds, it will provide about half of the lawn's nutrient needs. Nitrogen can also be added by top-dressing with compost, composted manure or processed sewage sludge. Other sources of nutrients are alfalfa pellets, blood meal (rich in nitrogen) and bone meal (high in calcium and phosphorus). The nitrogen in these organic fertilizers is released slowly, and because the release is affected by temperature and moisture, more is available when the grass needs it most. If your soil has been neglected and has a low level of beneficial micro-organisms, it will benefit from the addition of compost tea. Repeated applications of compost will improve the texture and the nutrient- and water-holding capacity of the soil.

Returning grass clippings to the lawn also returns nutrients to the soil, providing up to half the lawn's requirement for nitrogen. Clippings do not contribute to thatch buildup (a layer of dead plant material that can build up at the soil surface) in a healthy organic lawn. Adequate levels of fertility will speed the breakdown of organic matter and help to control thatch buildup. You may, however, wish to remove leaves and clippings in the fall that might contribute to snow mould infections. These should be added to your compost pile or applied as mulch to perennial borders.

Water your lawn deeply but less frequently to promote a deep, healthy root system. A deeply rooted lawn will survive periods of drought, although watering during extended dry periods will help to keep the turf healthy and dense. Apply enough water each time to soak down below the root zone of the grass plants. Monitor rainfall and supplement if needed to ensure 2.5 to 3.75 cm (1–1.5 in.) of water per week from late spring until late summer. Sandy soils should be watered more frequently, with less water at each watering. Don't use automatic watering systems that water at set times. These systems waste water and can damage the lawn by oversaturating during wet periods. For more information, see the water and soil sections in Chapter 3, Growing Healthier Plants.

Thatch

Excessive accumulation of thatch predisposes a lawn to disease and may provide habitat for chinch bugs and sod webworms. Thatch can be removed by coring, vertical mowing with machines designed to remove plugs or cut vertical strips in the thatch, or raking with a rake designed for the purpose.

Cultural practices

Mowing

Cutting the grass removes part of its ability to manufacture food and to shade the soil. A high mowing height is crucial to maintaining a thick, vigorous turf. This requires more frequent mowing. Bluegrass lawns should be mowed to 6 to 7.5 cm (2.5–3 in.).

Return the clippings to the lawn as a source of organic fertility. If you mow frequently, the clippings will be short, will break down quickly and won't contribute to thatch formation. Mow the lawn with the bagging attachment in place before growth starts in the spring to remove excessive thatch. The clippings can be added to the compost pile. Also bag the clippings when dandelions are going to seed. The seeds should only be added to compost if you are confident that the pile will go to a temperature above 66°C (150° F). You should also bag the clippings to remove fallen leaves in the autumn, adding them to the compost pile unless there is an excess of weed seeds.

Soil modification

When weeds become established in a lawn, it often tells the gardener something about the soil. Compacted soil favours quack grass. Compaction combined with poor drainage favours plantain. Weed problems can be alleviated by aeration, improved drainage and the addition of organic matter in the form of compost.

Borax and sugar

We can't possibly eliminate ants from our lawns; they are everywhere and they provide a valuable service of aerating the soil. However, they sometimes become pests when they build mounds in the lawn. They can be controlled with a mixture of borax and sugar. The sugar attracts the ants, and they carry the borax back to the nest, where it kills the queen and brood, destroying the nest. Because the borax is harmful to humans and pets, it needs to be kept covered. One way to make a trap is to poke a few holes in the sides of a tuna can, put the borax and sugar mixture in it, and cover it with aluminum foil held in place with a rubber band. There are also commercial ant bait preparations with borax or boric acid as their active ingredient.

Weed control methods

Certain perennial weeds are significant problems in turf and should be controlled. Annual weeds may be a problem with newly seeded lawns, but in most instances they can be controlled by mowing. Once the grass becomes established, it will crowd them out, and if the grass shades the soil, few annual weeds will grow in the second or subsequent years.

The most important method of controlling weeds in a lawn is to grow a thick, healthy turf. It competes with weeds that germinate and it masks the few weeds that inevitably become established. Aim for close to perfect: If your lawn is 90 percent turf and 10 percent weeds, weeds are only noticed on close examination, and that should be good enough for the environmentally conscious gardener. Maintain a healthy lawn through proper fertilization, watering and mowing. Grass and other ground cover plants will compete better with weeds and will suppress them if their own growing conditions are optimal.

A dense turf shades the ground, preventing weed seed germination. Mowing grass too short leaves it vulnerable to weed infestation. Grass that is mowed at 6 to 7.5 cm (2.5 to 3 in.) will have sufficient leaf surface to maintain a healthy root system while shading the ground to discourage weed seed germination. Mow frequently and remove no more than one-third of the leaf surface at each mowing.

If you have patches of lawn where the grass has died or thinned over the

White clover in a lawn grass mixture will provide about half of its requirement for nitrogen.

winter, you should over-seed. If your soil is in good condition, over-seeding with quality seed in the early fall helps your lawn outcompete a number of troublesome weeds.

Weed problems can be alleviated by aeration, improvement of drainage and the addition of organic matter in the form of compost. If weeds are few in number or are concentrated in a small area, it may be practical to remove them by digging or pulling. If there are patches where weeds have taken over, you may want to kill the weeds and the grass by solarization before cultivating and reseeding.

Solarization

Solarization is a process that kills all vegetation, including the grass. (See Chapter 4, Controlling Weeds Without Chemicals.) Once the vegetation is killed, it's important to add compost, work it in and reseed as soon as possible before weeds have a chance to become re-established.

Biological and organic methods

At the recommended rate for weed control, corn gluten meal also supplies about half of the lawn's annual requirement for nitrogen in a slow-release form. If you return the clippings to the lawn as well, this may be all the fertilizer you need. A word of caution: corn gluten inhibits germination of all seeds, so if you're thinking of seeding or over-seeding with grass seed, you should take a year off from using corn gluten meal.

Recent research into biological weed control has had some success. Sarritor® is a new product registered for the control of dandelions. It's a strain of *Sclerontinia minor*, a fungal disease that is specific to dandelions and has no residual effect. It works within 5 to 7 days. It won't hurt grass, but avoid applying it to other broadleaf plants.

Diagnostic chart

Use the following diagnostic chart to help you identify what's troubling your lawn, then refer to the Insects or Diseases sections of this chapter for in-depth information on the problem and how to avoid, control or eradicate it.

DIAGNOSTIC CHART

Common insects and diseases of lawns

PLANT	PART AFFECTED	SYMPTOMS	LIKELY PROBLEM
Lawn grass	foliage, crowns	Areas browning off, poor growth	**Glassy cutworm** (Insects)
Lawn grass	foliage	Localized yellowing or browning	**Hairy chinch bug** (Insects)
Lawn grass	foliage	Small brown patches merge to form large brown patches	**Sod webworm** (Insects)
Lawn grass	foliage	Expanding dark green rings; mushrooms sometimes grow in the rings	**Fairy ring** (Diseases)
Lawn grass	foliage	Grey mouldy patches in the lawn in spring	**Grey snow mould** (Diseases)
Lawn grass	foliage, crowns	Mouldy patches that are pink, especially at the edges	**Pink snow mould** (Diseases)

Insects

Glassy cutworm

Glassy cutworm (*Apamea devastator*) is an occasional pest of prairie lawns. It attacks creeping red fescue and bluegrass. Adults are nondescript greyish miller moths with a wingspan of 35 to 40 mm (1.5 in.). They lay eggs here and there on blades of grass in August. The eggs are white when laid but darken as they develop. The larvae hatch, move underground and begin feeding in the fall. The glossy,

Glassy cutworms are most often a problem on newly seeded lawns or during drought.

semi-translucent larvae are white or grey, without body markings but with a reddish-brown head. They are normally about half grown by winter, and resume feeding in the spring.

Mature larvae are 35 to 40 mm (1.5 in.) in length. Once fully grown, they pupate, emerging as moths from July to early September.

WHAT TO LOOK FOR: Moderate outbreaks may not be noticed if growing conditions are favourable. Severe outbreaks under drought conditions can cause a serious reduction in the stand of grass plants. If you have areas of lawn that are browning off and show poor growth in the fall or spring, dig around damaged plants and look for cutworms.

SOLUTIONS:

Cultural methods:

- Under organic management, glassy cutworms are normally controlled by a host of predatory ground beetles, parasitic wasps and flies. If you have a severe outbreak during a drought period, there are biological methods of control.

Less toxic alternatives:

- Bt *kurstaki* (*Bacillus thuringiensis* var. *kurstaki*) works reasonably well for control provided it is applied with adequate irrigation water. It is most effective when the cutworms are small in early fall. Apply it in the evening as the cutworms are nocturnal. It works best if applied two to three weeks after a period of peak egg laying.
- Nematodes (*Steinernema carpocapsae*) can seek out and destroy caterpillars. Apply to moist soil in the evening and keep the soil moist for about two weeks after application.

Hairy chinch bugs

Adult hairy chinch bugs (*Blissus leucopterus hirtus*) are black or grayish-black bugs. Their front wings are white with a black spot. They are about 3.5 cm (1.25 in.) long. During their life cycle, they pass through five growth stages, or instars, with a different outer shell between moults. The first instar has a bright orange abdomen with a cream stripe across it and a brown head and thorax. Through the instar stages, the colour darkens to purplish and then to black. In some local populations, most will have short wings that reach only halfway down the abdomen.

Adult chinch bugs overwinter in the thatch and become active in the spring when temperatures reach 21°C (70° F). Adults mate and lay eggs. The eggs hatch in eight to thirty days, depending on temperature. By mid-July, the first generation matures and lays eggs to begin a second generation. By

Hairy chinch bug nymphs and adults do the most damage to lawns in late summer.

this time, damage is usually consider-able. The second generation normally matures in late August and into September. When cold weather arrives, the adults seek protected areas in the thatch to spend the winter.

WHAT TO LOOK FOR: Chinch bugs pierce grass leaf blades and stems at the crown and suck the sap, causing grass to wilt and yellow. Watch for localized yellowing and browning of grass, especially in areas prone to drying. Early damage appears as irregular patches of straw-coloured grass. These areas may be dead, and expand despite watering. To check for chinch bugs, cut both ends out of a large can (such as a coffee can). Push it down into the turf at the edges of the affected area and fill it with soapy water. If chinch bugs are present, they will float to the surface.

SOLUTIONS:

Cultural methods:

- Early infestations can be con-trolled by sucking up the bugs with a shop vacuum. Use this technique before an infestation gets out of control.

Less toxic alternatives:

- Use household soap.
- Diatomaceous earth - treat infested areas as well as the areas immediately adjacent at a rate of 1 kg/100 m² (1 lb/500 ft²). Do not treat the entire lawn.

Sod webworm

Sod webworms (several species in the genus *Crambus*) are larvae of several species of beige or grayish-white moths, approximately 1 cm (0.5 in.) in length, with a wingspan of 2 to 2.5 cm (0.8–1 in.). These may be seen flying in zigzag patterns across the lawn in the evening laying eggs. The green or greyish brown larvae are generally less than 2.5 cm (1 in.) in length. They feed on the grass at the level of the thatch by chewing off the leaf blades and pulling them into tunnels to eat. Sod webworms usually feed at night.

Chinch bug soap and sheet trap

(Health Canada version)

Mix 30 ml (1 oz) dishwashing soap with 7 l (1.5 gal) water and drench a small area of lawn, about 0.2 m² (2 ft²). A larger area of lawn can be treated by using a hose attachment. The chinch bugs will crawl to the surface to escape the soap.

Lay a flannel sheet over the treated area and wait ten to fifteen minutes. The chinch bugs will crawl onto the sheet, where their feet will become trapped in the flannel nap. They can then be vacuumed off the sheet or drowned in a bucket.

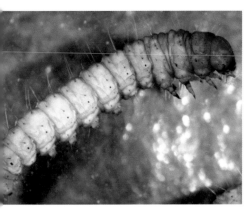

Sod webworm larvae spin tunnels in the thatch.

Some species have one generation per year, while others produce two.

WHAT TO LOOK FOR: Small brown patches, which can enlarge if the infestation is severe, merge and form large brown patches. If you suspect sod webworms, you can force the caterpillars to the surface by pushing a coffee can that has been cut open at both ends into the sod and filling it with soapy water. They will float to the surface of the water.

PREVENTION:

Cultural methods:

- Control thatch in the lawn.
- To reduce the severity of sod webworm infestations, implement appropriate fertilizer and irrigation practices. Water deeply but not too often, and maintain fertility by additions of compost, corn gluten meal or alfalfa pellets twice a year.
- Ground beetles and rove beetles are natural enemies of sod webworms. Preserve them by avoiding use of chemical insecticides.

SOLUTIONS:

Less toxic alternatives:

- Bt *kurstaki* is effective against young larvae.
- *Steinernema* nematodes are an effective control for sod webworms.
- Turf grasses containing fungal endophytes are resistant to webworms.

Sod webworm adults emerge to lay eggs. They can produce up to three generations per year in May, July and September.

Diseases

Lawn diseases fall into two groups: cool-season diseases, which are active during the fall, winter and spring, and warm-season diseases, which are active during the heat of summer. Damage from snow mould occurs during the winter when low-temperature organisms are active and ice limits gas exchange from the turf surface. Others, like dollar spot, attack during periods of excessive moisture when warm days and cool nights keep the grass wet for extended periods.

Well-maintained lawns are quite resistant to most diseases. Lawn diseases like anthracnose and basal rot (*Colletotrichum graminicola*), brown patch (*Rhizoctonia solani*) and damping off (*Pythium, Fusarium, Helminthosporium* and *Rhizoctonia*) are seldom evident if good cultural practices are followed. Conditions that promote disease are excessive moisture and excessive nitrogen fertilizer. If you have problems, improve the drainage, control thatch and don't apply excessive nitrogen and water to the lawn.

Attention to drainage is critical to disease resistance. Regrade to eliminate low areas where water accumulates on the lawn. Water your lawn in the morning to avoid water remaining on the grass overnight. Irrigate less frequently but deeply to encourage deep, healthy root systems.

Maintain good fertility, but avoid synthetic nitrogen. Apply compost tea, which enhances the number of beneficial bacteria in the soil, thus displacing pathogenic organisms.

Fairy ring

Fairy ring (*Marasmius oreades* and other fungal species) results from the breakdown of organic matter by various species of fungi in the soil. When the conditions are right, fungal fruiting bodies – mushrooms – develop. Fairy rings can appear in any species of grass used as lawn, and usually develop where there is undecayed wood in the soil. Although it is very difficult to

Fairy ring is characterized by rings of dark green grass with rings of dead grass beside them.

eradicate, there are ways to manage the lawn to minimize its effects.

WHAT TO LOOK FOR: Dark green, ever-expanding rings in the lawn. Mushrooms may appear in the rings.

SOLUTIONS:

Cultural methods:

- Fertilize and water the grass regularly to minimize the colour difference between affected and unaffected areas.

Fairy ring is a result of mushrooms breaking down organic matter in the soil.

- Spike the area with a long-tined manure fork to a depth of approximately 30 cm (1 ft) to improve water penetration, and water frequently for two weeks.

Snow mould

Snow mould appears as the snow melts in the spring. Grey snow mould (*Typhula*) and pink snow mould (*Fusarium nivale* and *Microdochium nivale*) are caused by different organisms and, although similar in appearance when exposed as the snow melts in the spring, they are quite different in seriousness. Grey snow mould only infects the leaves of the grass. Pink snow mould infects the roots as well as the leaves. It appears in the spring but can also appear as a *Fusarium* patch during cool, wet weather in the autumn.

WHAT TO LOOK FOR: Grey snow mould appears as grey mouldy patches in the lawn. Pink snow mould has a pinkish colour, especially at the edges of the mouldy patches.

SOLUTIONS:

Cultural methods:

- With grey snow mould, if the snow is raked to speed melting, the grass will recover as it begins to grow.
- Grey snow mould infections are usually diminished if compost is applied regularly.
- The first line of defence against pink snow mould is to improve drainage, control thatch and avoid over-fertilizing.
- Compost tea will help to displace pathogens with beneficial organisms and control disease.

Grey snow mould is seen as the snow melts. It only affects the leaves of the grass.

Pink snow mould attacks the crown and causes more serious damage.

Chapter 8

Vegetables

Growing organic vegetables is an extremely satisfying endeavour. Nothing beats digging those first new potatoes or brushing off the soil and eating a freshly pulled carrot in the garden. And since the price of supermarket organic produce is generally higher than non-organic produce, why not grow your own? The vegetables are closer and fresher, and you know that what your family is eating is chemical-free.

Granted, an infestation of Colorado potato beetles or an outbreak of aster yellows can make the experience less satisfying and more stressful, and the outcome less bountiful. But growing vegetables organically is no more difficult than it would be with chemicals – it's just a different approach, and a whole lot more environmentally friendly.

Nothing beats freshly dug carrots from your own garden.
A little cosmetic damage is always permissible.

The sheer number of insects, diseases and disorders that can occur in a vegetable garden can be daunting, but take courage! Prairie gardeners can garden for years without coming across the great majority of them. And since even conventional pesticides seldom offer a quick fix, preventative, non-chemical measures really are the best policy.

Many problems can be avoided by following the advice in Chapter 2, Getting Started and Chapter 3, Growing Healthier Plants. Use good sanitation and cultural practices as well as crop rotation, timing and barriers. Plant recommended, resistant or tolerant varieties. If problems do occur, try less toxic alternatives and natural predators and parasites. These ideas will help you bring a bountiful, chemical-free harvest to your table. Remember, extreme control measures are seldom warranted. A little cosmetic damage is always permissible.

Know your enemy!

Figuring out who is doing what to whom in a vegetable garden can be very obvious or downright difficult. A tomato hornworm is one of those in-your-face insects. Once you've seen one, you know them for life. Happily, that first encounter will likely be your last, as tomato hornworms are not that common. Colorado potato beetles and slugs are also easy to identify, but sadly you may develop an ongoing relationship with them. Sometimes, though, figuring out which pest is infesting your garden involves getting down to ground level and having a close look. When Sara was a child, her father would walk through the garden or the forest with her and play a game he called "Let's see who's home," as he turned over a log or a rock and proceeded to identify the insects "at home." Some insects are less obvious and require a bit of sleuthing. Some,

Rhubarb, a mainstay of prairie gardens, signals the first pie of spring.

Aphids are very small. Others, such as flea beetles or leafhoppers, jump or fly away at the least hint of disturbance. If you can't see it, you may have to identify the insect based on the damage it has caused.

Diseases can be even more difficult to identify. You may see the damage, but the culprits are microscopic. Yet some are easy: if your peas have a powdery white coating, you can be pretty sure the problem is powdery mildew, a fungal disease.

The culprit may, in fact, be you, or at least the weather. Many people think they have a insect or disease in their garden, but some plant problems are due to growing conditions or environmental stress such as too much, too little or uneven watering; nutrient deficiencies; or even cold temperatures. These are called disorders.

Cultural practices

Crop rotation

Rotating vegetables has two major benefits. First, it prevents the depletion of certain nutrients in the garden soil that would occur if the same vegetables were planted in the same place year after year. Second, it prevents the buildup of harmful insects and diseases.

Vegetables differ in their nutrient or fertilizer requirements. Corn and members of the cabbage family (cabbage, cauliflower, broccoli and Brussels sprouts) require a great deal of nitrogen. If planted continuously in the same area of the garden, they will quickly use up the nitrogen available in the soil. By grouping together vegetables that have similar nutritional needs and planting them in a different area of the garden each year, you allow the soil to replenish lost minerals.

Inoculants

If your garden is new, or if legume crops (peas and beans) have never been grown there, it may be necessary to "inoculate" or introduce *Rhizobium* so they can fix nitrogen. Inoculants are available commercially in granular form and are usually sprinkled in the furrow along with the seed as it is being sowed. Inoculants are also incorporated as a coating on some seed. Once peas and beans have been grown in a garden, *Rhizobium* will be present naturally in the soil, and it will no longer be necessary to apply the inoculant.

Peas that are supported off the ground have better air circulation and are less likely to succumb to disease.

If some vegetables are "depleters" and use a lot of minerals, others are "replenishers." Peas and beans belong to the legume family. Due to a unique relationship with certain soil bacteria called *Rhizobium,* legumes are able to "fix" nitrogen from the air, utilize it for their own growth and still produce some in excess for the crops to follow.

The root systems of plants also differ. Some are shallowly rooted (such as lettuce and radishes), while others (potatoes, tomatoes, parsnips, carrots, turnips and beets) are more deeply rooted. Those with shallow roots absorb nutrients from the upper layer of the soil; those with deeper, more extensive root systems absorb minerals from the lower depths of the soil. These types of plants should also be rotated.

The second major advantage of crop rotation is that it discourages the buildup of pest populations. Insect numbers tend to build up in soils repeatedly planted with the same crops. It's like providing pests with a guaranteed annual grocery basket. The basic idea of crop rotation is to grow plants susceptible to a particular pest or disease only once in a period of three or more years in a particular place in your garden.

Crop rotation is most effective when the organisms causing the problem live in the soil for only one or two years. In the absence of their host plants, most root-dwelling fungi (such as *Fusarium* of tomato, potato and strawberry) tend to die out. Crop rotation helps but is less effective against potato scab fungi, which may persist in the soil for many years.

Rotation is good at controlling insects that feed on only one type of vegetable and do not move very far or very fast. These insects will die soon after they emerge in the spring if their food plants are absent. It is seldom effective in controlling insects that are far-ranging (like cabbage butterflies or flea beetles). It is possible that if you scatter members of the cabbage family here and there throughout the vegetable garden, insects might not find them and damage will be less likely to occur, but in a small garden the scattering technique is unlikely to work.

Managing a rotation

Vegetables in the same family are generally infested by the same insects and infected by the same diseases. Thus, for the purpose of rotation, vegetables are generally grouped, and rotated, by family. Among these groupings are:

- Cabbage family: cabbage, cauliflower, Brussels sprouts, kale, broccoli, radish, turnip, rutabaga.
- Legumes: pea, bean.
- Vine crops: squash, pumpkin, cucumber, cantaloupe, watermelon.
- Corn.
- Onion family: onion, shallot, garlic, leek, chive.
- Potato family: potato, tomato, green pepper, eggplant.
- Goosefoot family: beet, Swiss chard, spinach.
- Umbellifera: carrot, celery, parsnip (These are added to the rotation which is most convenient in terms of available space).

Cabbage butterflies attack all members of the cabbage family including cauliflower, Brussels sprouts, kale, broccoli, radish, turnip and rutabaga.

Perennial vegetables such as rhubarb, asparagus and horseradish are not rotated, except if you are replanting the entire patch. Then move them elsewhere.

How do you manage the rotation? Depending of the size of your garden, vegetables may be divided into either four or six major groupings. If your garden is small, try the following four groups: cabbages; legumes; carrots, beets and onions; and vine crops. Divide your garden into four areas and plant a different group in each area every year, beginning the rotation again at the end of four years. If your garden is larger, it may be divided into six areas and rotated on a six-year basis, with the following groupings: cabbages, legumes, vines, corn, onions and potatoes. Goosefoot, umbellifera and herbs may be added to whichever group is convenient.

Vegetable varieties recommended by the University of Saskatchewan

The varieties listed below have been tested over two decades and are recommended based on superior yield, taste, disease and insect resistance, ease of culture and other factors. Although they were originally tested with market gardeners and commercial growers in mind, these varieties are of equal value in the home garden. They are generally available from retail outlets and seed catalogues across the prairies.

BEAN: Delinel, Matador, Strike, Goldrush, Gold Mine, Nash, Provider, Royal Burgundy, Tema

BEAN – BROAD: Broad Bean Express, Aquadulce

BEET: Red Ace, Alto, Merlin, Detroit Supreme, Moneta, Pablo, Formanova, Carillon, Cylindra, Ruby Queen

BROCCOLI: Arcadia, Captain, Eureka, Belstar

BRUSSELS SPROUTS: Diabolo, Jade Cross, Oliver

CABBAGE: Gonzales, Blue Vantage, Platinum Dynasty, Tobia, Huron, Loughton, Megaton, Multikeeper, Princeton, Cairo, Parcel, Bronco, Buscaro, Super Red, Copenhagen Market

CANTALOUPE: Athena, Jaipur, Passport, Aphrodite, Dove, Fastbreak, Goddess, Halona, Gourmet

CARROT: Bolero, Evora, Nantes Coreless, Vitana, Yaya, Royal Chantenay, Sunrise, Uppercut, Magnum, Sugarsnax, Eagle, Enterprize, Tendersnax, Apache, Arrowhead, Rainbow, Napoli, Nelson

CAULIFLOWER: Cumberland, Freedom, Artica, Caspar, Graffiti, Cassius, Minuteman, Wentworth, Sympathy

CELERY: Tango, Picador

CORN: Earlivee, Early Sunglow, Frisky, Polka, Revelation, Geronimo, Trinity, Navajo, Northern Extra Sweet, Passion, Awesome, Seneca Horizon, Fastlane, Optimum, Seneca Tomahawk

CUCUMBER: Cool Breeze, Cross Country, Eureka, Fancipak, Homemade Pickles, Fanfare, Dasher, General Lee, Indio, Marketmore, Speedway, Calypso, Raider, Salad Bush, Morden Early, Dasher II, Potluck, Zapata

EGGPLANT: Black Beauty, Black Bell, Night Shadow, Dusky

KALE: Blue Ridge, Winterbor

KOHLRABI: Early White Vienna

LETTUCE: Salad Bowl, Green Towers, Romulus, Freckles, Tibor, Green Forest, Little Gem, Paris Island Cos, Prizehead, Great Lakes, Cos, Bon Vivant, Buttercrunch, Green Bay, Two Star

ONION – BUNCHING: Alpine, Evergreen, Ishikura, Tokyo Long White, Talon

ONION – RED: Mars, Mercury, Red Beauty

ONION – SPANISH: Vision, Riverside Sweet Spanish, Kelsae Giant

ONION – WHITE: Sterling

ONION – YELLOW: Copra, Nebula, Frontier, Infinity, Fortress, Genesis, Rampart

PARSNIP: Andover, Harris Model, Hollow Crown

PEA: Bolero, Spring, Frosty, Wando

PEPPER – HOT: Cherry Bomb, Mucho Nacho, Thai Dragon, Chili Grande, Ring of Fire, Hungarian Wax

PEPPER – SWEET GREEN: Redstart, Socrates X3R, Fat n Sassy, Giant Marconi, Jumbo Sweet, Oriole, Red Dawn, Revolution, King Arthur, Super Heavyweight

POTATO – MISCELLANEOUS: Caribe, Snowden, Norchip, Penta, Banana, French Fingerling, Russian Blue, All Blue

POTATO – RED: Norland, Viking, Sangre, AC Peregrine

POTATO – RUSSET: Russet Burbank, Goldrush, Ranger Russet, Russet Norkotah

POTATO – WHITE: Shepody

POTATO – YELLOW: Yukon Gold, Bintje

PUMPKIN: Big Autumn, Spirit, Neon, Orange Smoothie, Rouge Vif d' Etampes, Autumn Gold, Jack of All Trades, Lumina, Magic Lantern, Mystic Plus, Prize Winner, Sorcerer, Cotton Candy, Racer, Jack O' Lantern

'Norland' potatoes are less susceptible to common scab and late blight.

RADISH: Crunchy Royale, Fireball, French Breakfast, Easter Egg, Mister Red, Rebel, Easter Egg II

SNOW PEA: Oregon Sugar Pod II, Super Sugar Snap, Sugar Lace, Sugar Ann

SQUASH: Cream of the Crop, Table Ace, Taybelle, Autumn Cup, Buttercup, Sweet Mama, Burgess Buttercup, Sunshine, Super Delight, Sweet Lightning, Delicata, Sweet Dumpling, Early Butternut, Celebration, Ambercup, Sunburst, Butternut, Table Queen

SPAGHETTI SQUASH: Stripetti, Pasta Spaghetti, Small Wonder, Vegetable Spaghetti

SPINACH: Melody, Tyee, Bloomsdale, Sardinia, Correnta

SWISS CHARD: Bright Lights, Large White Ribbed, Silverado, Fordhook Giant, Lucullus

'Shepody' is a white potato recommended by the University of Saskatchewan.

TOMATO: Celebrity, Matina Organic, Sunchief, Sunrise, Lemon Boy, Mama Mia, Roma, Viva Italia, Classica, Daiquiri, Hy-Beef, Mountain Fresh, Sunbrite, Ultra Sonic
TOMATO – HERITAGE: Black Prince, Black Russian, Red Currant, Oxheart
TURNIP: Purple Top White Globe
WATERMELON: Sangria, Sweet Favorite, Crimson Sweet, Sugar Baby, Lantha, Vista, Vanguard
ZUCCHINI SQUASH: Spineless Beauty, Bobcat, Payroll, Onyx, Sungreen

If you wait to sow your onion seeds until after caragana has begun to bloom, the onion maggot fly will have already laid her eggs on your neighbours' onions.

Timing

Timing works through avoidance. Sow seeds and put in transplants so that your vegetables develop when pest populations are at a low level. Use short-season varieties – varieties that require the fewest number of days from sowing or transplanting to harvest – recommended for your area. Try to plant a week or two earlier or later than "normal." This is not always easy on the prairies, where our season is already short.

The classic example of avoidance through timing is the onion maggot. The same number of heat units is required for the adult onion fly to emerge as for caragana and dandelion to begin to flower. Use onion sets or early-maturing onion varieties, and transplant or sow seeds *after* caragana and dandelion have begun to flower. By that time, the fly will have laid her eggs on your neighbours' onions.

If specific pests have been a problem in your garden, find out when they usually emerge in your area by consulting your local agricultural or horticultural extension specialist, Master Gardener Program liaison, or garden centre.

Trap plants

Trap plants are special treats that are of great interest to insects, and thus serve to lure the insects away from the plants in your vegetable garden. It's all a matter of taste – yours and the insects. Colorado potato beetles apparently prefer eggplants to potatoes. As long as you are more interested in potatoes than eggplants, the concept works.

The flip side? You must get rid of the eggplant in a timely fashion, along with its resident Colorado potato beetles, before they overflow the trap plant and spread elsewhere. And some trap plants will attract more insects into your garden than would normally find a home there. Trap plants are best monitored carefully.

Trap plants should be placed at least 3 m (10 ft) away from the desired vegetable, and should be sown or planted one to two weeks prior to the desired vegetable. In theory, the insects will collect on trap plants. Once insects are "in residence," pull out and destroy both the trap plants and the insects they are hosting.

Eggplant works as a "trap plant" for Colorado potato beetles, but might attract more insects into your garden than would normally find a home there.

Row covers

Row covers protect vegetables and fruit by excluding insects that attack food plants or transmit disease, and may also provide frost protection, enhance germination and extend the growing season. Row covers are made of a lightweight synthetic fabric, generally polypropylene, polyester or polyvinyl. Impenetrable to insects, they are available in various lengths and widths. Many gardeners place drip irrigation under the row cover.

"It is very satisfying, after finding cut off seedlings, to scratch around and discover the culprit and then feed it to the chickens."

Cedric Gillott, Professor Emeritus,
Department of Biology, University of Saskatchewan

Using fine mesh netting or row covers on cabbages prevents the cabbage butterfly from laying eggs on them.

Ideally, row covers allow a maximum amount of sunlight, water and air circulation. There is generally a trade-off: heavier fabrics provide more frost protection but less light entry. Lighter weight row covers screen out insects but offer no frost protection. Of course, home gardeners can always throw a blanket or tarp over the row cover if frost is predicted, so lighter weights may be best for non-commercial growers.

Cover plants that have a history of vulnerability to insects as soon as they have been sown or transplanted. On the prairies, row covers are often used to protect members of the cabbage family from the imported cabbage worm. Leave the row cover in place until danger of infestation is past. This may mean until the vegetable has been harvested.

Row covers can be supported with hoops or a frame, or laid directly over the crop they are protecting, in which case they are called "floating" row covers. Use floating row covers for prostrate vegetables such as pumpkins, cucumbers, squash and other vine crops. However, even a slight breeze can cause the growing points of upright plants to be rubbed and damaged by floating row covers, so these vegetables will require some sort of a frame or support. Row covers should be generous enough to allow for the upward and outward expansion of plants as they grow.

In either case, the edges of the row cover should be firmly secured with soil, boards, rocks, rebar or whatever is handy and works. It's critical that insect pests not be able to crawl under the row cover. It may be necessary to lift the edges of the row cover to weed or to allow for insect pollination of some crops during flowering.

Netting is useful to prevent insects such as the saskatoon bud moth or saskatoon sawfly from laying eggs on fruit trees and bushes. Ensure that the mesh size you select is adequate to do the job.

Like mosquito nets, both row covers and nettings should be checked periodically for holes. Store them in a dry place, out of sunlight, when not in use. Most should last a few growing seasons.

Insects

When insects consume our vegetables, it's usually fairly obvious. But sometimes their damage is more insidious. Some are also vectors, transmitting diseases with their mouthparts as they feed on one plant and then another. Aphids and leafhoppers sometimes transmit viruses, and therefore it's a good idea to keep track of what's eating your garden.

The best tools for identifying insects are a magnifying glass and a guide to prairie insects. Bring along a pail of soapy water, a piece of white paper and a resealable plastic bag. Look for damage first. Plants will give you clues to the insect

Aphid-infested dill makes for unappetizing pickles. Aphids are small and some are adept at camouflage, so you'll need to inspect carefully.

that's eating them. If the foliage is stippled or mottled, it's probably a rasping insect such as thrips. If there are obvious holes, it might be a flea beetle. If the leaf margins are ragged, it's probably a caterpillar. As the culprit grows, so will the extent of the damage. If the damage to plants is at a low level, it is generally due to disease keeping the insect population low.

Next, look for actual insects. They will generally be found on the undersides of leaves, the growing tips, the leaf axils and the soil near the base of plants. If you can't see anything but you suspect it's there, flick the leaf so "it" lands on the white paper for easier visibility. A portable yellow sticky trap is also useful. Disturb small jumpy insects in such a way that they'll fly into the trap, and then identify them at your leisure.

If you find an insect, don't automatically assume it's "bad". If you can't identify it, place it in the plastic bag and take it to someone who can: your local extension or agricultural office; Master Gardener office; or garden centre.

Diagnostic chart

Use the diagnostic chart as a starting point. It's organized alphabetically by vegetable, followed by the part of the plant affected, symptoms and likely problem. Follow up by looking up the specific insect, disease, or disorder in the next sections of this chapter.

DIAGNOSTIC CHART

Common insects, diseases and disorders of vegetables

VEGETABLE	PART AFFECTED	SYMPTOMS	LIKELY PROBLEM
Seedlings, many types affected	stem	topples over	Damping off (Diseases)
Asparagus	young spears	curved, bent, misshapen	Apsparagus beetle (Insects)
Bean	seedlings, transplants	cut at soil level	Cutworm (Insects)
Bean	foliage, stems	soft, beige-grey tissue rot	Grey mould (Diseases)
Bean	foliage	yellows, curls and puckers	Aphids (Insects)
Bean	foliage	water-soaked spots enlarge, turn brown; foliage dies	Common blight (Diseases)
	pods	grey, greasy lesions	
Bean	foliage, pods	purple, angular lesions; darken	Anthracnose (Diseases)
Beet	seedlings	stems cut at soil level	Cutworm (Insects)
Beet	foliage	small holes	Flea beetle (Insects)
Broccoli	seedlings, transplants	cut at soil level	Cutworm (Insects)
Broccoli	foliage	small holes	Diamondback moth caterpillar (Insects)
Broccoli	foliage	tiny shot holes	Flea beetle (Insects)
Broccoli	foliage	jagged, irregular holes; bright green frass	Imported cabbage worm (Insects)
Broccoli	foliage	stems elongate to form flowers	Bolting (Disorders)

Brussels sprouts	seedlings, transplants	cut at soil level	**Cutworm** (Insects)
Brussels sprouts	foliage	small holes	**Diamondback moth caterpillar** (Insects)
Brussels sprouts	foliage	tiny shot holes	**Flea beetle** (Insects)
Brussels sprouts	foliage	jagged, irregular holes; bright green frass	**Imported cabbage worm** (Insects)
Cabbage	seedlings, transplants	cut at soil level	**Cutworm** (Insects)
Cabbage	foliage	leaf tips and margins brown	**Tipburn** (Disorders)
Cabbage	foliage	yellows, curls and puckers	**Aphids** (Insects)
Cabbage	foliage	small holes	**Diamondback moth caterpillar** (Insects)
Cabbage	foliage	tiny shot holes	**Flea beetle** (Insects)
Cabbage	foliage	jagged, irregular holes; bright green frass	**Imported cabbage worm** (Insects)
Carrot	foliage	yellowing, witches' broom, bronze-red	**Aster yellows** (Diseases)
	root	hairy	
Cauliflower	seedlings, transplants	cut at soil level	**Cutworm** (Insects)
Cauliflower	foliage	small holes	**Diamondback moth caterpillar** (Insects)

Cauliflower	foliage	tiny shot holes	**Flea beetle** (Insects)
Cauliflower	foliage	jagged, irregular holes; bright green frass	**Imported cabbage worm** (Insects)
Cauliflower	head	yellow	**Yellow head** (Disorders)
Celery	foliage	yellowing, witches' broom, bronze-red	**Aster yellows** (Diseases)
Corn	seedlings	cut at soil level	**Cutwom** (Insects)
Corn	foliage	yellows, curls and puckers	**Aphids** (Insects)
Corn	foliage	shot holes or pinholes; later tunnels	**European corn borer** (Insects)
	ear	feeding, tunnelling	
Corn	ear	pouches filled with black spores	**Common smut** (Diseases)
Cucumber	seedlings, transplants	cut at soil level	**Cutworm** (Insects)
Cucumber	foliage	powdery white coating	**Powdery mildew** (Diseases)
Cucumber	foliage	wilting	**Bacterial wilt** (Diseases)
Cucumber	foliage	yellows, curls and puckers	**Aphids** (Insects)
Lettuce	foliage	leaf tips and margins brown	**Tipburn** (Disorders)

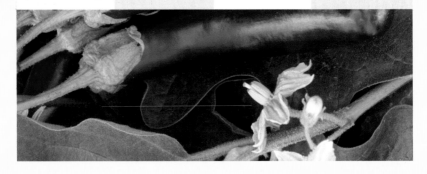

Lettuce	foliage	stems elongate to form flowers	**Bolting** (Disorders)
Lettuce	foliage	yellows, curls and puckers	**Aphids** (Insects)
Lettuce	foliage	large, irregular holes; slime trails	**Slugs** (Insects)
Lettuce	foliage	yellowing, witches' broom, bronze-red	**Aster yellows** (Diseases)
Melon	seedlings, transplants	cut at soil level	**Cutwom** (Insects)
Melon	foliage	powdery white coating	**Powdery mildew** (Diseases)
Melon	foliage	wilting	**Bacterial wilt** (Diseases)
Melon	foliage	yellows, curls and puckers	**Aphids** (Insects)
Melon	foliage	yellow spots, turn brown, fall out	**Anthracnose** (Diseases)
	fruit	dark spots, pink rot	
Onion	foliage	tip dieback, yellowing	**Basal rot** (Diseases)
	bulb	water-soaked, pink-brown rot	
Onion	foliage	wilting, yellowing	**Onion maggot** (Insects)
	bulb	tunnelling	

Pea	foliage, stems, pods	powdery white coating	**Powdery mildew** (Diseases)
Pea	foliage, stems, pods	grey-purple lesions	**Ascochyta leaf and pod spot** (Diseases)
Pea	seedlings	topples over	**Damping off** (Diseases)
Pea	foliage	yellows, curls and puckers	**Aphids** (Insects)
Pepper	foliage, fruit	water-soaked, beige-grey lesions	**Grey mould** (Diseases)
Pepper	fruit	white-yellow, papery spots	**Sunscald** (Disorders)
Potato	foliage	dark spots with concentric rings; plant dies	**Early blight** (Diseases)
Potato	foliage	leaves dark and brittle; plant dies	**Late blight** (Diseases)
Potato	foliage	large holes	**Colorado potato beetle** (Insects)
Potato	foliage	tiny shot holes	**Flea beetle** (Insects)
Potato	tubers	tunnelling	**Wireworm** (Insects)
Potato	foliage	lower leaves wilt, yellow, roll inward	**Bacterial ring rot** (Diseases)
	tubers	oozy, crumbly rot	
Potato	tubers	black "dirt" on skin	**Black scurf** (Diseases)

Potato	tubers	rough corky spots on skin	**Common scab** (Diseases)
Potato	tubers	skin and some flesh green	**Greening** (Disorders)
Potato	tubers	irregular shape	**Knobbiness** (Disorders)
Radish	seedlings, transplants	cut at soil level	**Cutworm** (Insects)
Radish	foliage	stems elongate to form flowers	**Bolting** (Disorders)
Radish	foliage	small holes	**Diamondback moth caterpillar** (Insects)
Radish	foliage	tiny shot holes	**Flea beetle** (Insects)
Radish	foliage	jagged, irregular holes; bright green frass	**Imported cabbage worm** (Insects)
Rhubarb	foliage	reddens, shoots spindly	**Red leaf** (Diseases)
	crown	rot, leaving cavity	
Squash	seedlings, transplants	cut at soil level	**Cutworm** (Insects)
Squash	foliage	powdery white coating	**Powdery mildew** (Diseases)
Squash	foliage	wilting	**Bacterial wilt** (Diseases)
Squash	foliage	yellows, curls and puckers	**Aphids** (Insects)
Spinach	foliage	small holes	**Flea beetle** (Insects)
Spinach	foliage	yellows, curls and puckers	**Aphids** (Insects)
Spinach	foliage	stems elongate to form flowers	**Bolting** (Disorders)
Swiss chard	foliage	tiny shot holes	**Flea beetle** (Insects)

Tomato	foliage	large holes	**Tomato hornworm** (Insects)
Tomato	foliage, fruit	irregular holes	**Slugs** (see Chapter 9, Flowers, Bulbs and Vines)
Tomato	foliage	dark spots with concentric rings	**Early blight** (Diseases)
	fruit	dark sunken area at stem end	
Tomato	foliage	small dark specks; foliage dies	**Bacterial speck** (Diseases)
	fruit	raised brown specks on green fruit	
Tomato	fruit	rot at blossom end	**Blossom end rot** (Disorders)
Tomato	fruit	yellow-white papery spots	**Sunscald** (Disorders)
Tomato	fruit	misshapen, scarred, lumpy	**Catface** (Disorders)
Turnip	seedlings, transplants	cut at soil level	**Cutworm** (Insects)
Turnip	foliage	small holes	**Diamondback moth caterpillar** (Insects)
Turnip	foliage	tiny shot holes	**Flea beetle** (Insects)
Turnip	foliage	jagged, irregular holes; bright green frass	**Imported cabbage worm** (Insects)
Watermelon	seedlings, transplants	cut at soil level	**Cutworm** (Insects)
Watermelon	foliage	powdery white coating	**Powdery mildew** (Diseases)

Insects

Aphids

AFFECTS: bean, cabbage, corn, cucumber, lettuce, melon, pea, spinach, squash

Among the aphids are both generalists and specialists. A cabbage aphid would seldom dream of dining on a pea, and vice versa. But given the right conditions, virtually all vegetables may succumb to aphid infestations at one time or another. In addition to the physical damage they inflict, aphids can transmit viral diseases. And their excrement or "honeydew" is perfect for the development of black mould.

Aphids are small, soft-bodied, pear-shaped insects. They can be white, green, pink or brown. Their piercing mouthparts suck sap from plant tissue, and they have a decided preference for succulent new growth.

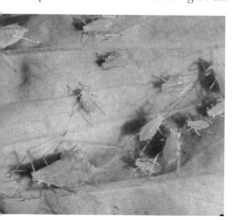

Aphids can be either generalists, feeding on a number of plant species, or specialists, eating only one type of plant. The pea aphid is a specialist.

Although their lifespan is short, they multiply quickly. Several generations of wingless females give birth to live young without the need for mating. When their population explodes, and conditions on the plant become overcrowded, they give birth to winged offspring that fly to another plant. In the fall, males are produced and sexual reproduction occurs. The eggs that are laid overwinter. Ants sometimes nurse aphids, attracted to the sugary honeydew that the aphids secrete.

WHAT TO LOOK FOR: Leaves yellow, curl and pucker, and plants weaken. Aphids may be present on both upper and lower leaf surfaces and on stems. Check new growth especially.

PREVENTION:

Cultural methods:

- Avoid high-nitrogen fertilizer, which stimulates lush growth that attracts aphids.
- Lay aluminum foil mulch on both sides of susceptible plants.

SOLUTIONS:

Cultural methods:

- Insert yellow sticky cards on sticks to trap winged aphids.
- Hose down plants with water every three days for two weeks.
- Avoid the use of chemical pesticides to encourage natural predators: lady beetles, lacewings.
- Avoid the use of chemical pesticides to encourage parasitic wasps.

Less toxic alternatives:

- Apply insecticidal soap.
- Apply diatomaceous earth.

Asparagus beetle

Although not a frequently occurring pest, occasional population buildups of common asparagus beetle (*Crioceris asparagi*) and spotted asparagus beetle (*C. duodecimpunctata*) can damage and disfigure newly emerging asparagus spears. We have an understandable aversion to eating the leftovers of a beetle, even a fairly attractive one such as this. These beetles are most active in the afternoon.

The common asparagus beetle is a small (1 cm/0.25 in.), oval, metallic beetle, varying in colour from blue to dark green to black, with reddish margins and six white spots. It could also be described as having a white back with a black cross and two prominent antennae. Small, shiny black eggs are laid singly or in rows on the emerging spears. The small

The grey to olive green larva of the common asparagus beetle also feeds on asparagus spears.

larvae are grey to olive green with black heads and legs. The adults overwinter in plant debris.

The spotted asparagus beetle is a little larger and is reddish-orange with very distinctive black spots. It eats the growing tips and foliage. The yellow-orange larvae feed inside the berries produced by female asparagus plants.

WHAT TO LOOK FOR: The larvae feed on the young spears and mature fronds. The spears are often curved, bent over or somewhat misshapen.

PREVENTION:

Cultural methods:

- Remove foliage from the aspara-gus patch in the fall to reduce overwintering sites.

The adult common asparagus beetle has distinctive markings as well as a distinct liking for young asparagus spears.

The spotted asparagus beetle eats the growing tips and foliage of asparagus plants. The larvae feed inside the berries produced by female asparagus plants.

- Cultivate in fall to prevent adults from overwintering.
- Use row covers when the spears are emerging.

SOLUTIONS:

Cultural methods:

- Cut the spears just below ground level daily as they emerge so as to remove the eggs of the common asparagus beetle before they hatch.
- Pick the berries produced by female asparagus plants while the larvae are within to control the spotted asparagus beetle.
- Hand-pick adults and larvae; remove or crush egg cases attached to the spears.

Less toxic alternatives:

- Apply insecticidal soap.
- Apply spinosad (Entrust 80 W), registered for the control of asparagus beetles.
- Avoid the use of chemical pesticides to encourage natural parasites: chalcid wasps, lady beetle larvae, *Tetrastichus asparagi.*
- Avoid the use of chemical pesticides to encourage natural predators: chickens and birds will do a good job in early spring or after harvest.

Colorado potato beetle

AFFECTS: eggplant, pepper, potato, tomato

Relatively large, easy to spot in all of its phases, and often occurring in large numbers, there is nothing subtle about the Colorado potato beetle (*Leptinotarsa decemlineata*). Early control, while the larvae are still small,

with proportionately smaller appetites, is your best bet. Large larvae eat more than younger ones.

The adult is an oval, black-and-orange striped beetle that overwinters about 20 to 25 cm (8–10 in.) below the soil surface. Adults emerge in late spring, conveniently at the same time that potato shoots appear, and immediately begin munching foliage. The bright orange-yellow eggs are laid on the undersides of potato leaves. The humpbacked larvae are red with rows of black spots along their sides, and black headed.

WHAT TO LOOK FOR: Holes in leaves, dark excrement on the foliage.

PREVENTION:

Cultural methods:

- Clean up in fall and cultivate to 20 cm (8 in.).
- Cultivate in early spring to expose insects to cold and birds.

Colorado potato beetles are all too common a problem, but they're easy to identify and hand-pick.

The humpbacked larvae of the Colorado potato beetle are red with black spots along their sides and are black-headed. Hand-pick and squash them.

The bright orange-yellow eggs of the Colorado potato beetle are laid on the undersides of potato leaves. Squash them within the leaf.

- Apply barriers: Potato beetles generally walk to work. Adults overwinter in the soil and walk on the soil surface. Mulching with 10 cm (4 in.) of straw makes their movement more difficult. A trench surrounding the potato patch, 10 cm (4 in.) deep and 30 cm (12 in.) wide, lined with plastic and filled with water, is also a deterrent. A low plastic or wooden barrier (like a two-by-four), 10 to 12.5 cm (4-5 in.) high, surrounding the potato patch also works, as they are poor climbers.
- Use row covers.
- Use a three-year rotation.

- Plant early-maturing varieties as early as possible. Larger plants incur relatively less damage.
- The Colorado potato beetle prefers to eat the more expensive and difficult to grow eggplant, so as long as eggplant is not on your list of favourites, it can be used as a trap plant. Remember to remove the trap plants (and the beetles) once they have attacked the eggplant and before they wander further afield to the potatoes.

SOLUTIONS:

Cultural methods:
- Hand-pick, squishing or dumping them in soapy water.

Less toxic alternatives:
- Apply diatomaceous earth.
- Avoid chemical pesticides to encourage natural predators such as ground beetles and the two-spotted stinkbug. Both adults and larvae of the Colorado potato beetle are poisonous to most predators due to the large amount of solanines (a glycoalkaloid poison found in species of the nightshade family) they consume as they feed on the potato foliage.

Cutworm

AFFECTS: almost all vegetables, especially at the transplant or seedling stage

There are many species of cutworms on the prairies, but the variegated cutworm (*Peridroma saucia*) and glassy cutworm (*Apamea devastator*) are among the most common. Contrary to garden folklore, cutworms do not curl around the stems of young plants to squeeze them off, they chew them. These insects can be especially severe in new gardens that were formerly lawn or pasture.

Adults are dull grey to brownish night-flying miller moths that lay small white eggs on the foliage of host plants. The larvae or cutworms are smooth, somewhat "greasy-looking," translucent, brownish-grey caterpillars about 5 cm (2 in.) long, with mottled, diamond-like markings. They curl up to form a C when disturbed. Feeding at night, they chew through the stems of seedlings and transplants at soil level. There are also climbing cutworms that feed on foliage. By day, cutworms hide just beneath the soil surface.

WHAT TO LOOK FOR: Plants are found cut off at soil level. Most damage is done in early spring. Later in the season, cutworms will consume foliage or even fruit.

PREVENTION:

Cultural methods:

- Cultivate the soil in early spring to expose larvae to birds.

Adult variegated cutworms are dull grey to brownish night-flying moths.

The larvae of variegated cutworms are brownish-grey with mottled, diamond-like markings. They curl up to form a C when disturbed.

Sinking a coffee or juice can, with ends removed, around new transplants is an easy way to reduce cutworm damage.

Cutworms do not curl around the stems of young plants to squeeze them off. They chew them.

- Cultivate again, to a depth of 20 cm (8 in.), in the fall.
- Use collars or row covers as barriers.

SOLUTIONS:

Cultural methods:
- Hand-pick directly from plants or soil.

Less toxic alternatives:
- Avoid chemical pesticides to encourage natural parasites: wasps.
- Avoid chemical pesticides to encourage natural predators: ground beetles.
- Apply Bt *kurstaki.*
- Apply diatomaceous earth.

The mature larvae pupate by spinning a cocoon on the foliage of the host plant.

Diamondback moth caterpillar

AFFECTS: broccoli, Brussels sprouts, cabbage, cauliflower, kohlrabi, radish, turnip

The appearance of the diamondback moth caterpillar (*Plutella xylostella*) in our gardens is weather related. They are rarely present during periods of cool, rainy weather. They do not overwinter in Canada, but are blown

Diamondback moth larvae are small, green, with a brown head and a noticeable V on their rear.

Adult diamondback moths blow up from the south in early spring and are particularly troublesome where canola and mustard are grown.

up from the south in early spring and are particularly troublesome where canola and mustard are grown. They eat related weeds before their crops of choice are sown.

The adult moth is small (2 cm/0.75 in. wingspan) and dark brown with white, diamond-like markings on its wings. Females lay yellow eggs singly on host plants in the spring. The small (1 cm/0.5 in.), pale green larvae have a brown head, a noticeable V on their rear and may sometimes be seen suspended by a silk-like thread.

WHAT TO LOOK FOR: The larvae eat the leaves and flowers of cruciferous (cabbage family) plants, leaving small holes in the foliage.

PREVENTION:

Cultural methods:

- Destroy and remove any refuse of cabbage family crops from the garden in fall.
- Apply barriers: Floating row covers are very effective.
- Plant resistant varieties: 'Mammoth Red Rock' cabbage, 'Purple Top White Globe' turnip.

SOLUTIONS:

Cultural methods:

- Hose off the caterpillars with a strong stream of water.

Less toxic alternatives:

- Apply Bt *kurstaki*.
- Avoid chemical pesticides to encourage parasitic wasps.

European corn borer

AFFECTS: sweet corn

The larvae of the European corn borer tunnel through emerging leaves and the husk into the developing ear.

The adult European corn borer is a nocturnal, pale yellow-brown moth that lays eggs on the leaves of the corn.

The European corn borer (*Ostrinia nubilalis*) is closely related to the sod webworm. This might strike us initially as odd, but corn and turf, their preferred hosts, are both grasses. Corn just happens to be edible and a bit taller.

Although its damage is off-putting, one can take consolation from the fact that the European corn borer is not a pest one comes across every summer.

The adult is a nocturnal, pale yellow-brown moth with a 2 cm (0.75 in.) wingspan. Flat, white egg masses are laid on the undersides of the leaves of host plants. The larvae are light brown to grayish-pink caterpillars with a dark spot on each segment and a dark head. There is one generation per year. Larvae overwinter in corn stalks and stubble, pupating in the spring.

WHAT TO LOOK FOR: Initially, there are shot or pinholes in the foliage; later, tunnels appear through emerging leaves and the husk into the developing ear. Look for "sawdust" around and below the stalk. Check the ears for frass (excrement).

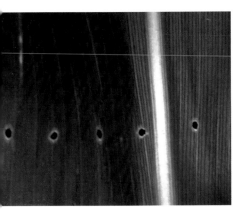

The first signs of damage from the European corn borer are shot or pinholes in the foliage.

PREVENTION:

Cultural methods:

- Clean up the garden in fall, followed by tilling to 20 cm (8 in.).
- Plant resistant varieties: Those with very tight wrapper leaves on the ears may be less likely to be infested.
- Use barriers: Cover ears with old pantyhose to reduce entry of larvae. They are flexible and will expand with the growth of the ears.
- Practice a three-year rotation.

SOLUTIONS:

Cultural methods:

- Hand-pick: Split the stalks below the entry point and remove the borers to interrupt their life cycle.

Less toxic alternatives:

- Apply Bt *kurstaki*.
- Avoid chemical pesticides to encourage natural parasites, such as parasitic wasps and tachinid flies.

Flea beetle

AFFECTS: arugula, beet, broccoli, Brussels sprouts, cabbage, cauliflower, kohlrabi, radish, potato, spinach, tomato

Here is an insect that more than makes up for its small size with its active lifestyle. Disturb the flea beetle (*Phyllotreta cruciferae*, and other species), and it jumps like a flea, hence its common name. Where there is one, there are usually many.

Besides the physical damage they do, flea beetles transmit viral and bacterial diseases, including early blight of tomatoes. Flea beetles are especially a problem in rural areas where canola and mustard are grown. They feed early, when plants are smaller and more vulnerable. Healthy, fast-growing transplants generally outgrow flea beetle damage. Seedlings and stressed plants are most vulnerable.

Flea beetles are very small (3 mm/ 0.1 in.). Shiny, dark brown or black, with curved yellow or white stripes, they look like tiny black dots. Adults

The presence of flea beetles is generally obvious: tiny shot holes in the foliage of members of the cabbage family.

lay eggs at the base of the host plant. These develop into slender white grubs, about 2 cm (0.75 in.) long with brown heads. The larvae feed on roots, the adults on foliage. Adults overwinter in soil or garden debris, within the garden or in nearby bush, emerging in early spring.

WHAT TO LOOK FOR: Tiny shot holes in foliage.

PREVENTION:

Cultural methods:

- Directly seeded plants are more vulnerable. Use transplants where possible.
- Cultivate between rows.
- Clean up in fall and cultivate to expose overwintering sites of adults.
- Close planting (with leaves touching) promotes shade, which flea beetles do not like.
- Use resistant varieties that generally have a thick waxy "bloom" on their foliage.
  Cabbage: 'Copenhagen Market', 'Early Jersey Wakefield', 'Ferry's Round Dutch', 'Mammoth Red Rock'.
  Broccoli: 'Atlantic', 'Coastal', 'Gem', 'Italian Green Sprouting'.
  Cauliflower: 'Early Snowball'.
  Radish: 'Champion', 'Sparkler'.
- Apply barriers: Use row covers immediately after sowing or planting.
- Practice a three-year rotation.
- Timing: Set out transplants after the spring infestation of flea beetles has finished feeding.
- Trap plants: Sow mustard or

Crucifer flea beetles are very small and look like tiny black dots.

arugula seed 3 m (10 ft.) from desired crop, two weeks prior to emergence or transplanting of desired crop. Flea beetles will be attracted to these. Dispose of the mustard or arugula plants – and the flea beetles – once they are infested.

SOLUTIONS:

Cultural methods:

- Apply overhead irrigation during the heat of the day to avoid moisture stress on plants while stressing adult flea beetles which prefer it hot and dry.
- Hand-pick with a hand-held vacuum.

Less toxic alternatives:

- Apply insecticidal soap.
- Apply diatomaceous earth.

Grasshoppers

AFFECTS: almost anything green when grasshopper populations are high

Grasshoppers (*Melanoplus* and many other genera) are all too familiar to prairie gardeners and hardly need an

Grasshoppers are large, fast, far-ranging and have voracious appetites.

grasshoppers that they are staggering and can hardly walk. (The downside? Their egg yolks are an unappetizing olive green.)

Adults are 2.5 to 5 cm (1–2 in.) long, with jumping hind legs, prominent eyes and shorter antennae. Colouring ranges from brown through yellow to green. Egg clusters are laid in the soil in fall, hatching in the spring. Some overwinter as mature larvae or adults. The larvae are wingless but otherwise resemble the adults.

Their damage is worse in late summer and fall. Provincial departments of agriculture develop annual grasshopper maps forecasting the severity of damage to field crops. Gardeners (especially in rural areas) would be prudent to have a look at these for their area. Hot dry springs and long hot summers generally indicate an increase in numbers for the coming year. Damp cool springs often mean that grasshoppers will succumb to disease and be fewer in number that summer.

WHAT TO LOOK FOR: If grasshoppers are present, you will see them jumping out of your way, and the fruits of your labour steadily diminishing. Grasshoppers eat almost everything. They will begin with foliage, but as their size and numbers increase, they may also eat fruit. Grasshoppers are more effectively controlled when small.

PREVENTION:

Cultural methods:

- Fall tilling exposes eggs to cold and birds, but the mobility of grasshoppers means they will fly in from elsewhere.

introduction. In most seasons, they are present but not problematic. When they're bad, they're very bad. Although the biblical hoards of migratory grasshoppers are not found on the prairies, those that are here can still travel far and wide, and are practically uncontrollable. They are generally more of a problem in rural areas than in urban areas, so the best bet may be a small flock of bantam hens, confined by snow fencing to the area in which you want control. We've seen bantams eat so many

- Mow surrounding grassy areas as low as the lawns will tolerate.
- Use barriers: Row covers made of fine wire mesh are preferable as grasshoppers can chew through fabric.

SOLUTIONS:

Cultural methods:

- Confine hens to the garden area.
- Avoid chemical pesticides to encourage natural parasites. Larvae of blister beetles and bee flies feed on grasshopper eggs. The bee flies lay eggs adjacent to grasshopper egg pods.

Less toxic alternatives:

- Apply insecticidal soap.

Imported cabbage worm

AFFECTS: broccoli, Brussels sprouts, cabbage, cauliflower, kohlrabi, radish, turnip

Cabbage worms (*Pieris rapae*) are the larvae of the ubiquitous white butterflies, found throughout North America, that hover around members of the cabbage family from mid-May to fall. While the adult butterflies do no damage, they can be faulted for their inexhaustible fertility.

Prairie gardeners are all too familiar with the white cabbage butterfly. While adults do no damage, their ability to reproduce is frightening.

The adult white cabbage butterfly has a wingspan of 3 to 3.5 cm (1–1.25 in.) and several black dots on its forewings. The white, ridged, bullet-shaped eggs are laid singly in late May. Velvety, light green caterpillars, with yellow stripes on their backs, emerge soon after, with several generations hatching per season. Adept at camouflage, they often seem aligned with the midribs of the leaves. But their damage is obvious. They overwinter as chrysalides in garden debris.

WHAT TO LOOK FOR: The caterpillars feed on the leaves, leaving jagged, irregular holes, and later tunnel into the edible portions of the vegetable. They also

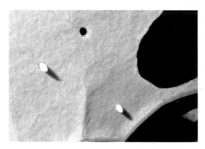

The eggs of imported cabbage worms are white, ridged, bullet-shaped and laid singly. Simply squash them against the leaf.

The larvae, called imported cabbage worms, are a velvety light green with a yellow stripe.

leave a distinctly unappetizing dark green excrement on or near the plants they eat.

Cultural methods:

- Cultivate in fall to destroy chrysalides.
- Clean up all cabbage family debris in the fall.
- Remove cruciferous weeds such as stinkweed, shepherd's purse, mustard and flixweed, which serve as egg-laying sites.
- Plant resistant varieties: Red or purple cabbages (such as 'Mammoth Red Rock') are less attractive to the caterpillars than white ones.
- Use barriers: Cover with row covers as soon as transplants are put outdoors, leaving covers in place until harvest.
- Use a three-year rotation.
- Timing: Plant as early as possible, before the eggs hatch.

SOLUTIONS:

Less toxic alternatives:

- Apply insecticidal soap.
- Apply Bt *kurstaki.*
- Apply diatomaceous earth.
- Avoid chemical pesticides to encourage natural parasitic wasps.

Onion maggot

AFFECTS: garlic, leek, onion, shallot

The only serious pest of onions on the prairies, the onion maggot (*Delia antiqua* syn. *Hylemya antiqua*), can do considerable damage in years when there are population buildups. Unfortunately, we seldom realize they are present until our onions wilt or fall over. Closer inspection reveals the culprit, by this time happily gorged on the bulb you were hoping to harvest.

Adults – anthomyid flies – look like grey-brown, hairy houseflies with a humped back and long legs. They are attracted to the onions by their smell.

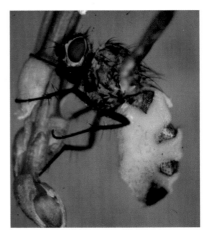

The path of destruction wrought by imported cabbage worms can be devastating.

Anthomyid flies, the adult form of the onion maggot, look like grey-brown, hairy houseflies with a humped back.

Females can lay up to two hundred eggs just under the soil at the base of newly planted or seeded onions. The younger the plant, the greater the damage will be. Small, off-white, tapered larvae bore narrow holes into the bulb. They are legless and about 1 cm (0.4 in.) long. Infestations can be severe when the weather is cool and wet.

WHAT TO LOOK FOR: Wilting and yellowing are the initial symptoms. Early severe damage can lead to death. Look for tunnels in the onions just below the soil surface. The lower stem and neck of the onion are often damaged, leading to secondary rot in storage.

PREVENTION:

Cultural methods:

- Fall cleanup is essential as damaged onions left in the garden are a major food source.
- Avoid close planting, which makes it a bit easier for maggots to move from one onion to another.
- Plant resistant varieties: Onion maggots prefer white varieties over yellow ones. Red varieties

sustain the least damage. Japanese bunching onions are resistant.

- Use barriers: Cover with row covers.
- Use a three-year rotation.
- Timing: Plant onion sets or transplants after caragana or dandelions begin to bloom.

SOLUTIONS:

Cultural methods:

- Remove and destroy infested plants.

Less toxic alternatives:

- Apply diatomaceous earth.
- Avoid chemical pesticides to encourage natural parasites: nematodes, parasitic wasps.
- Avoid chemical pesticides to encourage natural predators: ground beetles, rove beetles.

Slug

For information on slugs, see Chapter 9, Flowers, Bulbs and Vines.

Tomato hornworm

AFFECTS: eggplant, pepper, potato, tomato

Tomato hornworms (*Manduca quinquemaculata*) are very large and very obvious, once you see them. They are also very well camouflaged, which is why you sometimes don't see them. Their appetite is commensurate with their size. On a positive note, they are not gregarious and are very few in number. In many years of gardening, you may encounter fewer than a dozen.

Onion maggots attack onions, leeks, shallots and garlic. This freshly pulled garlic bulb is maggot-free, ready for cleaning and drying.

The adult tomato hornworm is a large, furry, mottled brownish-grey hawk moth with a large wing span that hovers at dusk like a hummingbird.

The tomato hornworm is large, lovely, solitary and has an enormous appetite.

The adult is a large, furry, mottled brownish-grey hawk moth with five orange-yellow spots along the sides of its body and a 12 cm (5 in.) wing-span. It feeds at dusk, hovering like a hummingbird. Greenish-yellow eggs are laid singly on the undersides of leaves. The larvae are 10 cm (4 in.) in length, green, with seven or eight oblique or V-shaped white lines along their sides. A harmless though unattractive black horn projects from their rear. Pupae overwinter 8 to 10 cm (3–4 in.) under the soil.

Its frass (excrement) is commensurate with its size and appetite.

WHAT TO LOOK FOR: Large portions of leaves and green fruit eaten. Dark frass (droppings) is often found on the foliage of the plant or on the soil beneath the site of damage. Leaves are sometimes left with only their midribs.

PREVENTION:

Cultural methods:

- Fall cleanup and tillage to a depth of 20 cm (8 in.) exposes pupae to birds and cold.

SOLUTIONS:

Cultural methods:

- Hand-pick.

Less toxic alternatives:

- Apply Bt *kurstaki*.
- If you see a hornworm with rice-like projections, your problem has been solved and there is no need to take further action. These projections are caused by the pupae of parasitic wasps. Simply leave the wasps to multiply.

Wireworm

AFFECTS: potato

We've all seen narrow tunnels winding through potatoes and wondered who was there before we were. Wireworms are the larvae of the click beetle. While there is no easy solution once dusky or European wireworms (*Agriotes obscurus* and other species) are present, prevention is straightforward: Simply wait three years before planting potatoes in gardens that were formerly pasture or lawns.

Wireworms overwinter deep in the soil where temperatures are more moderate. Adults are click beetles, slender, dark brown or black, 1 cm (0.4 in.) long. If flipped on their backs, they make a clicking sound as they right themselves, thus the common name. Adults lay eggs at the base of plants. Their larvae, wireworms, are 3 to 4 cm (1–1.5 in.) long, cylindrical, segmented and brownish-orange or yellow. They take their time maturing and can spend five or six years as larvae, feeding on potato roots and tubers in the soil. They are more plentiful on newly broken land that was formerly sod or pasture. In spring, they are attracted to germinating seeds or existing plants by the carbon dioxide the plants produce. Wireworms prefer cool, moist soil conditions and are generally found in the top 15 cm (6 in.) of soil during the growing season.

WHAT TO LOOK FOR: tunnelling in tubers.

PREVENTION:

Cultural methods:

- Cultivate deeply in the fall and again in spring.

One of the easiest ways of controlling wireworms is to wait 3 years before planting potatoes in gardens that were formerly pasture or lawns.

- If you have them, let chickens eat exposed insects before and after the growing season.
- Practice a three-year rotation.
- Timing: Wait three years before planting potatoes on land that was formerly pasture or lawn.
- Trap plants: Place pieces of potato on sticks buried 5 to 10 cm (2-4 in.) below the soil surface on the edge of your potato patch. Remove the potato pieces, wireworms and all, four weeks after planting your potato crop.

Diseases

Anthracnose

AFFECTS: bean, cucumber, melon, watermelon

Anthracnose (*Colletotrichum lindemuthianum* on bean, *C. lagenarium*, syn. *C. orbiculare* on melon, watermelon and cucumber) is a widespread disease of foliage and fruit, generally appearing late in the growing season.

There are several strains or races, and they can cause severe losses. Although anthracnose can be devastating, if you use clean seed and resistant varieties, chances of infection are low.

The fungus overwinters on seed and in infected plant residue. It is spread by water, rain, wind, tools and people walking or working in the garden when the foliage is wet. High relative humidity and "free water" on the foliage are needed for spore germination and infection.

WHAT TO LOOK FOR:

Bean: Small, angular lesions appear on the undersides of the leaves along the veins. At first purplish red, they later turn dark brown to black and may spread to the upper leaf surface. On pods, the lesions begin as dark dots, later enlarging and becoming sunken.

Melon, watermelon, cucumber: Yellow or water-soaked areas appear on the leaves, enlarge, turn brown and fall out, leaving holes in the leaves. The disease is worse on older foliage and may result in total defoliation. Stems are discoloured. Sunken dark spots develop on the fruit, later oozing a pink, gooey substance.

PREVENTION:

Cultural methods:
- Use clean seed.
- Plant resistant or tolerant varieties: There are six races of anthracnose, and few cultivars are resistant to all, but resistant cultivars are better than susceptible varieties.
  Bean: 'Bush Bean Modus', 'Nomad', 'Sonesta', 'Caprice', 'Rocdor', 'Carson', 'Scarlet Runner'.
  Cucumber: 'Dasher II', 'Diva', 'Fanfare', 'Pepi II', 'Summer Top', 'Intimadator', 'Speedway', 'Talladega', 'Thunder', 'Stonewall', 'Cobra', 'Indio', 'Sweet Slice', 'Jackson Classic', 'Cross Country', 'Lafayette', 'Fancipak', 'Sassy', 'Eclipse', 'Zapata', 'Pioneer'.
  Melon: 'Passport'.
  Watermelon: 'Vanguard'.
- Space plants generously and provide good air circulation.
- Avoid working in the garden when foliage is wet.
- Remove plant residue immediately after harvest.
- Practice a three-year rotation.

On bean pods, anthracnose shows up as dark spots that later enlarge and become sunken.

Anthracnose on cucumbers has sunken dark spots on the fruit that later ooze a pink gooey substance.

Ascochyta leaf and pod spot

AFFECTS: pea

Very common, and often seen on the lower leaves as plants mature, ascochyta leaf and pod spot (*Ascochyta pisi* and other closely related species) is favoured by rainy weather. The fungus survives on infected seed and plant residue and in the soil. It is spread by wind and splashing rain or irrigation water.

WHAT TO LOOK FOR: Peas can be infected at all stages of growth. Seedlings can be seriously weakened or killed. Grey to purple lesions, sometimes with concentric rings, appear on the leaves, stems and pods of mature plants. Stems will show purplish streaks both above and below the soil line that will eventually girdle them.

PREVENTION:

Cultural methods:

- Provide good air circulation.
- Avoid high nitrogen levels.
- Irrigate early in the day so foliage dries quickly.
- Sanitation: Remove all plant debris immediately after harvest.
- Practice a four-year rotation.

Grey to purple lesions appear on the leaves, stems and pods infected with ascochyta leaf and pod spot of peas.

Aster yellows

AFFECTS: carrot, celery, lettuce

Aster yellows (phytoplasma virus) occurs on a wide range of plants, from annual and perennial flowers to vegetables. It shows up when leafhopper populations are high and is seen more often on carrots harvested late in the season.

Transmitted by the aster leafhopper and other leafhoppers, the disease is carried northward as these insects migrate into the prairies from the south in spring. Leafhoppers pierce

There is often a witches' broom proliferation of foliage from the crown of carrots

Carrots infected by aster yellows are hairy, often with four vertical rows of tiny rootlets.

and suck plant tissue and transmit the virus into the phloem tissue of other plants. Aster yellows can be patchy within a garden because it spreads where the insects feed. The virus can overwinter on perennial weeds such as dandelions and thistles. There are no resistant varieties.

WHAT TO LOOK FOR: Initial symptoms are yellowing of younger leaves in the centre of the crown. This is followed by a witches' broom proliferation of small unhealthy shoots from the crown. Older leaves turn white and then bronzy-red, leaf stalks are twisted and hairy rootlets appear in four vertical rows on the carrot itself. Plants affected by aster yellows are poor in flavour.

PREVENTION:

Cultural methods:

- Use early-maturing types that may avoid aster yellows.
- Avoid planting carrots next to lettuce.
- Eradicate weeds like quack grass, plantain, knotweed, stinkweed, lamb's quarters and sow thistle, which are hosts to aster yellows.
- Control leafhoppers with row covers.
- Remove and destroy affected plants immediately; remove crop residues after harvest.

Bacterial speck

AFFECTS: tomato

The specks after which this disease is named occur on both the foliage and the green fruit of the tomato plant. Interestingly, the pH on ripe tomatoes is 5.2, too acidic for bacterial growth. Bacterial speck (*Pseudomonas syringae*

pv. tomato) is worse after heavy rains, when the bacteria are spread by splashing. The bacteria are also transferred on seeds, transplants and infected tomato plants left in the garden. During cool, rainy weather it can spread rapidly.

WHAT TO LOOK FOR: Dark brown to black specks of 2 mm (0.08 in.) diameter appear on the leaves. Surrounded by a yellow halo, they gradually merge. The leaves die and fall off. Slightly raised brown specks appear on the skin of green fruit.

PREVENTION:

Cultural methods:

- Use hot-water-treated seeds sown in sterile medium or disease-free transplants.
- Plant resistant or tolerant varieties: 'Window Box Roma', 'Muriel'.
- Avoid working in the garden when it is wet.
- Irrigate early in the day so plants will dry quickly.
- Clean up and remove all tomato plants from the garden immediately after harvest.
- Practice a three-year rotation.

Small black specks on the green fruit of tomatoes generally indicate the presence of bacterial speck.

Bacterial ring rot

AFFECTS: potato

Bacterial ring rot (*Clavibacter michiganensis* subsp. *sepedonicus*) is a serious and highly infectious disease of potatoes in Canada. Easily spread by tools and machinery, it causes tuber rot both in the garden and in storage. It's most easily identified by the milky substance that oozes from infected potatoes and stems when they are squeezed.

The bacteria overwinter in tubers, containers and garden tools. The Colorado potato beetle may be a vector.

WHAT TO LOOK FOR: Symptoms appear first on foliage. Soon after flowering, the lower leaves on a single or many stems will wilt and roll inward. They will turn from pale green to yellow and will be worse in hot, dry weather. If stems are cut, the vascular tissue appears brown. The eyes of infected tubers are red, while the vascular rings of infected tubers (near the stem end) are creamy yellow. The interior texture of the tubers is crumbly or cheese-like, and they may ooze when squeezed, but they are odourless. Subsequent infection by secondary bacteria can totally destroy tubers in storage.

PREVENTION:

Cultural methods:

- Plant only disease-free, certified seed pieces or small uncut potatoes.
- Disinfect tools if disease has been a problem.
- Clean up all potato debris in the garden immediately after harvest.
- Control Colorado potato beetles.
- Practice a three-year rotation.

Bacterial wilt

AFFECTS: all vines – cucumber, melon, pumpkin, squash, watermelon

Bacterial wilt (*Erwinia tracheiphila*) is a common disease, especially on cucumber, and is spread by the spotted and striped cucumber beetles as they feed. The beetles are less active in wet

A serious storage disease of potatoes, bacterial ring rot is most easily identified by the milky substance that oozes from the infected potatoes and stems when they are squeezed.

Bacterial wilt affects all vines and has no cure. Leaves develop dull green patches that quickly enlarge, followed by wilting of the entire plant and death.

weather. Once the bacteria are in the vascular tissue, the plants are pretty well doomed.

WHAT TO LOOK FOR: Leaves develop dull green patches that quickly enlarge, followed by wilting of the entire plant and death. The bacteria block the vascular system, preventing the uptake of water and nutrients.

PREVENTION:

Cultural methods:

- Control the beetles through the use of row covers.

Basal rot

AFFECTS: all *Allium* – chives, garlic, leek, onion, shallot

Although not a major problem, basal rot (*Fusarium oxysporum*) can affect onions both in the garden and in storage. The fungus is worse during periods of prolonged moisture when temperatures are high, not a frequent phenomenon on the prairies. Examine onions carefully before putting them into storage.

The fungus can be spread by wind, rain, insects and tools, and can persist in the soil for three or more years. It often enters the onions where onion maggots have tunnelled.

WHAT TO LOOK FOR: Tip dieback and yellowing of leaves. The roots decay, allowing the plants to be pulled out easily. The scales of the bulb first appear water-soaked. A pink to brown rot begins at the base of the bulb and moves upward. It is later covered with a white fungal growth.

Fusarium basal rot of onions often enters the bulb where onion maggots have tunnelled.

PREVENTION:

Cultural methods:

- Plant in well-drained soil.
- Use disease-free sets.
- Plant resistant/tolerant varieties: 'Frontier', 'Mountaineer', 'Nebula', 'Lasalle', 'Joliet', 'Pulsar', 'MacKenzie', 'Infinity', 'Verrazono', 'Nicolet', 'Vespucci', 'Green Banner', 'Cortland', 'Red Zeppelin', 'Mercury', 'Grateful Red', 'Sterling'.
- Control onion maggots.
- It is very important to cure or dry onions properly after harvest.
- Practice sanitation – remove plant debris from the garden immediately after harvest.
- Practice a three-year rotation.

Black scurf or canker

AFFECTS: potato

We all know it's healthy to eat the skin, but if your potatoes have black scurf it might not be appetizing. Black

Black scurf is "the dirt that won't wash off" the skin of potatoes.

- Plant shallowly (5 cm/2 in. deep) in warm soil (avoiding cold, wet soil) to encourage rapid growth and emergence.
- Hill after emergence.
- Do not irrigate until after sprouts have emerged from the soil.
- Harvest early, as soon as the tubers are mature.
- Practice sanitation – clean garden of potato plant debris immediately after harvest.
- Practice a three-year, or longer, rotation.

scurf or canker (*Rhizoctonia solani*) is a soil-borne fungus with many strains or races found all over the world. Sometimes called "the dirt that won't wash off," it invades plants at or below the soil level and is worse in cold or wet soils. The above-ground symptoms are caused by a toxin, a growth regulator produced by the fungus. The fungus persists indefinitely in the soil and on crop residue.

WHAT TO LOOK FOR: Small, rough black bumps on the potato skin that will not scrub off are the most obvious sign. Other symptoms may include: off-coloured reddish-brown roots; swollen stems; small, misshapen underground tubers; cankers on stems and stolons; aerial tubers; and leaves thickening, rolling, wilting and purpling. Sprouts may fail to emerge. Greyish-white, threadlike mycelium may be seen on stems near soil level.

PREVENTION:

Cultural methods:

- Use clean, black scurf-free, certified seed potatoes.

Common blight

AFFECTS: bean

When it's bad, it's really bad. In 1987, 70 percent of Manitoba's commercial bean crop was destroyed by common blight (*Xanthomonas* spp.). Since then, largely through the use of clean, inspected seed, the incidence of this bacterial disease has been greatly reduced. It affects green and yellow bush and pole beans.

Using clean inspected seed is a good way to avoid common blight of beans.

The bacteria survive in the soil and plant debris and are spread by infected seed, insects, tools, water and people. It's worse during periods of wet, windy, warm weather.

WHAT TO LOOK FOR: Water-soaked spots on leaves gradually enlarge, turn brown and are surrounded by a yellow halo. The foliage has a scorched or shot hole appearance and dies. Pods develop grey greasy lesions, eventually becoming red- brown and sunken.

PREVENTION:

Cultural methods:

- Use clean seed.
- Sow into well-drained soil once temperatures are warm.
- Avoid working in the garden when foliage is wet.
- Remove all plant debris immediately after harvest.
- Practice a three-year rotation.

Common scab

AFFECTS: beet, potato, radish, rutabaga, turnip

Common scab (*Streptomyces scabies*) occurs most frequently on potatoes, and the causal organism is present in small populations in most prairie soils. While it does not affect yield, it does affect quality. The potatoes are perfectly edible but unattractive, and it's wasteful because they require deep paring to remove the scabby skin.

Scab bacteria are found in former grasslands or recently broken pasture with a high pH – most of the prairies! The disease is favoured by warm, dry soils. While lowering the pH of our highly basic soils is impractical, maintaining moisture is doable. Scab is spread by rain, wind-blown soil and infected tubers.

WHAT TO LOOK FOR: Rough, blotchy, corky, dark tissue on the surface of tubers, generally less than 1 cm (0.4 in.) across. There are no symptoms on the foliage. It is found only sporadically on beets, radishes, rutabagas, and turnips; look for superficial tan to dark raised lesions with pitted and sunken centres.

PREVENTION:

Cultural methods:

- Plant less susceptible red potato varieties: 'Red Ruby', 'Chieftain', 'Norland', 'Viking'.
- Use resistant russet varieties: 'Russet Burbank', 'Goldrush', 'Gemstar', 'Umatilla', 'Cherokee', 'Norking', 'Norgold Russet'.
- Maintain high moisture levels from the initiation of tuber set to when they begin to increase in size, about four to six weeks after planting.
- Avoid applying fresh manure.
- Add well-rotted organic material to soil to help maintain moisture.

Common scab is easily avoided by keeping the soil evenly moist and using resistant varieties.

- Incorporate alfalfa pellets, or generous amounts of peat moss, which will tend to slightly acidify the soil.
- Green manure crops are believed to encourage soil micro-organisms that discourage the development of scab. They are grown in and plowed under to add organic matter and nutrients to the soil. Some are legumes, such as peas, beans, alfalfa and clover. Fall rye is also used.
- Practice a five-year rotation.

Common smut

AFFECTS: corn

We've only seen it once, but it's not easily forgotten. Common smut (*Ustilago maydi,* syn. *U. zeae*) is large, ugly and in-your-face. Favoured by warm, dry growing seasons, the spores can persist in the soil or on contaminated seed for up to a decade. It enters the plants through wounds caused by insects, tilling and hail.

Common smut of corn is not a common occurrence in spite of its name, but once observed, it is not easily forgotten.

WHAT TO LOOK FOR: Galls are initially white and spongy, but soon look like large pouches of dusty black spores covering the ear and tassel. The cobs lack kernels and silks and have a brush-like appearance. Irregular galls may also develop on the leaves and stems.

PREVENTION:

Cultural methods:

- Practice a three-to-four year rotation.
- Practice sanitation – immediately remove any infected plants.

Damping off

AFFECTS: all seedlings

Damping off (*Pythium* and other fungi) is primarily a disease of seedlings, especially those of vine crops. It can survive in the soil for up to ten years. It is at its worst under humid conditions when seedlings are overcrowded.

WHAT TO LOOK FOR: If your seedlings suddenly topple over and stems appear girdled, damping off is the suspect. Leaves yellow and wilt, beginning with those closest to the ground. The interior of the roots is discoloured, generally a yellow-orange red. This may extend into the stem. Pink fungal spores may be found at the base of the stem.

PREVENTION:

Cultural methods:

- Plant on well-drained, non-compacted soils.
- Avoid over-irrigating.
- Provide generous spacing.

- Cover the growing media with a thin layer of sand, perlite or vermiculite to encourage a dry surface.
- Ensure good fertility, especially phosphorus and nitrogen.
- Remove crop residue immediately after harvest.
- Practice a four-to-five year rotation.
- Also see Chapter 9, Flowers, Bulbs and Vines.

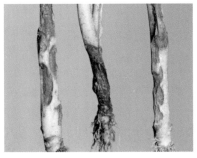

If your seedlings suddenly topple over, the chances are good (or bad) that they have succumbed to damping off, a fungal disease affecting many plants.

Early blight/leaf or target spot

AFFECTS: eggplant, pepper, potato, tomato

Early blight (*Alternaria solani, Alternaria alternata*) is a common foliage disease of potatoes and tomatoes that appears later in the growing season, but usually earlier than late blight. It is worse during periods of warm, humid or wet conditions, and when plants are older or under stress from drought, a nitrogen deficiency or weed competition. On tomatoes, the two fungal organisms (*A. solani* and *A. alternata*) are usually found together, and their symptoms and prevention are similar. They first attack the foliage and later the fruit. Older plants with a heavy fruit load and poor nutrition are more vulnerable.

The fungal organism can overwinter on diseased plants for at least a year and is also seed borne. It can be spread by wind, rain and insects, or by foliage touching infected soil.

WHAT TO LOOK FOR:

Potatoes: Small, circular to oval, brown or black, pinhead-sized spots appear on older leaves, generally during flowering. These gradually enlarge and become more angular. They may form concentric rings (like a target) and unite. The infected leaves do not fall off. Eventually, the plants die. The earlier the disease shows up, the worse the damage. Tubers may have shallow lesions with raised edges. Symptoms may show up in storage.

Tomatoes: Dark spots surrounded by concentric rings (thus the name "target spot") appear on the oldest leaves and

Early blight affects all members of the potato family, showing up first on older foliage in the form of pinhead-sized spots that gradually enlarge and unite.

On tomatoes, look for dark spots with concentric rings on the foliage and/or black sunken spots near the stem end of the fruit.

stems, soon spreading upward into newer growth. The spots become larger and irregular and can lead to total defoliation, resulting in sunscald on the fruit. The symptoms resemble blossom end rot on the fruit, but are found at the stem end. The spots are black, leather-like, and sunken, often with the same concentric rings.

PREVENTION:

Cultural methods:

- Use disease-free tomato transplants.
- Plant resistant or tolerant tomato varieties: 'Big Beef', 'Applause', 'Champion II', 'Health Kick', 'Husky Red', 'Lemon Boy', 'Mykonos', 'Patio', 'La Roma II', 'Cupid', 'Husky Cherry', 'Jubilee', 'Celebrity', 'Better Boy'.
- Encourage plant vigour through even moisture and fertility.
- Water early in the day so plants will dry quickly.
- Avoid working in the garden when it is wet.
- Ensure good air circulation.

- Keep foliage off the ground.
- Allow tubers to mature fully before harvesting.
- Do not harvest potatoes when soil is wet. Harvest carefully, avoiding wounds.
- Remove all plant debris immediately after harvest.
- Practice a three-to-four year rotation.
- Remove and destroy dead plants and culled potatoes immediately after harvest.

Grey mould

AFFECTS: bean, lettuce, pepper, other vegetables

Widespread under wet, cool conditions, grey mould (*Botrytis cinerea*) is most often seen on newly planted succulent pepper plants or bean pods during flowering and pod development. It usually enters the flower first, through wounds in the tissue caused by frost, insects, hail, wind, handling or tools. Spores are airborne or water-borne and live on dead and dying plant material and in the soil.

Worse during wet, cool weather, grey mould appears as sunken, water-soaked areas on the bean pod.

A soft rot of tissue, lesions are first dark green and water-soaked, then beige-grey, sometimes surrounded by concentric circles. There is brown streaking on stems and petioles.

PREVENTION:

Cultural methods:

- Use cultivars with an upright, open canopy, small flowers that do not persist and pods held off the soil.
- Harden off seedlings before planting them out.
- Grow on well-drained soil with good ventilation.
- Avoid dense plantings or crowding.
- Avoid excessive nitrogen, which causes soft succulent tissue growth.
- Irrigate early in the day so that foliage dries quickly.
- Avoid working in the garden when it is wet.
- Remove plants immediately after harvest.
- Practice a three-year rotation.

Late blight

AFFECTS: eggplant, pepper, potato, tomato

Late blight (*Phytophthora infestans*) is a fungal disease with a grim history, having wrought a path of destruction, including the Irish potato famine, through many countries and many eras. It seems to occur on the prairies about once every eight to ten years and is usually not a problem, partially because our growing season is relatively short and our humidity is low. It generally shows up in late summer and fall and is favoured by cool temperatures and high humidity. Not common, but devastating when it occurs, late blight is especially infectious to tomatoes that are grown in close proximity to infected potatoes, and vice versa.

Late blight can only overwinter on living potatoes, which is why fall cleanup following harvest is so vital in its control. Spores are spread by wind and rain. Infections can spread extremely rapidly, leading to the death of the entire plant very quickly.

WHAT TO LOOK FOR:

Potato: Large, dark green, water-soaked areas appear on the tips of older leaves after flowering. The entire leaf may become dark and brittle, often within a few days. Grey-white fungal growth may develop under the lesions on the undersides of the leaves. An entire potato patch can be killed within a week. Tubers may develop brownish-purple lesions and reddish-brown granular flesh, and then rot.

Late blight on potatoes is seen as large, dark green, water-soaked areas on the tips of older leaves. An entire patch can be killed within a week.

Tomato: Late blight on tomatoes is characterized by defoliation and fruit rot. The leaf symptoms are similar to those of potato. Water-soaked, blackish-green, irregular lesions develop on the older leaves. They quickly enlarge. Brown cankers may appear on stems and leaf petioles. Green fruit develop a brown rot, particularly on the "shoulders."

Green tomato fruit infected by late blight show a characteristic brown rot on their shoulders that gradually spreads to the entire fruit.

PREVENTION:

Cultural methods:

- Never use tubers from infected plants as seed potatoes. Purchase disease-free, certified seed.
- Plant resistant or tolerant tomato varieties: 'Red Grape', 'Duchess'; less susceptible potato varieties: 'Red Pontiac', 'Red Norland', 'Kennebec', 'Norland'.
- Avoid working in your garden when the foliage is wet.
- Irrigate tomatoes early in the day so plants can dry off before evening.
- Remove all plant debris after harvest.

- Check compost for volunteer tomato and potato plants and remove and destroy.

SOLUTIONS:

Cultural methods:

- Cut and remove potato tops at first sign of infection in hopes that the spores on the foliage will not be splashed into the soil to infect the tubers. Remove and destroy all infected potato plant debris immediately.

Removing infected late blight foliage of potatoes as close to the soil as possible may prevent the spores from being washed into the soil to infect the tubers.

Potato viruses

AFFECTS: potato

The most common viral diseases of potatoes found on the prairies are potato leafroll virus, potato mosaic virus and potato virus Y. All are extremely destructive and are spread by infected potato seed or aphids. All of these viral diseases result in fewer tubers that are smaller in size.

WHAT TO LOOK FOR: Symptoms of the potato leafroll virus include chlorotic (light green) foliage, inward rolling of the leaflets and lower leaves that may be dry and stiff with a leathery texture. Tuber interiors have little brown flecks. Potato plants infected with the potato mosaic virus are stunted, with mottled light green to yellow foliage. Potato virus Y is characterized by yellow and mottled foliage with dead spots, leaf drop and premature death of the plants.

PREVENTION:

Cultural methods:

- Plant virus-free, certified potato seed. Do not use this year's small potato tubers as seed for next year's crop. Small potato tubers are generally small because they are virus-infected!

Symptoms of leafroll virus of potatoes include the inward rolling and yellowing of leaves.

Potato virus Y is characterized by yellow mottled foliage and premature death of the plant.

- Control aphids.
- Plant early and remove and destroy any virus-infected plants.

Powdery mildew

AFFECTS: pea, all vines – cucumber, melon, pumpkin, squash, watermelon

Powdery mildew (*Erysiphe cichoracearum, Erysiphe polygoni*) is widespread and unsightly and can reduce fruit yield and quality, but it is seldom devastating. There are so many cultivars that are either resistant or tolerant of this fungal disease that there is little excuse for its presence in our gardens. It's worse during periods of high temperatures.

It can be seed borne, but generally overwinters on diseased plants and is spread by wind. It's more prevalent in shade and under the crowded conditions of dense plantings. On peas, it often occurs later in the season after the peas have been picked. Although a film of water is not required for spore germination, high humidity seems to increase the incidence of powdery mildew.

WHAT TO LOOK FOR: Small white, talcum powder-like spots appear on the stems and foliage, gradually increasing in size and coalescing. Leaves yellow, then turn brown, and eventually may shrivel.

PREVENTION:

Cultural methods:

- Use resistant or tolerant varieties: Cucumber: 'Dasher II', 'Diva', 'Eureka', 'Fanfare', 'Marketmore 76', 'Marketmore Select', 'Summer Top', 'Sweeter Yet', 'Intimidator', 'Speedy', 'Pioneer', 'Zapata',

'Eclipse', 'Tasty Green',
'Sweet Slice', 'Lafayette', 'Indio',
'Fancipak', 'Jackson Classic',
'Cutter', 'Cobra', 'Thunder',
'Stonewall', 'Talladega',
'General Lee'.
Melon: 'Primo', 'Goddess',
'Aphrodite', 'Eclipse', 'Ariel',
'Athena', 'Odyssey', 'Crete',
'Doral', 'Fastbreak', 'Halona',
'Sugar Cube', 'Magician', 'Magic
Wand', 'Aladdin'.
Pumpkin: 'Earlichamp', 'Magic
Lantern', 'Mystic Plus', 'Gargoyle',
'Gladiator', 'Warlock', 'Iron Man',
'Cannon Ball', 'Field Trip'.
Squash: 'Bush Delicata', 'Honey
Bear', 'Golden Glory', 'Payroll',
'Autumn Delight', 'Tay Belle',
'Celebration'.

Squash foliage with powdery mildew.
The easiest way to avoid this disease
is to use resistant varieties.

Pea: (use early maturing varieties
as powdery mildew is more
prevalent in later maturing types):
'Oregon Giant', 'Cascadia', 'Sugar
Sprint', 'Knight', 'Legacy',
'Encore', 'Bolero', 'Super Sugar
Snap', 'Sugar Lace II', 'Mr Big',
'Maestro', 'Oregon Sugar Pod II',
'Ambassador', 'Sabre'.

Powdery mildew is unsightly but seldom
devastating. The powdery white coating
makes it easy to diagnose.

- Ensure that vines are grown
  under good light conditions
  with good air circulation; avoid
  dense plantings.
- Avoid excessive fertility
  (especially nitrogen).
- Seed early.
- Keep plants well watered, but
  avoid wetting the foliage. Use
  drip irrigation or a soaker hose.
- Mulch to conserve soil moisture.
- Remove crop residue immediately
  after harvest.
- Practice a three-year rotation.
- For more information, see Chapter
  9, Flowers, Bulbs and Vines and
  Chapter 10, Trees and Shrubs.

Red leaf disease/bacterial soft rot
AFFECTS: rhubarb

This is one of the worst – and perhaps the only – diseases of rhubarb
on the prairies. Although the bacteria
have been around for a long time, little is known of the disease's life cycle
or how it is spread.

The most obvious sign of red leaf disease of rhubarb is the appearance of bright red spots on the foliage.

WHAT TO LOOK FOR: Often called crown rot, red leaf disease, or bacterial soft rot, *Erwinia rhapontici* causes decay of the terminal bud and leaves a cavity in the crown. The foliage turns red and side shoots are spindly. Leaves wilt and die.

PREVENTION:

Cultural methods:

- Only plant or divide disease-free rhubarb.
- Do not plant in areas where infected plants have been removed.
- Control aphids and other insects that may be responsible for its spread.
- Dig up and destroy infected plants.

Disorders

These problems are not caused by disease organisms but by adverse environmental factors such as temperature, moisture, nutrition or improper handling.

Blossom end rot

AFFECTS: tomato

Blossom end rot is caused by a calcium deficiency during fruit formation due to uneven watering or drought stress. Like other nutrients, calcium enters the plant dissolved in the soil water. If there are fluctuations in soil moisture, the calcium does not get to where it is needed by the developing cells in the tomato fruit. *There is already ample calcium in most prairie soils.* Applying lime to add calcium will increase our already high soil pH and cause additional problems. It is not recommended.

Blossom end rot is a common disorder of tomatoes caused by an uneven supply of calcium in the developing fruit due to uneven watering. Irrigate regularly and mulch.

WHAT TO LOOK FOR: Water-soaked areas appear at the blossom end of the tomato fruit, later becoming black, sunken and leather-like. Early fruits, during periods of rapid growth, are more likely to be affected than later fruits. It is most prevalent during periods of hot dry weather, affecting green and immature fruit. In the worst-case scenario, use the good portions of the affected fruit to make green tomato relish or mincemeat.

PREVENTION:

Cultural methods:
- Plant after the soil has warmed up.
- Apply water regularly (2.5 cm/1 in. per week) so that there is even soil moisture and thus a constant supply of calcium reaching the developing tomato fruit.
- Ensure that your tomatoes have sufficient phosphorus and potassium, avoiding an excessive application of nitrogen.
- Mulch the soil to conserve moisture.
- Avoid root damage when cultivating as injured roots limit water uptake.

Bolting

AFFECTS: broccoli, lettuce, radish, spinach

Bolting is caused by high temperatures, generally exceeding 28°C (82°F), and increased day length. Some cultivars are more susceptible to bolting than others.

WHAT TO LOOK FOR: Plant elongates upwards as it forms a flower stalk.

PREVENTION:

Cultural methods:
- Plant susceptible vegetables in early spring when temperatures are cooler.
- Use bolt-resistant varieties:
  Lettuce: 'Summertime', 'Yucaipe', 'Green Forest', 'Sangria', 'Nevada', 'Simpson Elite', 'Vulcan', 'Brunia', 'Odyssey', 'Two Stari', 'Lasting

Green', 'New Red Fire', 'Crunchy', 'Emeralda', 'Red Salad Bowl'.
- Spinach: 'Tortoiseshell', 'Tyee', 'Santorini', 'Bloomsdale'.

Bolting of lettuce and other vegetables is caused by high temperatures and increased day length.

Catface

AFFECTS: tomato

Cool weather (several days below 15°C/59°F), 2,4-D injury, excessive nitrogen and excessive pruning interfere with early fruit development immediately after flower pollination.

WHAT TO LOOK FOR: Malformation of tomato fruit showing up as a flattened blossom end with large bands of scar tissue crisscrossing each other, resulting in numerous lobes and cavities. More often found on large-fruiting varieties of tomatoes.

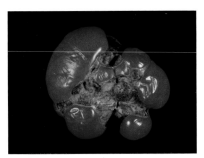

Caused by a number of factors, cat-facing occurs most often in larger fruiting tomato varieties.

Properly hilled potatoes seldom show greening. Remove all green portions prior to cooking and eating.

PREVENTION:

Cultural methods:

- Protect plants from unseasonably cool weather.
- Avoid high levels of nitrogen and excessive pruning.

- Avoid light in storage.
- Avoid susceptible varieties such as 'Kennebec.'

SOLUTIONS:

- Remove all green portions of the tuber prior to cooking and eating.

Greening

AFFECTS: potato

Greening is caused by chlorophyll formation due to exposure to sunlight in the garden or artificial light in storage. This causes an increase in the level of glycoalkaloids, which are toxic at higher levels and can cause stomach discomfort even at low concentrations. WHAT TO LOOK FOR: The skin of the potatoes is green and the outer flesh is green or yellowish-green. The taste is bitter. Cooking does not remove either the green or the bitterness, or the stomach discomfort that results from eating them.

PREVENTION:

Cultural methods:

- Ensure that potatoes are properly hilled so that the tubers are not exposed to sunlight.

Knobbiness

AFFECTS: potato

Knobbiness is caused by changes in soil moisture, usually a dry period followed by heavy rain or irrigation during the time of tuber formation. 'Russet Burbank' tubers are highly susceptible to knobbiness. WHAT TO LOOK FOR: The tubers have a very irregular form, with bumps and lumps and knobs. Some may be hourglass-like in shape.

PREVENTION:

Cultural methods:

- Ensure that potatoes receive even moisture, especially during tuber formation.
- Apply an organic mulch to conserve moisture.

Knobbiness of potatoes is caused by lack of even moisture. Not a problem as long as you're a patient peeler.

Sunscald

AFFECTS: pepper, tomato

Sunscald is caused by the sudden exposure of the developing fruit to direct sunlight, through pruning or defoliation, especially if weather conditions are hot and dry.

WHAT TO LOOK FOR: Sunscald generally occurs on the green fruit of tomatoes and peppers. A white or yellow patch develops on the side of the fruit facing the sun. It later becomes paper-like and sunken. Secondary rot organisms may enter.

PREVENTION:

Cultural methods:

- Maintain healthy, disease-free foliage and avoid excessive pruning.

Tipburn

AFFECTS: Brussels sprouts, cabbage, cauliflower, lettuce

Tipburn is caused by a calcium deficiency aggravated by uneven watering.

WHAT TO LOOK FOR: Brown dead spots on the leaf tips expand to the entire leaf margin. Tipburn also appears on the inner leaves of head-forming vegetables.

PREVENTION:

Cultural methods:

- Use resistant cultivars:
  Lettuce: 'Tiber', 'Yucaipe', 'Green Forest', 'Sangria', 'Nevada', 'Vulcan', 'Odyssey', 'Envy', 'Lasting Green', 'Caliente', 'Grand Rapids', 'Green Bay', 'Crunchy', 'Emeralda', 'Paris Island Cos'.

Sunscald is caused by the sudden exposure of the developing pepper to direct sunlight during hot dry weather.

Tipburn is seen on lettuce as well as Brussels sprouts, cabbage and cauliflower. Due to a calcium deficiency, it's easily avoided by using resistant varieties.

Cabbage: 'Melissa', 'Sweet Surprise', 'Megaton', 'Platinum Dynasty', 'Blue Vantage', 'Rondale', 'Red Dynasty', 'Artost', 'Atlanta', 'Novator', 'Bobcat'.

- Ensure balanced fertilization.
- Ensure even watering. Never let the plants dry out as this can exacerbate a calcium deficiency.
- Harvest early.

Yellow head

AFFECTS: cauliflower

We expect our cauliflower to be white, and so yellow-headed cauliflower is a bit disconcerting. This disorder can be due to sunburn or (less often) a boron deficiency (indicated by hollow areas within the stem). It can be avoided by tying the outer leaves with a bit of kitchen twine. 'Cheddar' is a new variety that's already yellow, and meant to be. Or you can try the purple varieties that do not require protection from the sun and turn a light green when cooked. If your heart's still set on white cauliflower, there are many self-blanching types whose leaves protect them and keep them white.

WHAT TO LOOK FOR: Heads appear yellow instead of white.

PREVENTION:

Cultural methods:

- Blanch by tying the outer leaves over the exposed head with twine or a rubber band, slack enough to allow for air circulation and expansion. This keeps heads white and provides moderate frost protection.
- Try self-blanching varieties with tight wrapper leaves that provide a built-in sun screen: 'Symphony', 'Freemont', 'Minuteman', 'Accent', 'Freedom', 'Attribute', 'White Sails', 'Apex', 'Wentworth', 'Casper'.
- Use a fertilizer with micronutrients including boron.

Tying the tops of the leaves over the head of the cauliflower protects it from the sun and yellowing.

Yellow head of cauliflower is not very appetizing. Plant self-blanching types with tight wrapper leaves.

Chapter 9

Flowers, Bulbs & Vines

One of the undervalued benefits of growing bulbs, vines and annual and perennial flowers on the prairies is the harsh climate. Our long, cold winters take their toll on insects and diseases (as well as the occasional well-beloved plant), and the dryness of our climate discourages many disease-causing organisms.

So take heart. In a good year, you'll probably not come across any problems. Even in a bad year, potential problems are few. We were able to come up with only a baker's dozen or so. Compare that to what gardeners face in southern Ontario or coastal British Columbia!

Observation and early detection are the keys to control. Possible problems could be the results of insects and diseases, or disorders caused by cultural or environmental problems. Use the diagnostic chart to help you identify what's troubling your particular plant, then turn to the appropriate section in this chapter – Insects, Diseases or Disorders – for in-depth information on the problem and how to avoid, control or eradicate it. For information on weed control see Chapter 4, Controlling Weeds Without Chemicals.

'Mrs. Perry' is a fine old heritage oriental poppy that does best in full sun on well-drained soil.

DIAGNOSTIC CHART

Common insects, diseases and disorders of flowers, bulbs and vines

PLANT	PART AFFECTED	SYMPTOMS	LIKELY PROBLEM
Seedlings, many types affected	stem	topples over	Damping off (Diseases)
Alyssum (annual and perennial)	foliage	tiny shot holes	Flea beetle (Insects)
Aster (as well as calendula, chrysanthemum, cosmos, delphinium, Echinacea, Erigeron, Gaillardia, marigold, petunia, Shasta daisy)	folliage	yellowing; witches' broom	Aster yellows (Diseases)
	flower	greenish tinge; misshapen	
Aster	foliage	white powdery coating	Powdery mildew (Diseases)
Clematis	stem, foliage	sudden dramatic wilting, blackening	Clematis wilt (Diseases)
Columbine	foliage	winding, white or tan trails	Columbine leaf miner (Insects)
Daylily	foliage	mottled, streaked	Thrips (Insects)
	flower	distorted; brown or silver; fails to open	
Delphinium (as well as larkspur)	foliage	tied together	Delphinium leaftier (Insects)
Delphinium	foliage	white powdery coating	Powdery mildew (Diseases)
Delphinium (as well as hosta, Veronicastrum)	foliage	distorted	Fasciation (Disorders)
	flower	flattened	
Fritillaria	flower, foliage, stem	eaten	Scarlet lily beetle (Insects)

Gladiola (as well as *Dianthus*)	foliage	mottled, streaked	**Thrips** (Insects)
	flower	distorted; brown or silver; fails to open	
Hollyhock	foliage	orange spots	**Hollyhock rust** (Diseases)
Hosta (as well as begonia, bleeding heart, cornflower, dahlia, delphinium, hollyhock, pansy, petunia and others)	foliage	large irregular holes; slime trails	**Slug** (Insects)
Hosta	foliage	"bleeding" of colour along veins; uncharacteristic puckering, twisting	**Hosta virus X** (Diseases)
Iris	stem, foliage	yellow-brown lesions; stems may break; fuzzy	**Grey mould** (Diseases)
	flower	fuzzy mass of grey spores	
Lily	stem, foliage, flower	eaten	**Scarlet lily beetle** (Insects)
Lily	stem, foliage	yellow-brown lesions; stems may break; fuzzy	**Grey mould** (Diseases)
	flower	fuzzy mass of grey spores	
Monarda	foliage	white powdery coating	**Powdery mildew** (Diseases)
Monkshood	foliage	tied together	**Delphinium leaftier** (Insects)

Peony	stem, foliage	yellow-brown lesions; stems may break; fuzzy	**Grey mould** (Diseases)
	flower	fuzzy mass of grey spores	
Peony	flower	no flowers	**Disorders**
Phlox	foliage	white powdery coating	**Powdery mildew** (Diseases)
Virginia creeper	foliage	yellowing and eventual browning	**Leafhoppers** (Insects)

Insects

Columbine leaf miner

AFFECTS: columbine

While it is aesthetically displeasing (although it might pass for an unusual form of variegated foliage!), the damage wrought by the columbine leaf miner (*Phytomyza aquilegivora*) is seldom devastating. It is present in most gardens where columbines are grown and has little effect on the plant's health or its ability to photosynthesize.

They tunnel or "mine" between the leaf surfaces, creating distinctive serpentine trails.

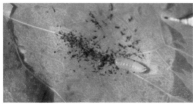

Columbine leaf miners are present in most gardens where columbines are grown.

The adult is a pale brown fly. Females lay eggs on the lower leaf surfaces of columbines in the spring. The pale larvae tunnel and eat the interior of the leaves, creating serpentine patterns before exiting through crescent-shaped slits to form brown pupae on the leaves. The flies emerge two weeks later. The last generation pupates in the soil.

The Japanese fan columbine (*Aquilegia flabellata*) shows greater resistance to columbine leaf miners than most other species and cultivars.

WHAT TO LOOK FOR: Winding white or tan trails through the foliage.

PREVENTION:

Cultural methods:

- Remove and destroy dead plant debris in the fall.

SOLUTIONS:

Cultural methods:

- Hand-pick and destroy infected leaves.
- Japanese fan columbines (*Aquilegia flabellata*) are more resistant than many columbines.

Delphinium leaftier, Delphinium worm

AFFECTS: delphinium, larkspur, monkshood

Native to the foothills of the Rocky Mountains, where the larvae consume wild larkspur, this moth (*Polychrysia esmeralda*, syn. *P. moneta*) has spread east, feeding on the monkshood and delphinium of our gardens. They have voracious appetites and can destroy newly emerging shoots within a few days.

No delphinium is immune to the delphinium leaftier, but if you're observant, and squash it early, little damage is done.

The adult is a dull-coloured, medium-sized (3.5 cm/1.5 in. wingspan), golden-brown moth that appears from late June to early August and feeds at twilight. Slow flying, in their native habitat the adults feed on the nectar of fireweed. Eggs are laid at the base of host plants, on which the larvae will eventually feed.

The small green larvae hatch in May as delphiniums are emerging. They climb the stems and begin eating the developing flower stem and leaves within the growing tip, generally when plants are about 15 to 30 cm (6–12 in.) in height. There is one generation per year. They overwinter as eggs or pupae.

WHAT TO LOOK FOR: Leaves of young stems are tied together. The culprit, along with a good deal of black frass (excrement), is within.

SOLUTIONS:

Cultural methods:

- Unroll the leaves and pick out the caterpillar, or simply pinch off the tips and discard the "package" – leaves, caterpillar and all. New stems will develop.

- A few birds are predators of the larvae.

The delphinium leaftier larvae hatch in May just as delphiniums are emerging.

. . . .

Leafhopper

AFFECTS: Virginia creeper, grape

. . . .

Leafhoppers are aphid-like insects that are distinguished by their hopping behaviour. Adults are pale whitish, wedge-shaped, about 5 mm ($\frac{3}{16}$ in.) long with a zigzag stripe down each wing. They fly from the undersides of leaves when disturbed and are often mistaken for whiteflies. They damage plants by sucking sap while injecting a toxin that causes "hopper burn," a yellowing of leaf tissues that eventually causes leaves to fall.

The Virginia creeper leafhopper (*Erythroneura ziczac*) occasionally damages Virginia creeper as well as grape plants. They emerge when temperatures are in the 15° to 20°C (60–68°F) range for several days.

WHAT TO LOOK FOR: Damage on the leaves of Virginia creeper appears as white blotches, and if the infestation is heavy the leaves will turn yellow, then brown and fall prematurely.

PREVENTION:

Cultural methods:

- Leafhoppers are naturally controlled by predators and parasites such as spiders, lacewings, parasitic wasps and birds.

Leafhoppers attack both Virginia creeper and grape, sucking sap from the foliage.

Typical "hopper burn" on the foliage of Virginia creeper.

- Populations can often be kept in check by cleaning up debris around susceptible plants and removing or mowing weeds from the adjacent garden areas.

SOLUTIONS:

Less toxic alternatives:

- Severe infestations may be controlled with insecticidal soap.

Flea beetle

AFFECTS: alyssum

Although especially a problem in rural areas where canola and mustard are grown, and often seen on members of the cabbage family in our vegetable gardens, crucifer flea beetles (*Phyllotreta cruciferae*) (and other species) also feed on annual and perennial alyssum in our flower borders. These tiny insects are most damaging when the plants are small.

WHAT TO LOOK FOR: Tiny shot holes in the foliage point to their presence.

PREVENTION:

Cultural methods:

- Using transplants rather than seeding directly is your best bet.
- For additional information, see Chapter 8, Vegetables.

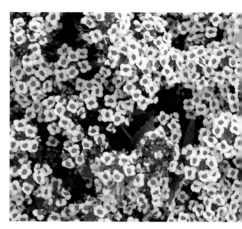

Annual sweet alyssum (as well as perennial alyssum) is much loved by flea beetles.

Scarlet lily beetle, red lily leaf beetle, lily beetle

AFFECTS: fritillaria, lily

Believed to have entered the prairies by hitchhiking a ride with lily orders from Ontario, the scarlet lily beetle (*Lilioceris lilii*) was first reported in Portage la Prairie in 1991 and in Winnipeg in

The scarlet lily beetle is attractive, fertile and lethal, feeding on all above-ground plant parts: leaves, stems, buds and flowers.

Flea beetles are tiny but in large numbers can do a lot of damage.

2006. Now in Alberta and Manitoba, it is only a matter of time before this devastating insect will be found throughout the prairies.

Native to Europe, the lily beetle has no natural predators in North America. They are fast-flying and are often difficult to see in the soil debris.

The adult is 6 to 9 mm (⅓ in.) long and is an attractive shiny red with a black head, antennae and undersides. Adults overwinter in the soil or under plant debris, preferring a shaded, cool, moist environment. They emerge from the soil and mate at the same time as lilies emerge from the soil. The females lay up to 450 reddish-orange eggs in clusters or uneven rows, often along the midrib on the undersides of the leaves. The eggs hatch in seven to ten days.

The larvae feed for two to three weeks and are capable of doing an enormous amount of damage in a very short time. They are light grey-brown and similar in size and form to larvae of the Colorado potato beetle. They hide by covering themselves with their own frass, or excrement, looking somewhat like a black slug.

Both lilies and fritillaria are consumed by the scarlet lily beetle. Check the soil of all incoming plants for eggs, larvae and adults.

The larvae pupate in the soil below lilies for two to three weeks, emerging as adults that feed in August and September, often moving on to new territory later.

WHAT TO LOOK FOR: Both the larvae and adults feed on all above-ground plant parts: leaves, stems, buds and flowers. Plants are left ragged and forlorn, and are sometimes consumed to ground level.

Thanatosis and Stridulation

Thanatosis is a defence mechanism of adult beetles triggered by danger. When this occurs, they first become motionless, fold their legs and wings, and then fall to the ground so their black "belly" is facing upwards, acting as camouflage against the soil. If they still feel vulnerable, they squeak (by rubbing their body parts together) in an attempt to startle their enemy into leaving. This is called stridulation.

"If the ground be strewed in the evening with fresh cabbage leaves, the slugs will hide under these and may be destroyed in the morning."

Samuel Orchart Beeton, *Beeton's Shilling Garden*, 1900

PREVENTION:

Cultural methods:

- Purchase lily bulbs from a reputable nursery or garden centre, lily grower or lily society.
- Avoid purchasing lilies already potted in soil.
- Ensure that newly acquired lily bulbs are clean and free of soil. Inspect them carefully for pests before planting.
- Check the soil of all incoming plants. Inspect lilies closely and regularly.

SOLUTIONS:

Cultural methods:

- Hand-pick adults; crush larvae and eggs against the foliage.
- Disturb the soil to expose adults and pupae, destroying any that are found.

Less toxic alternatives:

- Apply diatomaceous earth.
- Wash bulbs in a 2 percent bleach solution (20 ml/l (⅔oz/1 qt) of water) for twenty minutes, rinsing prior to planting.
- European predators include the parasitic wasp *Diaparsis jucunda*, as well as *Tetrastichus setifer* and *Lemophagus errabundus*. *Tetrastichus setifer* has recently been approved for release in Canada. Other predators may be available in Canada in the future.

Slugs

AFFECTS: primarily hosta, as well as begonia, bleeding heart, cornflower, dahlia, delphinium, hollyhock, pansy, petunia and others; lettuce, tomato

Slugs (Mollusca) are a common garden pest, but the problem could be worse. Prairie winters have their advantages. Banana slugs, found on the west coast, are much larger and capable of more extensive damage, but

Slugs have voracious appetites and attack many plants including hollyhock.

Slugs are hermaphroditic (each individual having both male and female parts), but to produce fertile eggs, an individual must mate with another slug.

Newer slug baits use iron phosphate that inhibits the slug's ability to eat, causing death in a few days.

to facilitate movement and prevent water loss. Their eyes are at the ends of tentacles. They lay round, translucent, jelly-like eggs in the soil or under plant pots or other shelters. They feed at night or during cloudy days on soft plant tissue, using their rasping mouth parts. There is one generation per year. Slugs overwinter in the soil and under plant debris.

WHAT TO LOOK FOR: Slugs leave slime trails and large, irregular holes in the leaves. When damage is severe, only the midribs remain. Slugs will also chew holes in tomato fruit, especially at ground level.

PREVENTION:

Cultural methods:

- Carefully inspect new plants, their containers and soil for slugs and their eggs, washing off all soil from plant parts if required.
- Keep the soil surface around susceptible plants clean and free of vegetation, creating a drier, less-hospitable environment and eliminating hiding places.
- Use drip irrigation to keep the surface soil drier. If using overhead irrigation, water early in the morning.

will not overwinter here. Slugs prefer dark, moist, cool situations and do poorly in sunny, open areas during hot, dry summers.

Slugs are best described as snails without an obvious shell. Generally cream coloured, dark brown or black, and less than 2.5 cm (1 in.) long, their soft bodies are coated in mucus

Slug recipes

Homemade remedies abound for slug control but many are more urban myth than garden solution. Drink your beer; don't give it to the slugs. Avoid salt – it ruins your soil. Egg shells, ashes and coffee grounds, even mini-fences made of copper flashing or galvanized zinc are all less effective than the options listed here.

- Mulch with materials abrasive enough to damage their tender bodies. Post peelings work well.
- Cultivate deeply in the fall to expose slugs to freezing temperatures.
- A three-year rotation is useful for susceptible annual bedding plants (as well as tender lettuce and salad greens). Rotate with bedding plants slugs do not enjoy, such as geraniums.

SOLUTIONS:

Cultural methods:

- Slugs are slow-moving and soft-bodied, and therein lies your advantage. Hand-picking works if done with consistency and determination. It is best done at dawn or dusk, or at night with a flashlight. Wear gloves if you are squeamish, and drop the slugs into a container of soapy water.
- Slugs will collect under boards, where it is dark, cool and damp; check these "traps" early each morning, dumping the slugs in soapy water.
- Lure slugs with a beerless "beer" bait made of yeast, sugar and water. Bury the small container so that the top edge is slightly higher than the soil surface. Slugs will crawl up, over and in, but most beneficial insects will not be drowned.
- Predators: centipedes; magpies, robins, downy woodpeckers and other birds; garter snakes, toads and salamanders; and the introduced ground beetle *Carabus nemoralis.*

Less toxic alternatives:

- Apply newer slug bait formulations which use iron phosphate. It inhibits the slug's ability to eat and perhaps to produce mucus. Slugs die within a few days.
- Apply diatomaceous earth.

Thrips

AFFECTS: primarily gladiola; also daylily, *Dianthus,* rose

These insects are so tiny (1.5 mm/ ¹⁄₁₆ in.), and generally so well hidden, deep in the flower or in a leaf crevice, that you need a magnifying glass to see them. Long and narrow, from pale yellow to black, gladiola thrips (*Taeniothrips simplex* and other species) resemble tiny dark threads. They can move quickly when disturbed. If you believe they are feasting on your gladioli, shake the flowers while holding a stiff piece of white paper under them. The thrips will show up on the paper. As well as feeding on plants, they also carry plant viruses. To their credit, they assist in pollination and some species are predators, killing harmful insects.

Thrips are extremely small and very well hidden. You're much more likely to see their damage.

Thrips feed by rasping plant tissue and sucking sap, leaving flowers and foliage mottled, streaked, brown, silvered and distorted.

Females can lay up to two hundred eggs in spring, either in slits in the leaf or flower tissue or on the leaf surface. Both the larvae and adults damage plants. There are several generations per year. Thrips are killed by low temperatures and only overwinter by hibernating in gladiola corms kept in storage. Infested corms are sticky from exuding sap and are rough and darker in colour.

WHAT TO LOOK FOR: Because thrips feed by rasping the outer epidermal layer of the leaves and then sucking the sap from the plant tissue, the foliage appears mottled and streaked. Flowers can be distorted, streaked and have brown or silver areas. Infested flower spikes may fail to bloom. Thrips are often found on the undersides of the leaves near the midrib.

PREVENTION:

Cultural methods:

- Mulch gladioli and mist them during dry weather; maintain even moisture.
- Aluminum foil mulch, placed on the soil around susceptible plants in early spring, is not attractive, but it disorients thrips, hopefully away from your gladioli.

Less toxic alternatives:

- Store gladiola corms at 4°C (40°F) in a fridge or cold room. Before planting, soak corms for three hours in 2 percent bleach solution (20 ml/l (²/₃ oz/1 qt) of water).

SOLUTIONS:

Cultural methods:

- Place blue sticky traps even with the plant canopy. Homemade sticky traps are messy but effective.
- Encourage predators: minute pirate bugs, lacewings, big-eyed bugs, ground beetles, birds.

Less toxic alternatives:

- Use insecticidal soap.
- Apply diatomaceous earth to the foliage.
- Apply sulphur to the foliage.
- *Beauveria bassiana* is a microorganism found in soils. It is slow acting and needs a moist environment, but will kill thrips.
- Spinosad, derived from *Saccharopolyspora spinosa*, an actinomycete (a kind of bacteria) works on the nervous system of thrips. They stop feeding fairly quickly, but it takes them a few days to die. It has good residual activity.

Diseases

Aster yellows

AFFECTS: aster, as well as calendula, chrysanthemum, cosmos, delphinium, *Echinacea, Erigeron, Gaillardia,* marigold, petunia, Shasta daisy; other plants such as carrot

A widespread disease of many plant families, aster yellows got its name because annual China asters (*Callistephus chinensis*) succumbed to it in droves in the early 1900s. There is more than one strain, and all are transmitted by feeding insects. Fortunately, it is only seen occasionally in prairie gardens. There is no cure. Perennials infected with aster yellows become weakened and are more prone to winterkill.

Although aster yellows overwinters on perennial host plants, its spread is mainly dependent on leafhoppers. It is not seed borne, nor does it persist in the soil. This is a virus-like disease caused by a phytoplasma, a single-celled organism without cell walls. It overwinters in the insects or on perennials, including weeds such as dandelions, thistle and plantain.

WHAT TO LOOK FOR: Vein clearing (the conspicuous lack of chlorophyll) in parts of younger leaves, causing them to turn from green to yellow. Foliage may have a purplish cast. Flower petals lose their characteristic colour and take on a green tinge. The flowers are misshapen, often resembling a mass of tiny leaves. Long, thin branches develop from the leaf axils, a proliferation known as witches' broom. In contrast, the main stem is stunted.

PREVENTION:

Cultural methods:

- Control weed hosts.

The spread of aster yellows, a virus-like disease, is mainly dependent on leafhoppers that carry it from one plant to another as they feed.

When infected with aster yellows, flower petals lose their characteristic colour and take on a greenish tinge. They are often distorted.

Less toxic alternatives:
- Apply insecticidal soap to control insect vectors

SOLUTIONS:

Cultural methods:
- Pull and destroy infected plants.

Clematis wilt can occur overnight, causing the vines to turn black with purple veins.

Aster yellows can overwinter on perennial weeds such as Canada thistle.

Clematis wilt

AFFECTS: clematis

Clematis wilt (*Phoma clematidina, Ascochyta clematidina*) is most common on young plants and is more likely to kill newly transplanted vines. It typically attacks flower buds and new growth first. The pathogens clog the vascular tissue of the plant, causing wilt. Fortunately, this disease does not infect the roots.

WHAT TO LOOK FOR: Wilting of clematis stems may also be caused by mechanical damage due to wind or slugs chewing on stems, but with clematis wilt it is dramatic and can happen overnight. The affected vines will turn black with purple veins.

PREVENTION:

Cultural methods:
- Plant resistant varieties. As a rule, small-flowered clematis types such as *Clematis alpina, C. macropetala* and *C. viticella* are not susceptible to wilt. If you are purchasing large-flowered hybrids, make sure you only buy and plant healthy nursery stock.
- Plant clematis with roots in shade and tops growing up into the sun.
- Provide good growing conditions: the soil should have plenty of organic matter and good drainage; water regularly to keep the soil moist; and top-dress with compost or other organic fertilizers.
- Plant clematis deeply enough so that a crown will develop below the ground.

Damping off, a fungal disease, can affect almost all seedlings. Seedling stems first show water-soaked lesions (generally unnoticed) and then collapse at soil level.

Use resistant cultivars developed from species such as *Clematis alpina*, *C. macropetala*, and *C. viticella*. 'Polish Spirit' is one of these.

SOLUTIONS:

Cultural methods:

- Prune affected stems to ground level. Disinfect pruners after each cut. Destroy infected stems; do not compost them.

Damping off

AFFECTS: seedlings, transplants

Damping off (species of *Fusarium, Pythium, Rhizoctonia solani*) is a common cause of seedling death in both greenhouses and gardens. It is caused by a variety of fungi and usually encountered during periods of high humidity. It is worse when seeds are slow to germinate, generally under cool, wet conditions. The fungi rapidly infect plant tissue if a film of water is present. Prevention is the best cure.

WHAT TO LOOK FOR: Seedling stems first show water-soaked lesions (generally not even noticed) and then very quickly collapse at soil level. Some fail to emerge.

PREVENTION:

Cultural methods:

- Use sterilized or pasteurized growing media, and clean containers and tools when sowing seeds indoors.
- Water early in the day, and avoid overwatering.
- Provide good air circulation, good light and soil drainage, and avoid overcrowding seedlings; use a fan indoors.
- Cover the growing media with a thin layer of sand, perlite or vermiculite to encourage a dry surface.
- Outside, seed into warm soil to encourage rapid germination.

Less toxic alternatives:

- Biological seed treatments: *Trichoderma* (a fungus, sold under the product name RootShield®); *Bacillus subtilis* and *Streptomyces griseoviridis* (bacteria, sold under the product names Serenade© and Mycostop©).

SOLUTIONS:

Cultural methods:

- Use compost in vegetable gardens and for directly seeded annual flowers; it generally contains beneficial fungi able to suppress *Pythium*.
- See Chapter 8, Vegetables.

Grow seedlings with adequate spacing and good light in a well-drained mix, covering it with a layer of sand, perlite or vermiculite to encourage a dry surface.

Grey mould

AFFECTS: iris, lily, peony

Botrytis or grey mould (*Botrytis* species) is probably the most serious and widespread of the lily diseases, attacking other perennials as well. Like many fungal infections, it is highly weather dependent – it is worse under wet conditions. Plants with spring frost damage are more vulnerable. The spores require moisture and a temperature range of 15° to 20°C (60–68°F) to germinate.

The fungus overwinters in the soil and plant debris. Spores are windborne and germinate during wet weather on a film of water or on droplets.

WHAT TO LOOK FOR: Grey mould can affect all above-ground parts: the emerging stem, foliage and flowers. It generally does not penetrate the bulb scale. Water-soaked lesions develop; they are circular to oval in shape and yellow to reddish brown in colour, generally with a yellow "halo." These coalesce under humid conditions. Lower leaves may yellow and

Grey mould on iris can begin as small water-soaked lesions on foliage, often with a yellow halo.

On lilies infected with grey mould, lower leaves may yellow, brown and shrivel.

Peony foliage infected by grey mould often turns brown and shrivels.

To reduce the incidence of grey mould, plant susceptible species in full sun on well-drained soil, allowing generous spacing for good air circulation.

shrivel. Infected stems may break at the point of infection. Buds and flowers may appear abnormal and brown. Lesions on flowers enlarge rapidly, turning from brown to black and finally to grey with a fuzzy mass of spores.

PREVENTION:

Cultural methods:

- Avoid wetting the foliage; avoid overhead irrigation; water earlier in the day so foliage dries quickly.
- Provide good air circulation; avoid overcrowding.
- Plant in full sun in well-drained soil.
- Avoid monoculture or practice rotation.
- Mulch to prevent water splash of soil or spores onto foliage.

SOLUTIONS:

Cultural methods:

- Remove and destroy infected foliage during the growing season by hand-picking infected leaves.
- Remove and destroy infected plant debris in fall.
- Replant lily bulbs in full sun in well-drained soil.

Less toxic alternatives:

- Dust lily bulbs with sulphur prior to planting or replanting.
- Apply a copper-based Bordeaux mixture.

Hollyhock rust

AFFECTS: primarily hollyhock, as well as *Abutilon, Lavatera, Malva*

If you've grown hollyhocks, chances are you've seen hollyhock rust. By the mid-1800s, hollyhock rust (*Puccinia malvacearum*) had been recorded in Chile, Australia and Europe. It's widespread, seldom very damaging, but not pretty to look at.

The rust overwinters on old leaves and stems. Fungal spores are spread by wind, rain and insects, and infection is worse during wet weather. Many rust diseases (such as saskatoon-juniper rust) require two distinct hosts, but hollyhock rust requires only hollyhocks.

WHAT TO LOOK FOR: The underside of new foliage shows brownish orange pin-head spots. The disease later spreads to the upper surfaces of leaves, where the lesions are larger, often with red centres. Lesions may coalesce and parts of the leaf surface may dry up and fall out. Premature leaf drop may occur.

PREVENTION:

Cultural methods:

- Provide good air circulation and adequate spacing of plants.
- Keep foliage dry.
- Do not work among hollyhocks when they are wet.
- Remove and destroy old plant debris.
- Remove round-leafed mallow weeds, which are also affected by this disease.
- Plant *Alcea rugosa* which is resistant to hollyhock rust.

SOLUTIONS:

Cultural methods:

- Remove and destroy infected leaves.

Less toxic alternatives:

- Apply sulphur or lime sulphur.

Remove and destroy all round-leafed mallow, a weed which is also affected by hollyhock rust and can harbour fungal spores.

Hosta virus X

AFFECTS: Gold-leafed hostas seem particularly susceptible but hosta virus X also affects other favourites: 'Birchwood Parky's Gold', 'Blue Cadet', 'Gold Edger', 'Goldrush', 'Gold Standard', 'Honeybells', 'Royal Standard', 'So Sweet', 'Stiletto', 'Striptease', 'Sum & Substance', 'Sweet Susan', and the species *Hosta undulato* 'Albomarginata', *H. ventricosa* and *H. venucosa*. This list is not complete but indicates plants to be aware of.

Hollyhock rust is first characterized by brownish orange pin-head spots on the undersides of new foliage, later spreading to the upper surface and becoming larger.

A popular shade plant easily propagated by division, hostas have long been regarded as pest-free (except for slugs) and virtually indestructible. Weird mottling is not unusual in hostas and is generally due to simple

The most common symptom of hosta virus X is "bleeding" of colour along the leaf veins associated with blue or green mottling of the leaves.

colour mutation. But all of this changed with the appearance of hosta virus X, first described in 1996.

Although many viruses are either soil-borne or spread by insects, hosta virus X is believed to be spread by the movement of sap from an infected plant to a healthy one, generally through division or by bruising or breaking a leaf or other plant part.

The virus itself may be present for years without the plant dying and may be spread to other hostas during this period.

WHAT TO LOOK FOR: "Bleeding" of colour along the leaf veins, associated with blue or green mottling of the leaves, is the most common symptom. Also look for puckering and twisting that is not characteristic of the species or cultivar and the development of mosaic ring spots. Dead areas may occur within a leaf, or entire leaves may die.

PREVENTION:

Cultural methods:

- Clean tools and hands between working with each hosta plant.
- Leave dead leaves and spent flowers on your hostas.
- Be observant. Look for the symptoms.
- Be discerning as to where you purchase hostas, buying from reputable nurseries, although even this is no guarantee your hosta will be virus-free.

"Hostamania"?

In the 1600s, at the height of "Tulipmania" in Holland, fortunes were won and lost in the trade of tulip bulbs. Although highly prized, tulips with unusual striping and stippling were seldom long lived. With the hindsight of four centuries and a liberal dose of modern plant pathology, we now recognize that the striping was due to a virus that was also the cause of their untimely death.

Botanical history is now repeating itself, this time with *Hosta*. New hosta cultivars, with characteristics now known to be caused by hosta virus X, were actually introduced and sold, thus rapidly spreading the virus far and wide. Among these were 'Blue Freckles', 'Breakdance', 'Eternal Father', 'Kiwi Watercolours', 'Leopard Frog' and 'Lunacy'. Lunacy, indeed!

Be discerning as to where you purchase hostas, buying from reputable nurseries, although even this is no guarantee your hosta will be virus-free.

A white powdery coating on the leaf surface indicates powdery mildew. To reduce its incidence, give delphiniums generous spacing with good air circulation.

SOLUTIONS:

Cultural methods:

- If you suspect a hosta is virus-infected, remove all of it (including root pieces), and place it in a plastic bag in the garbage. Do not compost it. Use bleach to disinfect the tool used to dig it up.

Powdery mildew

AFFECTS: aster, delphinium, *monarda*, phlox, others

Powdery mildew is a fungal disease with fairly obvious symptoms. It is caused by various genera and species and is highly weather dependent. Although it seems like a contradiction, most powdery mildews are promoted by high humidity but low rainfall. The reason? The conidia (asexual spores) are easily damaged by raindrops.

Spores of powdery mildew are spread by wind and air currents in spring. The disease appears worse during periods of warm days and cool nights when dew is present, or when plants are under moisture stress. It is generally worse in shaded areas. Bee balm (*Monarda*) and garden phlox are among the most susceptible perennials, but fortunately many resistant cultivars have been introduced in the last few decades.

WHAT TO LOOK FOR: A white powdery coating on the leaf surface. On severely infected plants, leaves will drop and plants will be weakened.

PREVENTION:

Cultural methods:

- Use resistant varieties. The following are hardy to zone 3: Monarda: 'Coral Reef', 'Grand Marshall', 'Grand Parade',

Many newer varieties of Monarda have been bred with powdery mildew resistance.

'Gardenview Scarlet', 'Jacob Cline', 'Marshall's Delight', 'Mohawk', 'Petite Delight', 'Petite Wonder', 'Raspberry Wine', 'Violet Queen'.

Phlox: 'Purple Flame', 'Spinners', 'Laura', 'David', 'Delta Snow', 'Franz Schubert', 'Nora Leigh'.

- Grow plants in full sun.

Older varieties of garden phlox may be more susceptible to powdery mildew.

- Water the soil rather than the foliage; ensure even moisture; irrigate early in the day so foliage dries quickly.
- Ensure adequate spacing for good air circulation.

SOLUTIONS:

Cultural methods:
- Clean up and destroy fallen leaves and infected plant material.

Less toxic alternatives:
- Apply sulphur.
- Apply baking soda (sodium bicarbonate) or potassium bicarbonate.
- For additional information, see Chapter 8, Vegetables, Chapter 10, Trees and Shrubs and Chapter 11, Fruit.

Disorders

Fasciation

AFFECTS: delphinium, hosta, *Veronicastrum* (culver's root)

Generally a "once in the life of the plant" occurrence, fasciation is almost always due to cold weather in early spring that caused irregularities in cell division. Fasciation has also been attributed to viral infection, heavy manuring or a soil bacterium, *Corynebacterium fascians*. It seldom repeats itself. If it shows up continually in the same plant, it's due to a genetic mutation. Such was the case with *Veronicastrum virginicum* 'Fascination', now a much sought-after cultivar!

WHAT TO LOOK FOR: Distorted growth: fused and flattened stems; or misshapen, off-coloured, curled, split flower heads. Often, only a single stem is affected.

SOLUTIONS:

Cultural methods:

- The simple solution is to cut out the distorted stem.

Fasciation is a disorder that results in distorted growth with fused and flattened stems and misshapen flowers as seen in this delphinium.

Fasciation can also be found in hosta. Cutting off the affected stem is the easiest solution.

Peonies not blooming

AFFECTS: peony

Peonies fail to flower for a number of reasons. The most common is that they have been planted too deep. The tops of eyes or buds should be no deeper than 5 cm (2 in.) below the soil surface. Deeper planting results in an absence of light on the buds, inhibiting flowering. Other possible reasons for not blooming include:

- Plants are immature.
- Plants are too old or overcrowded.
- Plants have been moved and divided too frequently.
- Plants are in too much shade. Plant peonies in full sun in well-drained soil.
- Plants have been given too much nitrogen fertilizer.
- Buds have been killed by frost or grey mould.

Planting peonies too deep is the most common reason for their failure to bloom.

Chapter 10

Trees & Shrubs

Woody plants form the "bones" of the landscape. They give us shade and shelter, provide privacy, define space, hide undesirable views and frame ones that enhance our landscapes. They grow for many years in one place and, if we provide conditions for healthy growth, they will thrive.

Stress reduces the ability of trees and shrubs to resist or overcome pests and disease. A healthy plant that has an adequate supply of moisture and nutrients and is growing under favourable conditions will be much more likely to survive an attack by pathogens or insects.

Choosing appropriate species and varieties, proper planting and good cultural practices will contribute to our success in discouraging or controlling pests and diseases. When, despite our efforts, a valuable tree or shrub is attacked by disease or insects, there are a variety of techniques and products that we can use. We should choose those that do the least harm to the environment and the beneficial organisms in our gardens, and target them at specific problems.

Trees and shrubs provide background and framing and define spaces in the landscape.

Some problems are merely cosmetic. For example, eriophyid mites make unsightly little bumps on the leaves of such tree species as American basswood, but they don't do significant harm to the tree. Other problems are so devastating as almost to rule out planting the affected species. The bronze birch borer will kill an infested tree over a period of a few years. The wise gardener will not choose the most susceptible species, cutleaf weeping birch. And despite our efforts to save our elm trees, diseases like Dutch elm disease are essentially incurable. Once trees are infected, they should be removed to reduce its spread.

Cultural practices

Choosing the right tree or shrub

Choose plants that are suited to the growing conditions of the planting site. A list of trees and shrubs that are suitable for prairie conditions, along with characteristics and growing requirements, can be found in *Best Trees and Shrubs for the Prairies* by Hugh Skinner and Sara Williams. You may be able to observe trees growing under local conditions in arboretums or other public gardens. If there are wet areas that are prone to occasional flooding, choose plants that will tolerate those conditions. Select shade-tolerant trees or shrubs for shaded areas. When planting in an area with existing large trees, choose woodland species that are tolerant of shade and competition. Narrow areas along walks and driveways are better suited to low-growing shrubby ground covers than to larger specimens. These are well described in *Best Groundcovers and Vines for the Prairies* by Hugh Skinner and Sara Williams.

Plant trees like 'Delta' hackberry that are disease resistant and well-adapted to city conditions.

Preparing the bed

Like other plants, trees and shrubs only thrive if conditions are favourable. Grasses, weeds or other trees and shrubs compete with your prized specimens for space, nutrients, water and light. Pruning to thin the canopy of overhanging trees allows more light to penetrate. Judicious removal of trees that are past their prime will open a site for new or replacement plantings.

Perennial weeds such as Canada thistle, quack grass and dandelion should be removed. Quack grass is a particular priority for control because its roots produce chemicals that restrict the growth of nearby trees. Tree and shrub growth can also be severely limited by competition with grass. Keep an area around trees free of grass to the edge of the branches (the drip line) when trees are young. Alternatively, group them in grass-free, mulched beds, or use noncompetitive perennial groundcovers or annuals.

Half of a tree or shrub is below the surface of the soil. Healthy roots are required to support a healthy tree. Preparation of the planting site is therefore critical. Roots need water to grow and take up nutrients, but they also need air. Good drainage is essential. When preparing a planting bed, slope it so that water drains away from the site. In low-lying areas or where drainage is poor, plant on berms. By raising the planting bed 15 to 30 cm (6–12 in.) above the high-water level, you provide drainage for the roots. If the soil is heavy clay or sandy, improve it by adding liberal quantities of compost or composted manure. This improves aeration and adds a slow-release nutrient source to the roots and soil micro-organisms that helps to protect the tree roots from disease.

After you plant

The first line of defence against disease is to provide growing conditions favourable to the plant.

In soils that have a healthy level of organic matter, soil-borne disease organisms are often displaced by beneficial bacteria, fungi and other organisms. The regular addition of compost will offer significant protection against many diseases.

Adequate water will reduce stress. Trees and shrubs should be watered deeply to encourage deep rooting. Water regularly through dry periods during the growing season, applying 2.5 to 5 cm (1–2 in.) of water each time. Don't forget that roots need air as well as water to thrive. Allow the soil to dry on top between waterings.

Trees should be supported by a stake until roots are established. Be sure to check ties regularly to ensure that they aren't girdling the trunk, and remove them after two years.

Staking protects the tree from wind damage until roots are established.

Mulching gives many advantages to a newly planted tree. The mulch suppresses competitive weeds and conserves water. It prevents bark damage from string trimmers and lawn mowers, a common reason for failure among newly planted trees.

Organic mulch should be applied to a depth of 10 cm (4 in.). Leave an unmulched area about 15 cm (6 in.) from the trunk to prevent the bark from being damaged by moisture.

Planting trees in a mulched bed conserves moisture and reduces weed problems.

Planting ground covers around tree trunks lessens competition from grass and protects the trunk from mower and string trimmer damage.

Pruning

New gardeners are often reluctant to prune, and not without reason. Poor pruning techniques or dirty pruning tools can spread disease. But proper pruning is essential to the health of your trees and shrubs for a number of reasons.

1. When a bare-rooted tree or shrub is transplanted, roots are severed or damaged. Cut back these roots to healthy tissue so that they can heal and regrow. To compensate for the loss of roots, gardeners often prune back the top to reduce stress on the newly transplanted tree, but be careful not to reduce the top too much – leaves are also required for the development of new roots.

2. Young trees and shrubs are often pruned to encourage a desired growth form. Early pruning can help develop the desired form without removal of large branches. Trees with good form are less prone to breakage or rubbing wounds that allow disease organisms to enter.

3. Prune to remove dead, damaged or diseased wood. The health of a tree or shrub can often be improved and its life extended by properly pruning broken branches or diseased wood. When pruning diseased wood be particularly careful to disinfect tools after each cut to prevent the spread of pathogens.

4. Pruning is sometimes necessary to accommodate human activities or to remove dangerous branches such as those that are low hanging, storm damaged, or overhanging roofs and damaging shingles. Collisions can damage trees as well as people and property.

A well-pruned Japanese tree lilac develops into an attractive low headed tree.

A general rule is to prune back to a larger stem at or just above a bud. The branch stub beyond the bud or branch will die back. If a short stub is left, the tree can heal over the cut with bark. A long stub cannot heal over and provides an entry point for disease. A rule of thumb is not to leave a stub that you can hang a hat on. Be careful not to damage the branch collar, a ridge of tissue at the base of a branch. It is the site of growth from which a callus will form over the wound.

Pruning tools should be disinfected periodically with a 5 percent bleach solution (10 ml of bleach to 200 ml (⅓ oz / 7 oz) of water) or with 70 percent isopropyl alcohol (rubbing alcohol). Tools should be dipped in the solution or wiped clean with a cloth soaked in the solution. If you're pruning diseased wood, tools should be disinfected between cuts.

Insects

Trees and shrubs are attacked by many different insects, but most of these only occasionally cause serious damage. Insects chew leaves, suck or siphon sap, or bore in wood, and in doing so may weaken the plant and spread viral, bacterial or fungal diseases. Healthy plants generally resist limited attacks, and harmful insects are usually kept under control by the predators and parasites that follow them. However, there are a number of serious insect problems that we can control or avoid entirely with a little knowledge of their habits and life cycles.

Diagnostic Chart

Use the diagnostic chart to help you identify what's troubling your tree or shrub, then turn to the appropriate section in this chapter – Insects, Diseases or Disorders – for in-depth information on the problem and how to avoid, control or eradicate it. Observation and early detection are the keys to control.

DIAGNOSTIC CHART

Common insects, diseases and disorders of trees and shrubs

PLANT	PART AFFECTED	SYMPTOMS	LIKELY PROBLEM
All	branch, trunk	broken branches, bark injuries, trees not vigorous after nearby construction	**Mechanical injury** (Disorders)
All	foliage, stem, branch	leaves distorted, silvered, streaked or spotted; stems twisted or brushy growth	**Chemical injury** (Disorders)
Many	foliage, branch, trunk	small leaves, browned needles; dieback of top; split or blistering bark	**Winter Injury** (Disorders)
Many	foliage, wood	leaves small with interveinal discolouration; dark staining of wood	**Verticillium wilt** (Diseases)
Many	stem, branch, trunk	sunken bark; discoloured stinking wood; black or orange dots on dead bark	**Cytospora canker** (Diseases)
Many, commonly alpine currant, hawthorn, lilac, rose	foliage, stem	powdery white coating	**Powdery mildew** (Diseases)
Many	foliage, stem	dark or white bumps on needles; yellowing leaves	**Scale insect** (Insects)
Many	foliage	fine webbing catches dirt; leaves turn pale or bronzed	**Spider mite** (Insects)
Many	foliage	leaves distorted, may become covered with clear liquid then black fungus	**Aphids** (Insects)
American elm	foliage	leaves chewed; severe infestation will defoliate trees	**Cankerworm** (Insects)
American elm	trunk	reddish dust piles at base of trunk	**Elm bark beetle** (Insects)

Amur maple	foliage	yellowing leaves with dark green veins starting with newest leaves	**Lime-induced chlorosis (Disorders)**
Apple	foliage	yellowing leaves with dark green veins starting with newest leaves	**Lime-induced chlorosis (Disorders)**
Ash	stems	dieback; serpentine galleries below the bark; D-shaped exit holes	**Emerald ash borer** (Insects)
Ash	stems	holes with sawdust and weeping sap at the base of the stems	**Lilac (ash) borer** (Insects)
Ash	male flowers	black masses where flowers should be	**Ash flower gall mite** (Insects)
Ash	foliage	trees are defoliated; caterpillars move and rest in large numbers	**Tent caterpillar (forest) (Insects)**
Aspen	foliage	trees are defoliated; caterpillars move and rest in large numbers	**Tent caterpillar (forest) (Insects)**
Basswood	foliage	finger galls on leaves	**Eriophyid mite** (Insects)
Birch	foliage	trees are defoliated; caterpillars move and rest in large numbers	**Tent caterpillar (forest) (Insects)**
Birch	foliage	finger galls on leaves	**Eriophyid mite** (Insects)
Birch	stems, trunk	dieback; vein-like swellings on trunk	**Bronze birch borer** (Insects)
Cherry	foliage	finger galls on leaves	**Eriophyid mite** (Insects)
Cherry, ornamental	branches	black swellings on branches	**Black knot** (Diseases)
Chokecherry	foliage	trees are defoliated; silky tents built in trees	**Tent caterpillar (Eastern) (Insects)**
Chokecherry	branches	black swellings on branches	**Black knot** (Diseases)

Cotoneaster	foliage, branches	leaves wilt, turn brown and hang on; branch tips develop crooks	**Fireblight** (Diseases)
Cotoneaster	foliage	yellow spots, then appear bleached	**Pear sawfly** (Insects)
Crabapple	foliage, branches	leaves wilt, turn brown and hang on; branch tips develop crooks	**Fireblight** (Diseases)
Crabapple	foliage	trees are defoliated; silky tents built in trees	**Tent caterpillar (Eastern)** (Insects)
Crabapple	foliage, fruit	orange spots on leaves and fruit that develop horn-like projections	**Cedar-apple rust** (Diseases)
Elm	foliage, entire tree	yellowing and dying leaves, followed by death of tree within the year	**Dutch elm disease** (Diseases)
Elm	foliage	leaves roll over; aphid-like insects covered with waxy strands	**Woolly elm aphid** (Insects)
Green ash	foliage	leaves chewed; severe infestation will defoliate trees	**Cankerworm** (Insects)
Hawthorn	foliage	yellow spots, then appear bleached	**Pear sawfly** (Insects)
Hawthorn	foliage	orange spots on leaves and fruit that develop horn-like projections	**Cedar-apple rust** (Diseases)
Honeysuckle	foliage, branches	leaves curled; dense distorted purplish growth	**Honeysuckle aphid** (Insects)
Honeysuckle	foliage, twigs	finger galls on leaves	**Eriophyid mite** (Insects)
Juniper	stems	brown galls develop gelatinous orange horns	**Cedar-apple rust** (Diseases)
Lilac	stems	holes with sawdust and weeping sap at the base of the stems	**Lilac (ash) borer** (Insects)

Manitoba maple	foliage	leaves drip honeydew	**Box elder bug** (Insects)
Manitoba maple	foliage	leaves chewed; severe infestation will defoliate trees	**Cankerworm** (Insects)
Maple	foliage	trees are defoliated; caterpillars move and rest in large numbers	**Tent caterpillar (forest)** (Insects)
Maple	foliage	finger galls on leaves	**Eriophyid mite** (Insects)
Mountain ash	stems	holes with sawdust and weeping sap at the base of the stems	**Lilac (ash) borer** (Insects)
Mountain ash	foliage, branches	leaves wilt, turn brown and hang on; branch tips develop crooks	**Fireblight** (Diseases)
Mountain ash	foliage	yellowing leaves with dark green veins starting with newest leaves	**Lime-induced chlorosis** (Disorders)
Oak	foliage	yellowing leaves with dark green veins starting with newest leaves	**Lime-induced chlorosis** (Disorders)
Oak	foliage	trees are defoliated; caterpillars move and rest in large numbers	**Tent caterpillar (forest)** (Insects)
Plums, ornamental	branches	black swelling on branches	**Black knot** (Diseases)
Poplar	roots	tumour-like growth near the soil surface	**Crown gall** (Diseases)
Poplar	foliage	finger galls on leaves	**Eriophyid mite** (Insects)
	flowers	clump galls replace flowers	
Rose	foliage	black spots on leaves; early defoliation	**Black spot** (Diseases)
Rose	roots	tumour-like growth near the soil surface	**Crown gall** (Diseases)

Rose	foliage	yellowing leaves with dark green veins starting with newest leaves	**Lime-induced chlorosis** (Disorders)
Rose	foliage	bushes are defoliated; silky tents built in bushes	**Tent caterpillar (Eastern)** (Insects)
Saskatoon	entire plant	poor growth on young plants	**Woolly elm aphid** (Insects)
Silver maple	foliage	yellow leaves with dark green veins starting with newest leaves	**Lime-induced chlorosis** (Disorders)
Spirea	foliage, branches	leaves wilt, turn brown and hang on; branch tips develop crooks	**Fireblight** (Diseases)
Spruce	branches	dying lower branches; white gum on and below affected branches	**Cytospora canker of spruce** (Diseases)
Spruce	foliage	pineapple-shaped galls at branch tips	**Eastern spruce adelgid** (Insects)
Spruce	foliage	chewed needles beginning at the top of the tree; can progress to complete defoliation	**Yellowheaded spruce sawfly** (Insects)
Spruce	foliage	needles turn purple to brown on current year's growth; usually begins at tree bottom	**Rhizosphaera and lophodermium needle cast** (Diseases)
Willow	roots	tumour-like growth near the soil surface	**Crown gall** (Diseases)

Insects

Aphids

AFFECTS: birch, cotoneaster, crabapple, cranberry, dogwood, elm, hawthorn, honeysuckle, maple, plum, poplar, rose, snowball, willow

There are many species of aphids. Some are specific to a particular species or genus of plant, while others are generalists and infest many different types of plants. They are small, soft-bodied, from pinhead-size to about 2.5 mm (0.1 in.) long, and may be yellow, green or black depending on species. True aphids have two cornicles (little horns) on their posterior end. They feed by sucking sap from leaves, stems or roots.

Aphids normally overwinter as eggs in crevices in bark or in buds. These eggs hatch in spring and the aphids begin feeding on the undersides of leaves. They reproduce asexually by giving birth to live offspring. Their numbers can increase exponentially in a short time to colonize a plant. In response to various environmental conditions (crowding, shortening day length, etc.), winged males and females seek out mates and fly away to form new colonies.

WHAT TO LOOK FOR: Parts of the plant where aphids are feeding may become disfigured, and leaves that are infested may become pale in colour and curled. Aphids excrete a clear fluid (honeydew) that accumulates on objects near feeding sites and supports the growth of black fungus. Some ants feed on the honeydew and will move and protect aphids to obtain it.

PREVENTION:

Cultural methods:

* Encourage natural enemies of aphids, including lady beetles, green lacewings, syrphid flies and parasitic wasps.

Large numbers of aphids damage new shoots.

Lady beetle larvae are voracious predators of aphids.

SOLUTIONS:

Cultural methods:

- Minor infestations can be discouraged by spraying them with a strong stream of water every two to three days, or by squashing aphids between your fingers.
- Control aphid-tending ants by coating branches with a sticky substance like Tanglefoot®.

Less toxic alternatives:

- Spot-spray insecticidal soap to control aphids with minimal effect on predatory insects.
- Apply diatomaceous earth to the infested leaves.
- If aphid populations were high in the previous season, consider spraying the bark of infested trees or shrubs with dormant oil in early spring before trees or shrubs leaf out to control eggs.

Ash flower gall mite

AFFECTS: ash (male)

Ash flower gall mites (*Eriophyes fraxiniflora*) infest male flowers of ash trees at bloom time, producing black growths. Ash trees normally have male and female flowers on separate trees, and it is only the male flowers that are affected. The galls do not appear to harm infested trees, but they are ugly.

WHAT TO LOOK FOR: Irregularly branched and fringed green masses form after flowering, then turn black. The galls become more visible as the trees lose their leaves in fall.

PREVENTION:

Cultural methods:

- Plant female ash trees.

SOLUTIONS:

Cultural methods:

- Some measure of control can be achieved by pruning off the unsightly galls early in the season.

Less toxic alternatives:

- Apply dormant oil to infected trees during late winter or early spring for control of mites.

Ash flower gall mite causes distorted growth of male ash flowers. These growths turn black in the fall and hang on the trees.

Poplar flowers can also be infected with an eriophyid mite similar to ash flower gall mite.

Box elder bug

AFFECTS: Manitoba maple (female)

Box elder bugs (*Leptocoris trivittatus*) are true bugs that undergo gradual metamorphosis from bright red nymphs to adults that are black with red markings. They pierce leaf tissue and feed on sap, but are not usually very harmful to the trees. If they are numerous, they tend to be an annoyance around houses as they will crawl up the walls and enter through cracks around doors and windows.

WHAT TO LOOK FOR: Sticky sap on objects below a maple tree; red and black bugs.

PREVENTION:

Cultural methods:
- Remove female Manitoba maples or plant only male trees.

SOLUTIONS:

Less toxic alternatives:
- Spray with insecticidal soap.

Box elder bugs are a nuisance insect that live on female Manitoba maple trees.

Bronze birch borer

AFFECTS: birch

All birch species are susceptible to attack by the bronze birch borer, but some are more attractive to the beetle than others. The European white birch (*Betula pendula*) and its cultivars are most susceptible. Native paper birch (*Betula papyrifera*) is moderately susceptible, and the river birch (*Betula nigra*) is rarely attacked.

The bronze birch borer (*Agrilus anxius*) is a jewel beetle, a member of the metallic wood-boring beetle family, *Bupretidae*. The adult beetle is black with a bronzy iridescence. Its larvae are legless white grubs that chew galleries in the phloem of birch. When these galleries girdle a branch or the trunk of a tree, the tree dies back above that point. The galleries are visible as ridges and swellings on the bark. With no intervention, a tree that is infested will usually die within about five years.

Bronze birch borers have caused devastating damage to many birch trees on the prairies.

The adult bronze birch borer lays eggs in crevices in the bark in June. The eggs hatch in about two weeks, and larvae immediately tunnel into the phloem of the tree to feed. In our climate, they take two years to complete their life cycle. They pupate at the end of the second summer, emerging by chewing a D-shaped hole in the bark in early summer to begin the cycle again.

WHAT TO LOOK FOR: Birch trees that are dying back at the top. Closer inspection will reveal vein-like swellings where larvae have tunnelled under the bark. After adults have emerged, you will find the D-shaped exit holes.

PREVENTION:

Cultural methods:

- Because the borer only attacks weakened trees, keep trees in good health by watering during periods of drought, mulching to conserve moisture and maintain cooler soil and avoiding wounds to the tree.
- In areas where the borer is a significant problem, plant trees other than birch.

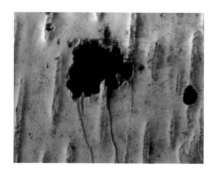

Bronze birch borer adults emerge from D-shaped holes in the bark.

When galleries of bronze birch borer larvae girdle branches, the branches die back.

SOLUTIONS:

Cultural methods:

- Remove heavily infested trees or ones that have recently died from borer injury.
- Prune dead and dying branches below dead wood and destroy the pruned branches.
- There are no effective controls against larvae that are established under the bark of a birch tree, but woodpeckers are one of the key predators for borer larvae.

Cankerworm

AFFECTS: prefers American elm, green ash, Manitoba maple

Spring cankerworm (*Paleacrita vernata*) and fall cankerworm (*Alsophila pometaria*) belong to a group of moth larvae called inchworms or measuring worms because of their habit of moving the back part of their body

Male cankerworm adults are
well-disguised winged moths.

The wingless female fall cankerworms
lay bands of eggs cemented to twigs.

Cankerworm larvae defoliate trees
when present in large numbers.

up in a loop and then launching forward a fixed distance. There are other inchworms that feed on ornamental and fruit trees, but the spring and fall cankerworms can cause significant damage.

Adult male cankerworms are grey or green mottled moths with a wingspan of about 2.5 cm (1 in.). The females are wingless and crawl up the tree trunks into the canopy of the tree to lay eggs, in the fall in the case of fall cankerworm, or in the spring for the spring cankerworm. The eggs hatch from egg masses when the trees are breaking bud in the spring. The caterpillars feed for three to four weeks, then fall to the ground and pupate. Larvae can move from tree to tree on silk threads with the help of the wind. Adult spring cankerworms emerge from the pupae in spring and fall cankerworm adults emerge in October to repeat the cycle.

WHAT TO LOOK FOR: Cankerworms can be recognized by their looping movement, and by the silken threads they use to drop to earth after they have finished feeding. If they are numerous, they may completely defoliate affected trees in early summer. Spring cankerworms can be various colours; fall cankerworms are black.

PREVENTION:

Cultural methods:

· The best way to control adult cankerworms is to encircle trees with Tanglefoot® bands to trap the wingless females as they crawl up the trees. To be truly effective, all trees in the neighbourhood should be banded, otherwise larvae can travel from unbanded trees to banded trees. Bands should be in place by mid-September to control fall cankerworm, and by mid-March to control spring cankerworm.

SOLUTIONS:

Less toxic alternatives:

- Cankerworm larvae can be controlled by spraying with products that contain Bt *kurstaki* as the active ingredient. This should be done in the early stages of infestation to be effective.

Eastern spruce adelgid

AFFECTS: black, Norway, red and white spruce

Eastern spruce adelgid (*Adelges abietis*) feeds at the base of needles. Female adelgids overwinter at the base of buds. When the buds are swelling in the spring, they deposit eggs that hatch in about ten days, and the nymphs migrate to the base of the expanding bud. Their feeding stimulates the bud to develop into a gall, which encloses the nymphs until it opens in late August or early September. The nearly mature nymphs become winged adults that mate and disperse. The following spring, they lay eggs to begin the cycle again.

WHAT TO LOOK FOR: Pineapple-shaped galls on the tips of spruce twigs. Usually damage to the tree is superficial, but in heavy infestations the tips of most of the tree's branches may be dead.

Eastern spruce adelgids form galls at the tips of branches that die and turn brown after the adults emerge.

SOLUTIONS:

Cultural methods:

- Minor infestations can be controlled by removing and destroying green galls before nymphs emerge in late summer.
- Prune brown galls to improve the appearance of the tree.

Less toxic alternatives:

- Apply horticultural oil and insecticidal soap in fall or early spring, when adelgids aren't protected by galls. Applications may remove the waxy coating that makes blue spruce blue, but the colour of subsequent new growth won't be affected.

Emerald ash borer

AFFECTS: ash

Emerald ash borer (*Agrilus planipennis*) is an introduced beetle that is having a devastating effect on ash trees in the United States and has moved into southern Ontario. It has not yet been detected in the Canadian prairies, but it attacks all species of ash grown here, including green ash, black ash, white ash and Manchurian ash. The adult is a slender, iridescent, dark green beetle about 12 mm (0.5 in.) long. Infested trees die back and will die within one to three years.

WHAT TO LOOK FOR: Serpentine galleries may be found by removing bark from the lower part of infested trees. Adults emerge through D-shaped holes.

SOLUTIONS:

Cultural methods:

- Be vigilant to identify infestations so that trees can be removed to prevent its spread.

Emerald ash borer larvae make serpentine galleries below the bark.

- By restricting the movement of ash trees and ash firewood, the invasion of this pest may be slowed.

Less toxic alternatives:

- There are currently no controls available for emerald ash borer, although research on parasitoids is being carried out.

This iridescent green beetle has the potential to devastate ash trees if it becomes established on the prairies.

Elm bark beetle

AFFECTS: American elm

Native elm bark beetle (*Hylurgopinus rufipes*) and the smaller European elm bark beetle (*Scolytus multistriatus*) are wood-boring insects and the vectors of Dutch elm disease. The damage they cause by wood boring is usually minor, but if they carry spores of *Ophiostoma ulmi* (syn. *Ceratocystis ulmi*) they can infect the tree. Virtually all infected trees die within a year. Reducing bark beetles will slow the progress of the disease.

The native elm bark beetle is tiny, 2.4 to 3.0 mm (0.1 in.) long, while the

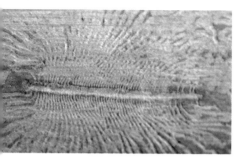

Elm bark beetles make distinctive galleries under the bark.

The smaller European elm bark beetle is an important carrier of Dutch elm disease.

European elm bark beetle is slightly smaller. The native beetle is black and rough, while the European species is reddish-brown and shiny.

WHAT TO LOOK FOR: Reddish dust piles may be found at the base of elm trees where the beetles have bored entry holes for overwintering in late September or early October, or where they have bored exit holes in the spring.

PREVENTION:

Cultural methods:

- Remove dead and dying elm trees, and debark and dispose of the wood to reduce breeding sites.
- Do not prune elm trees during the growing season as the cuts will attract

bark beetles. Pruning elm trees is prohibited between April 1 and September 30 in Alberta, between April 1 and July 31 in Manitoba and between April 1 and August 31 in Saskatchewan. If branches are damaged during the summer and pruning must be done, wounds should be covered with an appropriate wound dressing.

Eriophyid mite

AFFECTS: ash, American basswood (syn. linden), birch, cherry, elm, maple, poplar

These mites are specialists, with each tree species having its own mite species. The damage is primarily aesthetic but tends to be more severe on trees that are stressed.

WHAT TO LOOK FOR: Eriophyid mites are only visible with a microscope but make their presence known through flower galls on ash and poplar trees, and leaf galls on basswood, birch, cherry, elm, maple and poplar.

Many tree species host eriophyid mites that form finger galls on leaves.

'Dropmore' linden is a hybrid of American basswood that is immune to eriophyid mites.

PREVENTION:

Cultural methods:

- Provide adequate moisture and fertilizer.
- There are trees that are immune to mite infection.American basswood is susceptible to finger gall-forming leaf mites, but other lindens and the hybrids between American basswood and littleleaf linden, and American basswood and Manchurian linden, are practically immune. One such resistant cultivar is 'Dropmore' linden.

Honeysuckle aphid

AFFECTS: honeysuckle

Honeysuckle aphid (*Hyadaphis tataricae*) has been a devastating problem for many honeysuckle species.

Honeysuckle aphids distort new growth on susceptible honeysuckle species and cultivars.

WHAT TO LOOK FOR: Honeysuckle aphids infest new growth and cause a dense, distorted, often purplish growth known as witches' broom. Heavily infested honeysuckle shrubs can die.

PREVENTION:

Cultural methods:

- Grow resistant species and cultivars such as European fly honeysuckle, 'Albert Thorn' honeysuckle, sweetberry honeysuckle, and tatarian honeysuckle varieties: 'Arnold Red', 'Cameo', 'Honeyrose', 'Flamingo' and 'Sunstar'.

Lilac (ash) borer

AFFECTS: ash, lilac, mountain ash

Lilac (ash) borer (*Podosesia syringae*) is a species of clearwing moth. The adult, while technically a moth, resembles a wasp in both appearance and flight habits. There are many other similar clearwing moths whose larvae bore into apple, birch, clematis, cranberry, dogwood, elder, grape, hawthorn, maple, oak, pear, pine, poplar, raspberries, Virginia creeper and willow. Most have similar life cycles, but some borer species mature and lay eggs in late summer rather than in spring.

The lilac (ash) borer is difficult to control because it is protected within the tree for most of its life cycle. The moth lays eggs in rough bark at the base of a tree or shrub in the spring. When the eggs hatch, the larvae bore through the bark and begin feeding on the sapwood and heartwood of the infested plant until fall. In the spring, larvae feed, then pupate just beneath the bark in the feeding galleries. Adults emerge, leaving their pupal cases protruding from the tunnel. Females use pheromones to attract males for mating. Within an hour of mating, they begin to lay eggs in cracks and wounds in the bark of ash or other host trees.

WHAT TO LOOK FOR: Holes with sawdust and weeping sap appear at the base of the tree or shrub; leaves on affected stems wilt; often the stems break off at ground level.

PREVENTION:

Cultural methods:

- Remove and destroy badly infested shoots before May.
- Pierce larvae with a wire if tunnels are discovered.
- Keep plants healthy and vigorous.

SOLUTIONS:

Less toxic alternatives:

- Two nematodes carry pathogens that kill the host: *Steinernema carpocapsae* and *Heterorhabditis bacteriophora*. They have proven to be effective and safe and are available in Canada.

Although they resemble wasps, lilac (ash) borers are clearwing moths.

Lilac (ash) borers can cause dieback of young shoots or they may bore into wood at the base of older shoots.

Pear sawfly

AFFECTS: cherry, cotoneaster, hawthorn, pear, plum, rose

Pear sawfly (*Caliroa cerasi*), also called pear slug, is a small sawfly whose larvae can defoliate host trees or shrubs when populations are high.

Young larvae are dark in colour, about 1 cm (0.5 in.) long, with inconspicuous legs. As they mature, they become lighter in colour and come to resemble greenish-orange caterpillars. The adult is a nonstinging, 0.5 cm (0.4 in.) long, four-winged wasp. In the spring, after the leaves have expanded, adults emerge from the soil below infested trees or shrubs and lay eggs. The eggs hatch and the larvae feed for about a month, then fall to the ground and pupate. Adults emerge in late July or early August to begin a second generation. It is often this second generation that causes significant damage.

WHAT TO LOOK FOR: Yellow spots appear on leaves. As an infestation progresses, leaves will have a bleached or scorched appearance.

SOLUTIONS:

Cultural methods:

- Cultivate around infested trees or shrubs in the fall and spring to reduce the number of overwintering pupae.
- Hose pear sawfly larvae off the leaves with a strong stream of water.

Less toxic alternatives:

- Diatomaceous earth is effective against the larvae.
- Spray with insecticidal soap.
- Products containing the biological insecticide spinosad are effective against sawflies, but Bt products are not.

Pear sawfly (syn. pear slug) can defoliate cotoneaster if numbers are large.

Undamaged cotoneaster foliage is beautiful in fall colour.

Pine needle scale appears like white paint specks on pine needles.

Scale insect

AFFECTS: most trees and shrubs

Scale insects are sap-sucking insects that spend most of their lives under a shell that is either covered by a leathery body wall or by a waxy shell. Females live, feed and lay eggs, or give birth to live young, under the protection of this scale. Males develop under thin scales and emerge as winged adults without functional mouthparts; they mate and die.

Mobile young, called crawlers, emerge from their mother's scale to disperse on the plant by crawling or are carried by wind, humans or animals. Once they find a suitable place to feed, they begin to develop scales, which appear as brown or white bumps on the bark or needles of the infected tree or shrub. Scale insects are protected for most of their life cycle by the scale covering. This limits control strategies.

WHAT TO LOOK FOR: Round, oval or elongated bumps appear on stems or needles. Scales may be dark brown to black or white. Leaves may become yellow and drop prematurely.

SOLUTIONS:

Cultural methods:
- Light infestations are normally controlled by birds and predatory insects.

Less toxic alternatives:
- Severe infestations can be controlled by spraying with dormant oil before bud break in the spring.
- Summer horticultural oils or insecticidal soaps can be sprayed when the crawlers are active during the summer.

Spider mite

AFFECTS: many tree and shrub species

Spider mites are not insects but tiny creatures related to spiders. They have four pairs of legs, no antennae and a single oval body section. There are many species of spider mites that can attack plants, but the ones that

Spruce spider mites cause damage to the needles on new growth of a blue spruce.

Spider mites feed on leaf cell contents and give the leaves a yellowish or bronzed appearance.

most commonly cause damage are the two-spotted spider mite (*Tetranychus urticae*), the European red mite (*Panonychus ulmi*) and the spruce spider mite (*Oligonychus ununguis*). They pierce individual plant cells and feed on the contents.

Two-spotted spider mites and European red mites proliferate during warm, dry, summer weather. By contrast, spruce spider mite populations build up during cool spring and fall weather. During hot weather in midsummer, they produce resting eggs and become dormant. When the weather becomes cooler in the fall, the eggs hatch and adults resume activity. Most spider mites overwinter as eggs, but the two-spotted spider mites overwinter as adults in protected locations in the soil or on plants. A generation requires from twenty to as few as five days depending on weather conditions.

WHAT TO LOOK FOR: Most spider mites produce fine webbing. As numbers build up, the foliage takes on a yellowish or bronzed cast. Plants often drop damaged foliage prematurely. Heavily infested plants may be stunted or even killed. The foliage that is coated with silk collects dust and looks dirty.

SOLUTIONS:

Cultural methods:

- Moderate spider mite infestations can be controlled by a strong stream of water. This treatment knocks spider mites off while preserving natural predators.
- Spider mites are eaten by lady beetles and lacewings.
- Predatory mites are available for control of spider mites, but these are not usually as effective outdoors because they need moderate temperatures (below 28°C/82°F) and high humidity to thrive.

Less toxic alternatives:

- Horticultural oils at 1 to 2 percent solution in water can be used in the summer, while dormant oils at 3 to 4 percent are used to kill mite eggs during the winter.
- Insecticidal soaps can be used during the summer. Complete coverage is important if using oils or soaps for control of mites as they are killed only if they are contacted by the spray (either of the above treatments may remove wax that causes the blue colour in blue spruce).
- See Chapter 11, Fruit, for more information.

Tent caterpillar (forest)

AFFECTS: ash, aspen, birch, maple, oak

Tent caterpillar (eastern)

AFFECTS: crabapple, chokecherry, rose

Forest tent caterpillars (*Malacosoma disstria*) and eastern tent caterpillars (*M. americanum*) are very similar in appearance and differ mainly in their feeding habits. The larvae of both species are hairy brownish black caterpillars. Eastern tent caterpillars have a light stripe down their backs, while forest tent caterpillars have a white keyhole pattern. Both have yellow-brown lines with blue spots down the sides. The eastern tent caterpillar builds a silk nest in a tree or shrub. The larvae go out to feed during the day and return to the nest at night. The forest tent caterpillar goes on the move, and during outbreaks, large numbers will migrate

through the forest, defoliating their preferred food tree species. Resting larvae cluster in large numbers in trees or on buildings. Tent caterpillars don't directly kill trees, but repeated defoliation causes poor growth, weakens trees, and makes them susceptible to other insects and pathogens.

Tent caterpillar moths lay bands of eggs, cemented together and attached to small twigs on host trees in late summer. The eggs hatch in early spring.

WHAT TO LOOK FOR: Eastern tent caterpillars build distinctive silk tents in the branches of shrubs or small trees. Forest tent caterpillars are usually noticed by defoliation of trees and masses of migrating caterpillars.

SOLUTIONS:

Cultural methods:

- Nests of eastern tent caterpillars can be opened in the late evening and the insects squashed, or the nest can be pruned out and destroyed. Forest tent caterpillars do

Forest tent caterpillars (upper) have a white keyhole pattern down their backs. Eastern tent caterpillars (lower) have a light stripe.

not build nests, so this is not an appropriate control measure for them.

- Egg cases and pupae can be scraped off branches and burned.
- Burlap wrapped around the trunk of an infested tree will capture caterpillars as they migrate down the tree to pupate in the soil. Check the trap and destroy trapped larvae daily.

Less toxic alternatives:

- *Bacillus thuringiensis kurstaki* and products with Bt *kurstaki* as the active ingredient are effective against caterpillars. Larvae will die within five days of ingesting the bacteria.

Western ash bark beetle

AFFECTS: ash

Western ash bark beetle (*Hylesinus californicus*) is an oval, grey or brown, 2 to 3 mm (0.1 in.) beetle that overwinters in the bark near the base of ash trees. It will attack any ash species that is grown on the prairies but is most commonly found on green ash.

After mating, the female chews a gallery encircling a branch and lays eggs. Eggs hatch into white legless grubs with a black head. They tunnel away from the egg gallery, and grow from 2 to 4 mm (0.1–0.2 in.) in length. They pupate in mid-July and emerge as adults in late July and August. They then relocate, usually to a crotch of the tree, and chew their way in to feed on the phloem for several weeks before walking, falling or flying to the base of the tree. There, they chew overwintering sites in the lower 15 cm (6 in.) of the trunk.

Western ash bark beetles usually attack trees that are under stress. During drought or if trees are damaged due to storms, they may reach outbreak proportions and cause considerable dieback, and even death of trees if they infest the trunk.

WHAT TO LOOK FOR: Trees that are under attack can be identified by an accumulation of boring dust at their base. The egg gallery is sunken and discoloured and

Western ash bark beetle larvae chew galleries in the phloem of ash trees.

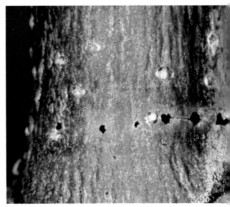

Western ash bark beetle females lay eggs in galleries that encircle branches.

has a distinctive row of ventilation holes, 1 mm (0.04 in.) in diameter and about 5 mm (0.2 in.) apart. Leaves on the branch with the egg gallery turn yellow in July or early August and the branch dies.

PREVENTION:

Cultural methods:

- Regularly prune ash trees to remove damaged and dying branches. Consider removing older, weakened trees.

SOLUTIONS:

Cultural methods:

- Prune out and destroy infested branches.

Less toxic alternatives:

- Wrap a sticky band around the trunk approximately 30 cm (12 in.) from the ground in early April to trap some of the emerging beetles. Repeat this procedure in September to intercept beetles walking down the trunk.

Woolly elm aphid

AFFECTS: American elm, saskatoon

Woolly aphids commonly have two hosts that are specific to this species of insect. Eggs usually overwinter on the primary host, the elm. They hatch into wingless females, begin feeding and produce one or two generations of live-born offspring. These then grow wings and fly to the secondary host, the saskatoon, where they continue to feed for the remainder of the summer. As fall approaches, another generation of winged females flies back to the primary host, where they give birth to tiny male and female aphids, which then mate. Each female then produces one large egg, which is deposited in a protected location on the bark.

The primary host of woolly elm aphid (*Eriosoma americanum*) is American elm. The aphid feeds inside folded-over elm leaves. In early summer, it flies to saskatoon bushes, where it moves into the soil to feed on the roots. It usually does light damage to established plants, but can be devastating to young saskatoons.

WHAT TO LOOK FOR: Woolly aphids are similar to true aphids but are covered with white waxy strands, which give them a cottony appearance. Often when they feed on leaves, the leaves curl to enclose them.

PREVENTION:

Cultural methods:

- Natural enemies such as lady beetles, lacewings and parasitic wasps normally keep woolly aphids under control. Encourage

Elm leaves are distorted and roll around woolly elm aphids.

these predators and protect them by avoiding chemical pesticides.

SOLUTIONS:

Less toxic alternatives:

- Dormant applications of horticultural oil can often reduce the population of overwintering woolly aphids.
- Contact insecticides such as insecticidal soap are usually not effective because woolly aphids are protected by the rolled elm leaves.

Woolly elm aphids can severly damage young saskatoon plants.

Yellowheaded spruce sawfly

AFFECTS: Native North American spruce species, including Colorado spruce, Norway spruce, white spruce

There are many species of sawflies that attack a wide variety of broad-leafed and coniferous trees. The larvae look like smooth, greasy caterpillars, but sawflies are in the same family as wasps. You can tell sawfly larvae from caterpillars by the number of prolegs (leg-like projections) on their abdomen: Caterpillars have two to five pairs, while sawfly larvae have six or more pairs.

Yellowheaded spruce sawflies (*Pikonema alaskensis*) overwinter in cocoons in the soil, emerging in spring just as buds on spruce swell. Females lay eggs at the base of new needles. Larvae emerge within two weeks and begin to feed. Larvae grow to 20 mm (0.8 in.) in length and have green bodies with six grayish-green stripes and brownish-orange heads.

WHAT TO LOOK FOR: The sawfly tends to attack young trees from 1 to 5.5 m (3-18 ft) in height. Damage begins with chewing of the needles at the top of the tree. A severe infestation can result in complete defoliation of the tree with only a few brown stubs of needles left.

PREVENTION:

Cultural methods:

- Trees grown in shade are less susceptible to attack.

Yellowheaded spruce sawflies can defoliate young spruce trees from the top down.

SOLUTIONS:

Cultural methods:

- Minor infestations on small trees can be controlled by hand-picking or by syringing the tree with a strong spray of cold water.

Less toxic alternatives:

- Spray with insecticidal soap.

Diseases

Black knot

AFFECTS: Members of the genus *Prunus*, most commonly native chokecherry, Schubert chokecherry and mayday tree; purple-leaved chokecherry cultivars; occasionally native plum species

Black knot (*Apiosporina morbosa*) is a fungal disease that overwinters in knots on infected trees. Spores are disseminated during wet weather in spring when temperatures rise above 16°C (61°F). They are spread by wind and splashing water and can penetrate the bark of elongating green shoots. During the first season a slight swelling develops in the infected twig. The following spring, the galls expand rapidly. They become greenish-brown and release asexually produced spores. The second spring after infection, knots enlarge, become black and erupt, releasing spores that can travel some distance from the initial infection.

WHAT TO LOOK FOR: Black swellings on branches and twigs.

Black knot erupts from chokecherry branches in the spring.

PREVENTION:

Cultural methods:

- Plant resistant varieties or species. No chokecherries or mayday trees are resistant. Choose trees such as flowering crabapple, hawthorn or mountain ash near an area where there is an infection.

SOLUTIONS:

Cultural methods:

- Infected branches should be pruned at least 10 to 15 cm (4-6 in.) below the gall before March 1 or after flowering. Be sure to sterilize tools with a 5 percent bleach solution or alcohol after each cut. Once pruned, branches should be buried or burned to prevent them from becoming a source of infection.

Less toxic alternatives:

- Apply lime sulphur spray in the spring before bud break. This treatment is only effective in combination with cultural treatments.

Black spot

AFFECTS: rose

Black spot (*Diplocarpon rosae*) is a common foliar disease of roses. Severe infestations on susceptible plants can defoliate a rose bush by midsummer. The fungus overwinters on fallen leaves and on the canes of infected bushes. Spores are released when conditions are warm and moist in the spring and need seven hours of moisture to germinate and infect new leaves. Within two weeks, infections produce more spores, which are dispersed on the wind.

WHAT TO LOOK FOR: Irregular dark spots surrounded by chlorosis (yellowing) of the adjacent leaf tissue.

PREVENTION:

Cultural methods:

* Grow resistant cultivars. Among the many resistant shrub and rugosa rose cultivars are: 'Hansa',

'Morden Belle' rose is resistant to black spot.

'Therese Bugnet' and other rugosa hybrids; 'Champlain', 'John Cabot' and most others in the Explorer series. There are also resistant cultivars within the hybrid tea and floribundas, including 'Chrysler Imperial', 'Electron', 'Love', 'Queen Elizabeth', 'Showbiz' and 'Sunsprite'.

* Keep the foliage of roses dry. Avoid overhead irrigation. Plant roses where there is good air circulation, in sunny locations where they will dry quickly after rain.

SOLUTIONS:

Cultural methods:

* Remove black spot-infested foliage from the plants and debris from under rose bushes as frequently as possible.

Black spot infects rose leaves and can cause early defoliation.

Less toxic alternatives:

- Spray foliage with potassium bicarbonate fungicide every seven to ten days during wet weather in the summer. A good strategy is to alternate an acidic lime sulphur spray with the basic potassium bicarbonate.
- Use copper hydroxide or copper salts, applied in the same manner.
- Dust the leaves of infected plants with sulphur to prevent further infection.
- If you have a problem with black spot on susceptible varieties, you may need to begin applications in spring as soon as the foliage emerges and continue every seven to ten days during wet weather throughout the summer. Fungicide applications should be made before disease is evident as a preventative measure. They will not cure an existing infection but will only halt the development of new infections.

Cedar-apple rust can infect the fruit of crabapples.

Cedar-apple rust

AFFECTS: **Juniper family hosts** – eastern red cedar, some varieties of creeping juniper and some varieties of Rocky Mountain juniper. **Rose family hosts** – apple, flowering crabapple and hawthorn.

Cedar-apple rust (*Gymnosporangium juniperi-virginianae*) is a fungal disease that alternates between infecting junipers and members of the rose family. In eastern North America, the alternate host is commonly eastern red cedar (*Juniperus virginiana*), hence the name cedar-apple rust.

Susceptible cultivars of both hosts must be present for the disease to proliferate.

Hard, woody galls on infected juniper branches give rise to bright orange gelatinous spore-bearing growths in spring. The spores move to and infect rose family hosts, developing into yellow or orange spots on leaves or fruit. From these lesions, spore-bearing structures called aecia grow in late summer. In turn, these produce spores that can infect a juniper host. The fungus overwinters in the galls on juniper plants.

WHAT TO LOOK FOR: Woody galls on junipers develop gelatinous orange horns; orange spots on leaves and fruit of crabapple, hawthorn or saskatoon develop horn-like projections.

PREVENTION:

Cultural methods:

- There are resistant varieties of juniper, apple and hawthorn. Resistant cultivars of *Juniperus sabina* include: 'Arcadia', 'Blue Danube', 'Broadmoor', 'Buffalo', 'Calgary Carpet™', 'Moor-Dense', 'Skandia' and var. *tamariscifolia.*
- Because susceptible cultivars of both hosts need to be present for proliferation, avoid planting junipers in close proximity to susceptible members of the rose family to interrupt the disease cycle. However, spores can travel up to 1 km (0.6 mi), so it's difficult to ensure isolation.

SOLUTIONS:

Cultural methods:

- Prune the galls from susceptible juniper cultivars before they can produce spores, destroying them by burning or burying.

Less toxic alternatives:

- Apply sulphur to junipers according to label directions.

Cedar-apple rust forms woody galls on its juniper hosts.

Crown gall

AFFECTS: a wide range of hosts, including fruit; most common on poplar, rose and willow

Crown gall (*Agrobacterium tumefaciens*) is a bacterial disease common around the world, usually entering the plant through wounds on the roots caused by pruning, cultivating, insect injury or winter damage. The bacteria can survive in the soil for two years without infecting plant roots.

WHAT TO LOOK FOR: A tumour-like growth, usually occurring near the soil surface. Plants that are infected often fail to thrive.

PREVENTION:

Cultural methods:

- Grow resistant species; conifers are not affected by the disease.
- Avoid planting susceptible types for at least two years after an infected plant has been removed.

Crown gall can produce a tumour-like growth at the soil level on a rose.

- Plant only healthy nursery stock that have no visible tumours on the roots or at the root collar (where root meets stem).
- Avoid wounding roots when cultivating or hoeing.

Less toxic alternatives:

- *Agrobacterium radiobacter* (Dygall™) is a bacterial control agent that prevents infection by crown gall. It will not control existing infections. It is usually used as a dip when plants are being transplanted.

SOLUTIONS:

Cultural methods:

- Dig out and discard plants that are infected.

Cytospora canker

AFFECTS: balsam poplar, crabapple, large-tooth aspen, mountain ash, Norway maple, poplar hybrids, Schubert chokecherry, silver maple, sugar maple, trembling aspen, water birch, white birch, willow species

Orange fruiting bodies erupt through dark sunken bark of a mountain ash killed by Cytospora canker.

Cytospora canker (*Cytospora* spp., *Leucostoma cincta*) of deciduous trees commonly infects a wide variety of hosts. The primary ones are poplars and willows, but it can also damage birch, fruit trees, maples, mountain ash, and oak. Typically, the tree develops areas of dark, sunken bark. Under the bark the wood is discoloured. These infections often girdle the branch or trunk and result in death of the portion above the canker. The fungus is often present on the bark of healthy trees but only causes disease on trees that are stressed or have bark injuries.

Spores infect limbs of trees through pruning wounds, leaf scars, winter injury sites or bruises from hail. As the infection progresses, the bark becomes sunken and the wood beneath it becomes discoloured, with an unpleasant odour. Small black or orange fruiting bodies develop on the infected area. During periods of high humidity, these exude orange, hair-like spores that are spread by wind, splashing water or animals.

WHAT TO LOOK FOR: Sunken bark; discoloured, stinking wood; black or orange dots on dead bark.

PREVENTION:

Cultural methods:

- Plant resistant cultivars or species.
- Maintain trees in a healthy, vigorous state.
- Prune in late winter when inoculum (infectious material) levels are low. Prune in dry weather and allow cuts to heal before irrigating.
- Use trickle or microsprinkler irrigation instead of overhead sprinklers.
- Protect trees from winter injury, sunscald, rodent damage and insect injury.
- Do not plant new susceptible trees next to old infected trees.

SOLUTIONS:

Cultural methods:

- Remove and burn diseased plant material as soon as you encounter it. Disinfect pruning tools with 70 percent rubbing alcohol or a 5 percent bleach solution between cuts.

Cytospora canker of spruce

AFFECTS: black spruce, Colorado spruce, Douglas fir, fir, Norway spruce, white spruce

Cytospora canker of spruce, caused by *Cytospora kunzei* var. *piceae* is a widespread and severe disease of spruce trees. Millions of spores are produced in pimple-like structures on infected branches. These are spread by wind, splashing water, animals or

Cytospora canker of spruce infections ooze white gum.

pruning tools. Most infections take place in the spring and occur on trees that are stressed or injured.

WHAT TO LOOK FOR: Generally, the first symptoms are dying lower branches. As the disease progresses, it affects branches higher in the tree. Cankers that appear at the base of infected branches ooze sap that builds up as white gum.

PREVENTION:

Cultural methods:

- Plant resistant species and cultivars.
- Avoid injuries to branches or stems.
- Prune in late winter before active growth in spring.
- Keep trees healthy and vigorous. Space trees at appropriate distances to reduce competition, mulch to moderate moisture levels and minimize stress by avoiding soil compaction.

SOLUTIONS:

Cultural methods:

- Remove and destroy infected branches, sterilizing pruning tools between cuts to prevent disease spread. Prune in dry weather to minimize spread.

- Control insects that may act as vectors for disease.

Dutch elm disease

AFFECTS: American elm, Siberian elm

Dutch elm disease is a fungal disease of elms caused by *Ophiostoma ulmi* (syn. *Ceratocystis ulmi*). The disease is spread by the native elm bark beetle or the smaller European elm bark beetle (see page 176). It can also move through boulevard plantings or shelterbelts through root grafts between adjacent trees. It commonly infects American elm (*Ulmus americana*), and once a tree begins to show symptoms, it will die within one to two years. It can also infect Siberian elm (*Ulmus pumila*), and while not all Siberian elm trees die, those that survive can act as reservoirs for the disease organism. The disease has been spread over long distances by people moving infected firewood. Some high-value trees have been protected from infection by the injection of fungicides into the tree, but this is costly and must be repeated regularly.

WHAT TO LOOK FOR: Trees that are infected through root grafts often die quickly. They may leaf out with small leaves in the spring, and as the weather warms up these leaves wilt, turn brown and hang on the tree. If a tree is infected by beetles, it may first show yellowing of leaves on a branch in the crown, called "flagging." This progresses over the summer, and often the tree will leaf out

"Flagging" branches, with leaves turning colour and dying in mid-summer, is one of the early signs of Dutch elm disease.

with small leaves the following spring, then wilt and die.

PREVENTION:

Cultural methods:

- In urban areas of Manitoba and Saskatchewan, the spread of the disease has been slowed by programs for the removal of infected trees. So far, Dutch elm disease has not become established in Alberta.

- Elms should not be pruned during spring and summer (banned in Alberta from April 1 to September 30, in Manitoba from April 1 to July 31, and in Saskatchewan from April 1 to August 31).

- Keeping trees healthy and vigorous makes them less attractive to beetles.
- Work is progressing on the selection of resistant varieties of Japanese elm (*Ulmus davidiana*) and varieties and hybrids of American elm. This is a lengthy process, as trees must mature to prove their resistance. Selections introduced until now are hardy to zone 3.

Less toxic alternatives:

- Inoculation of trees with Dutch Trig®, a vaccine that stimulates the tree's natural defences, is being tested in prairie cities. It is used to protect healthy trees from infection. This treatment must be carried out by a certified arborist.

Fireblight

AFFECTS: cotoneaster, crabapple, hawthorn, mountain ash, spirea

Fireblight (*Erwinia amylovora*) is a bacterial disease that can be spread by insects or weather events, or on a gardener's tools, hands or clothing to infect other susceptible plants. Infections usually occur on flowers, succulent young shoots, wounds caused by improper pruning or injuries caused by hail.

Fireblight overwinters in cankers in the bark of infected trees. When the weather turns warm and moist in the spring, the bacteria multiply. Typically, the bacteria are spread to flowering trees by pollinating insects

Brown dead leaves hang on a branch of mountain ash killed by fireblight.

such as honeybees. Following this, secondary infections take place when bacteria are moved to wounds or infect lush young shoots.

WHAT TO LOOK FOR: New shoots, flowers or flower clusters appear water-soaked, wilt and turn brown. Leaves and flowers remain on the tree or shrub but appear as if they have been scorched by fire. Tips of infected branches become hooked or curved, like a shepherd's crook. As the infection progresses, the bark below the infected leaves becomes dark brown or black and sunken. The edges of the infection may produce an amber ooze.

PREVENTION:

Cultural methods:

- Plant resistant varieties.
- Lush growth is most susceptible to infection, so avoid fertilizing susceptible plants with high levels of nitrogen.
- Avoid working around trees when it is wet.
- Clean pruning tools with disinfectant after every cut, especially if used for pruning diseased trees.

Less toxic alternatives:

- Control leaf-feeding insects such as leafhoppers and aphids to help contain the spread of disease.

SOLUTIONS:

Cultural methods:

- Prune infected branches about 15 cm (6 in.) below the lowest signs of infection. Destroy the infected branches. Be sure to disinfect your tools after each cut.

Less toxic alternatives:

- Bacterial strains *Pseudomonas fluorescens* 506 (Blightban© 506), *Pantoea agglomerans* C9-1 (Blightban© C9-1) or *Bacillus subtilis* QST 713 (Seranade®) will colonize flowering shoots and reduce the incidence of fireblight infection.
- Before bud break, copper sulphate sprayed with superior horticultural oil will significantly reduce infectious material from cankers on infected trees.
- From bud break until the emerging shoots grow to 1 cm (0.4 in.), use a fixed copper fungicide for this purpose.

Powdery mildew

AFFECTS: almost all plants, but commonly alpine currant, hawthorn, lilac, rose

Powdery mildew (caused by a number of fungal species in the *Erysiphales* order) is an easily recognized disease that can infect almost any plant. Some types of powdery mildew infect a variety of plants, while others are specific to one species. It generally diminishes the vigour of plants and affects their appearance. However, it can sometimes severely weaken plants, making them susceptible to winterkill.

Infections usually become worse in late summer because the high humidity created near leaf surfaces when warm late summer days are followed by cool nights encourages spores to germinate. Spores are carried by wind to other susceptible

Powdery mildew can infect a variety of trees and shrubs especially those planted in the shade.

plants. Most powdery mildew species overwinter at the sexual reproduction stage, and remain on infected foliage or falls to the ground. Some types, such as those that infect apple, hawthorn, plum and rose, overwinter by infecting buds.

WHAT TO LOOK FOR: White powdery spots on leaves and stems.

PREVENTION:

Cultural methods:

- Plant resistant varieties, particularly in shaded areas. Resistant varieties include: rugosa roses such as 'Hansa' and 'Blanc Double de Coubert'; Explorer series roses such as 'John Cabot', 'John Davis' and 'Henry Kelsey'; and Parkland series roses like 'Cuthbert Grant', 'Morden Centennial' and 'Prairie Joy'; lilac species and varieties such as Japanese tree lilac, 'Miss Kim' Manchurian lilac, dwarf Korean lilac, Preston hybrid lilacs such as 'Miss Canada' and 'Donald Wyman', 'Pocohantas' early lilac, common lilacs such as 'Sensation', 'Madam Lemoine', 'Katherine Havermeyer' and 'Charles Joly.'

SOLUTIONS:

Cultural methods:

- Prune to promote good air circulation and to open canopies of trees and shrubs to sunlight.
- If practical, remove and destroy infected leaves.

Less toxic alternatives:

- Spray with bicarbonate (NaHCO$_3$ or KHCO$_3$). Use a solution of 20 ml (4 tsp) baking soda and 15 ml (1 Tbsp) horticultural oil mixed with 4.5 l (1 gal) water, or fungicides with potassium bicarbonate as the active ingredient.
- See Chapter 11, Fruit, for additional information.

Rhizosphaera and lophodermium needle cast of spruce

AFFECTS: many species of pine and spruce

These fungal needle diseases show similar symptoms, but rhizosphaera is usually seen on Colorado spruce, while lophodermium can be found on many species of spruce and pine. Lophodermium is more common on young seedling trees, while rhizosphaera is more common on more mature trees. Rhizosphaera normally infects needles on new growth in May and June, while lophodermium can infect the current year's needles at any time during the summer and fall.

WHAT TO LOOK FOR: Infected needles turn purple to brown in the late fall or winter. In winter and spring, needles develop yellow or reddish-brown spots,

Needles turn brown on the lower branches of a spruce tree infected with Rhizosphaera needle cast.

then turn reddish brown. Lower branches are normally affected first, and under epidemic conditions they may be killed.

PREVENTION:

Cultural methods:

- Plant only healthy nursery stock.
- Do not plant seedlings next to windbreaks of susceptible trees, particularly if the disease has been present.
- Provide trees with good growing conditions and pay particular attention to mulching and improving heavy, compacted soils.
- Irrigate in the morning to prevent needles from staying wet for long periods of time.

Less toxic alternatives:

- Consider spraying trees with copper oxychloride in early June if there have been problems in previous years.

SOLUTIONS:

Cultural methods:

- Prune trees during dry weather to remove infected branches. Disinfect tools with 70 percent rubbing alcohol, which will remove pitch as well as kill spores. Destroy the pruned branches.
- Remove needles from the base of infected trees to reduce infectious material.
- Improve drainage and soil aeration in the vicinity of infected trees.

Less toxic alternatives:

- Spray trees with copper oxychloride in early June.

Verticillium wilt

AFFECTS: ash, barberry, boxwood, Ohio buckeye, cherry, currant, dogwood, elder, elm, gooseberry, lilac, linden, maple, oak, plum, rose, Russian olive, saskatoon, spirea, sumac, viburnum, weigela. Affects over three hundred species of broad-leaved plants.

The list of plants, both woody and herbaceous, that are susceptible to verticillium wilt is long. Most plants are similarly affected. Trees or shrubs infected with Verticillium and showing wilting of twigs at the end of one season may die the following year, or may not show symptoms for several years before the disease reappears. It can be spread on seeds, on tools or tillage equipment and by flowing water.

Verticillium wilt is caused by the soil-borne fungi *Verticillium dahlia* and *V. albo-atrum*. Both species overwinter as black, thick-walled masses

Verticillium wilt usually infects trees that are under stress.

that can survive in the soil for several years without infecting a host plant. Strains vary in their virulence and their ability to infect specific host plants. When a host is encountered, the fungi can infect the roots and progress upward through the vascular system of the plant.

WHAT TO LOOK FOR: Interveinal discolouration of leaves, wilting, defoliation and sometimes death of the plant. Infected trees may display small leaves, thin crowns and poor vigour. Infected wood often has dark staining.

PREVENTION:

Cultural method:

- Healthy trees and shrubs that have adequate water and fertility are better able to resist infection by Verticillium.

SOLUTIONS:

Cultural methods:

- If suspected, verticillium should be confirmed by a pathology lab as it can be mistaken for *fusarium* wilt or bacterial wilt. Verticillium is very difficult to eradicate from the soil. In a garden plot where plants have succumbed to verticillium, use resistant species or cultivars and don't plant susceptible plants in the area for at least five years. Species resistant to verticillium include birch, crabapple, hackberry, hawthorn, larch, mountain ash, pine, poplar, spruce and willow.
- In the garden, there is no effective way to eradicate verticillium spores. If starting plants in a greenhouse or for potted plants, use sterilized soil or medium.

- If a tree or shrub shows symptoms, fertilize to promote health, using alfalfa pellets as the source of nitrogen. Water regularly, applying 2.5 to 5 cm (1–2 in.) of water each time.
- Prune and destroy branches that show signs of infection. Cut well below where branches show signs of internal discolouration. Clean pruning tools between each cut with 70 percent rubbing alcohol or a 5 percent bleach solution.
- If the plant dies, remove it with as much of the root as possible and destroy it.

Disorders

Some conditions are the result of environmental factors or human activity, not diseases. These are referred to as disorders.

Chemical injuries

Herbicides are poisons that don't distinguish between weeds and valuable trees or shrubs. Careless use of herbicides commonly damages or kills trees. Chemical injuries can happen when a gardener (or a gardening neighbour) uses volatile products like 2,4-D, allows drift from Roundup® to hit the foliage on a tree or shrub, uses a herbicide like dicamba that is active in the soil, or allows soil sterilants to come in contact with roots. Damage from drift might be mild, but at certain times of the year and with certain tree species, one spray-drift

2,4-D causes distortion of growth on Manitoba maple.

incident can kill a tree. If soil sterilants are used in areas where tree roots grow (roots often reach at least as far from the tree as it is tall) or where it can be leached to the tree roots by runoff water, the result can be lethal.

Properties that are adjacent to farmland are particularly prone to drift from field spraying if farmers are careless and spray when wind can carry chemicals onto trees. Injuries can also happen from the dumping of construction materials, motor oil, salts and other toxic products. These products can contaminate the soil and may require costly removal of the contaminated soil before replanting.

Acid rain and other forms of pollution can injure leaves of plants. Our prairie atmosphere is usually relatively free of pollution, but the function of leaves can be impaired by soot and grime if trees are planted along major streets or in industrial areas. Tree species vary in their ability to tolerate these chemicals. More resistant species include crabapple, elm, hackberry, Japanese tree lilac and oak.

Salt applied to roads can harm trees, particularly those growing on the boulevards of high traffic streets where salt is used frequently. If the soil becomes saline, trees may decline and die. Salt spray from the roadway can kill buds and cause distorted witches' broom growth. Salt-tolerant trees include Colorado spruce, green ash, Japanese tree lilac and largetooth aspen.

WHAT TO LOOK FOR: Leaves may be silvered, streaked or speckled due to pollution. Herbicide damage can be seen as distorted, sometimes twisted, growth or as yellowing of the leaves. Salt damage can cause scorch on the edges of leaves and distorted brushy growth.

PREVENTION:

Cultural Methods:

- Avoid the use of harmful chemicals such as soil sterilants.

- Make sure that adjacent landowners are aware of the potential injury that can occur from spray drift.
- Plant salt-tolerant species near streets to which salt is frequently applied.

Lime-induced chlorosis

AFFECTS: Amur maple, apple, mountain ash, oak, rose, silver maple

Lime-induced chlorosis is usually seen where soils are high in lime ($CaCO_3$). It is aggravated by poor drainage or wet soil conditions.

WHAT TO LOOK FOR: Yellowing of leaves between the veins, with the veins remaining dark green.

SOLUTIONS:

Less toxic alternatives:

- Apply chelated iron, either as a foliar spray mixed with water or applied to the soil and watered in.

Lime-induced chlorosis first appears as yellowing of the newest leaves with the veins remaining dark green.

Foliar applications will have a more immediate effect, while soil applications will have longer-lasting results.

Mechanical injuries

Branches in the canopy of a tree can be broken and damaged by severe weather (hail, early or late snowfall or wind) and other, accidental, causes. If branches are broken, they should be pruned to remove damaged wood, eliminate hazards and allow the tree to heal.

The bark at the base of trees is often injured by mowers and string trimmers. Protect young trees with collars made from split plastic drain tile sections or with plastic tree protectors. Eliminate the need to cut grass up to the base of trees by mulching around trees or planting groundcovers in tree wells at the base of the trunks.

Injuries to older trees are common on construction sites (such as a home addition or garage). If excavation is necessary, it may be possible to dig beyond the drip line around the outer branches of the tree, or to tunnel under the tree rather than trench through the roots. Roots can also be damaged by compaction of the soil. Avoid equipment traffic over the roots and, if possible, restrict foot traffic over them.

The most important part of a tree or shrub in terms of its health and vigour is below ground. Trees can be injured or killed if soil is deposited

Damage to bark from string trimmers can kill newly planted trees.

Leaving branch stubs when pruning can create entry points for disease organisms.

over the roots. The severity of the injury will depend on the depth of the fill, the texture of the fill (gravelly fill that allows infiltration of air and water will be much less damaging than clay fill that is impermeable) and the species or type of tree. Oak, pine and spruce will be more severely injured than poplar, willow and elm. If you need to raise the grade around a valuable and healthy tree, construct a dry well around the trunk of the tree with drain tile radiating out to the drip line of the tree. Fill the dry well at the trunk of the tree and around the drain tile with coarse crushed rock to allow air to penetrate the soil. If you lower the grade near a tree, terrace the cut and, if possible, make the change outside the drip line of the tree.

WHAT TO LOOK FOR: Bark split or cut at the base of the tree, branches broken, poor vigour after construction work near the tree.

PREVENTION:

Cultural methods:

- Protect trees from injury by fencing during construction.
- Use collars to protect newly planted trees.
- Provide for aeration if backfilling over roots.

SOLUTIONS:

Cultural methods:

- Prune damaged branches.
- Protect damaged trunks to allow them to heal.
- Aerate compacted soil over the roots.

Winter Injury

Winter injury can take a variety of forms. Bark injuries and frost cracks occur when there are rapid changes in temperature in late winter, when the warm sun heats the south side of the trunk of a tree, then the temperature drops rapidly when the sun goes down. Frost cracks can occur due to heating and cooling of the trunk or sometimes due to extreme cold. They are not as injurious to the tree as sunscald, but the split in the bark can provide an entry point for disease organisms.

Needle browning often happens on evergreen trees or shrubs in late winter as water evaporates from the needles when the root ball is frozen. There are other causes for winter browning, including salt spray, insects and male dogs urinating on lower branches.

People often get alarmed when inner needles of evergreen trees turn brown and drop in midsummer, but it's natural for an evergreen to drop a portion of its needles each year. Most coniferous trees hold needles for three to four years, so each year a quarter to a third of the needles drop from the inner portions of the branches.

WHAT TO LOOK FOR: Dieback of branches or tops. Sometimes injured parts of the plant will produce small leaves, and examination will show a ring of brown, damaged tissue below the bark.

Sunscald can appear as blistered or sunken dead areas of bark on the south or west side of a tree. Sometimes vertical frost cracks develop up one side of the trunk of a tree.

PREVENTION:

Cultural methods:

- Protect trees by wrapping the trunks with burlap or plastic wraps or by painting them with white latex paint that has been diluted by half with water to reflect sunlight. Plant evergreens where they are protected from late winter sun to help alleviate winter burn. Cedars are particularly susceptible to winter browning. Newly transplanted plants are most prone to winter injury and can be protected by making a screen. Staple burlap to stakes on the southwest side of the tree or shrub.

- The most winter-hardy varieties will not usually have sunscald injury. More tender varieties may avoid it if they are planted in sheltered locations where they are protected from wind and late winter sun.

- Mulch to lessen the effects of freezing and thawing and to keep winter soil temperatures warmer.

- Provide good growing conditions but don't fertilize in late summer or early fall.

- Make sure that evergreens are well-watered before winter.

Extreme winter browning on Scots pine.

Cultural practices go a long way towards preventing harmful infestations and diseases in fruit plantings. Begin by planting insect- and disease-free stock, and, where possible, using resistant cultivars. Cultural control of insects includes cultivation to disturb overwintering sites, weed control to eliminate other hosts and timely irrigation to prevent drought stress which makes plants more vulnerable to insect attack.

A variety of insects feed upon the roots, foliage, flowers and fruit. Heavy infestations may delay cold hardening in the fall, leaving plants more vulnerable to winter injury. Insects also spread viruses and other diseases. To decrease the incidence of disease, grow fruit in full sun with good air circulation and good soil drainage. In low-lying areas, use raised beds. Provide wide spacing of plants for greater air circulation.

Probably because of their prickles, it's only recently that gooseberries have gained popularity with prairie gardeners.

Fruit growers who object to paying a "bird tax" resort to netting. A finer mesh will exclude a host of insect pests as well.

Good weed control eliminates overwintering sites for insects and alternate hosts for disease organisms as well, and also increases air circulation. Avoid planting into the same soil where diseased plants have been previously located.

Also avoid the use of excess nitrogen fertilizer that encourages denser foliage and softer fruit that is more vulnerable to disease entry. Irrigate at a time of day when the fruit and foliage will dry quickly. Avoid working in the fruit garden or picking fruit when it is wet. Using an organic mulch prevents the fruit from touching the soil and fungal spores from the soil from splashing onto the fruit.

Harvest early in the day as soon as the fruit is ripe and avoid bruising it. Remove diseased and dead plant debris immediately after harvest.

We have mentioned several low-risk commercial products that are not yet sold to home gardeners but may be in the future. At the time of publication, these are only available in large quantities and, depending on provincial and municipal bylaws, in some cases may only be applied by commercial applicators.

Diagnostic Chart

Use the diagnostic chart to help you identify what's troubling your fruit, then turn to the appropriate section in this chapter – Insects, Diseases or Disorders – for in-depth information on the problem and how to avoid, control or eradicate it.

DIAGNOSTIC CHART

Common insects, diseases and disorders of fruit

PLANT	PART AFFECTED	SYMPTOMS	LIKELY PROBLEM
Apple	foliage	brown, retained through winter	Fireblight (Diseases)
	stems	curled at end	
Apple	foliage	silver sheen	Silverleaf (Diseases)
Apple	foliage	yellow blade, dark green veins	Lime-induced chlorosis (Disorders)
Apple	fruit	round, corky lesions	Apple scab (Diseases)
Apple	fruit	winding trails through flesh but not core	Apple maggot/railroad worm (Insects)
Cherry	fruit	prematurely red, shrivelled; exit holes	Cherry fruit fly (Insects)
Chokecherry	shoots, foliage	silken tent in crotch, caterpillars within	Tent caterpillar (eastern) (Insects)
Chokecherry	stems, branches	dark encircling growths; dieback beyond	Black knot (Diseases)
Chokecherry	fruit	red, swollen, pear-shaped; fall prematurely	Fruit gall midge (Insects)
Currant	shoots, foliage	stunted, yellow; dieback; late to leaf out	Currant borer (Insects)
Currant	foliage	defoliation	Imported currant worm (Insects)
Currant	fruit	blotched; ripens prematurely	Currant fruit fly (Insects)
Pear	foliage	brown, retained through winter	Fireblight (Diseases)
	stems	curled at end	
Plum	fruit	enlarged, hollow	Plum pocket (Diseases)

Raspberry	crown, roots	cream to brown galls, turn black, hard, warty	**Crown gall** (Diseases)
Raspberry	roots, canes	interior red-brown; stunted; decay	**Root rot** (Diseases)
	foliage	yellow	
Raspberry	canes	purple-brown lesions below leaf attachment; dieback, breaking	**Spur blight** (Diseases)
	foliage	black triangular spots	
Raspberry	foliage	curled, stippled; may turn grey, bronze, dry up	**Two-spotted spider mite** (Insects)
Raspberry	foliage	wilting, distortion, stunted	**Aphids** (Insects)
Raspberry	foliage	yellow leaf, dark green veins	**Lime-induced chlorosis** (Disorders)
Raspberry	fruit, foliage	powdery white coating	**Powdery mildew** (Diseases)
Raspberry	foliage	yellow, puckered, downward curling	**Mosaic virus** (Diseases)
	fruit	dry, seedy, crumbly	
Raspberry	fruit	misshapen, crumbled	**Tarnished plant bug** (Insects)
Raspberry	fruit	powder-like growth, brown rot	**Grey mould** (Diseases)
Saskatoon	seedlings, young plants	weak, yellowing; white-purple growth on roots	**Woolly elm aphids** (Insects)
Saskatoon	shoots, branches	early fall colouration; dieback; bark drying, splitting	**Cytospora dieback and canker disease** (Diseases)
Saskatoon	shoots, foliage	silken tent in crotch, caterpillars within	**Tent caterpillar (eastern)** (Insects)
Saskatoon	shoots, flower buds	webbed together in early May; larvae in buds	**Saskatoon bud moth** (Insects)

Saskatoon	foliage	brown, retained through winter	**Fireblight** (Diseases)
	stems	curled at end	
Saskatoon	foliage	leaves roll downward; felt-like growth on underside, turns black	**Black leaf** (Diseases)
Saskatoon	foliage	angular yellow-brown spots on new leaves	**Entomosporium leaf and berry spot** (Diseases)
Saskatoon	foliage	powdery white coating	**Powdery mildew** (Diseases)
Saskatoon	foliage	raised yellow-orange spots; tiny spiny projections below	**Saskatoon-juniper rust** (Diseases)
	fruit	raised yellow-orange spots	
Saskatoon	fruit	slit-like scar on berry near calyx	**Saskatoon sawfly** (Insects)
Saskatoon	fruit	felty grey growth	**Grey mould** (Diseases)
Saskatoon	flowers	pierced, leak amber sap; flowers die	**Tarnished plant bug** (Insects)
Strawberry	crown, roots	tunnelling	**Strawberry root weevil** (Insects)
	leaves	red	
	fruit	small	
Strawberry	foliage	yellow leaf, dark green veins	**Lime-induced chlorosis** (Disorders)
Strawberry	foliage	powdery white coating	**Powdery mildew** (Diseases)
Strawberry	fruit	felty grey growth	**Grey mould** (Diseases)
Strawberry	flowers	flower stem cut; flower hanging by thread	**Strawberry clipper/ bud weevil** (Insects)

Insects

Aphids

AFFECTS: raspberry

Aphids are small, soft-bodied insects, often light green in colour, that suck sap from leaves of many types of plants, including those of fruit. There are many species of aphids and they have an amazing ability to reproduce, mostly without sex. They overwinter as glossy black eggs on raspberry canes, hatching in the spring. Outbreaks are worse under cool, moist conditions. Because the raspberry aphid (*Amphorophora agathonica*) is the primary vector of several viral diseases of raspberries, controlling it is critical.

WHAT TO LOOK FOR: Wilting, leaf distortion, stunting.

SOLUTIONS:

Less toxic alternatives:

- Apply insecticidal soap.

The large raspberry aphid not only sucks sap from the foliage, but is a carrier or vector of viral diseases.

- Apply diatomaceous earth.
- Avoid chemical pesticides to encourage natural parasites: wasps.
- Avoid chemical pesticides to encourage natural predators: lady beetles, lacewings.

For additional information, see Chapter 8, Vegetables and Chapter 10, Trees and Shrubs.

Apple maggot/railroad worm

AFFECTS: apple

Apple maggot/railroad worm (*Rhagoletis pomonella*) is the worm or maggot most often found on prairie apple trees. The common name, railroad worm, describes the winding tunnels that trace the maggot's route within the fruit.

Adults, resembling small houseflies, emerge from the leaf litter or soil beneath apple trees from early July to early August. Females soon begin laying eggs just beneath the skin of the apples. Their fecundity is frightening: up to three hundred eggs in a lifetime of only two to four weeks. The yellowish-white, wedge-shaped and legless maggots hatch within five to ten days depending on temperature. They eat their way through the fruit, tunnelling as they go. Soon after the fruit drops to the ground, the larvae exit and burrow into the soil, where they pupate for the winter.

WHAT TO LOOK FOR: Fruit infested by apple maggots have numerous small winding tunnels throughout the flesh but not into the core or seeds. The skin may show raised dimples, depressions or bumpiness.

Apple maggots tunnel throughout the flesh, but not into the core or seeds of the fruit.

Adult apple maggots resemble small houseflies and can be immobilized using traps.

PREVENTION:

Cultural methods:

* Traps immobilize the adult flies prior to egg laying and can be homemade or purchased. They should be in place by the last week in June. Yellow traps covered in a sticky substance such as Tanglefoot® proved more effective in trapping adults at the University of Saskatchewan research plots than those resembling apples (about 7.5 cm/3 in. in diameter, round, painted red). Place the traps where they are visible on the edge of the canopy and reapply Tanglefoot® as needed. An attractant (ammonium acetate or ammonium carbonate) greatly enhances the effectiveness of these traps.
* Apply netting with a fine mesh on dwarf apple trees.

SOLUTIONS:

Cultural methods:

* Rake up, remove and destroy all fallen fruit about twice a week to interrupt the fly's life cycle. If you wait too long, the larvae will have left the fruit and entered the soil. Do not compost the fallen fruit. Send it to the landfill or bury it to a depth of at least 30 cm (12 in.).

Less toxic alternatives:

* Organic commercial orchardists are now using GF-120 NF Naturalyte® Fruit Fly Bait or Entrust™ 80W to control apple maggots. Both contain spinosad. Spinosad GF-120 Naturalyte is also registered commercially. An attract-and-kill bait, it also works for the cherry fruit fly, another *Ragoletis* species.

Cherry fruit fly

AFFECTS: cherry

One of the few problems encountered with the new dwarf sour cherries developed by Dr. Bob Bors of the University of Saskatchewan, the cherry

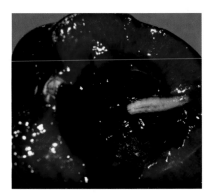

Small cherry fruit fly larvae feed around the pit before exiting from the fruit.

The adult fruit fly resembles a small black and yellow fly.

fruit fly (*Rhagoletis cingulata*) is only an occasional pest. Observations in other regions suggest that later-ripening cherries are more vulnerable.

Similar to the apple maggot, the adult is a small, black and yellow fly that emerges in late spring. Females cut small slits and lay their eggs in the young cherries. The larvae are white, legless and 5 to 6 mm (0.25 in.) long. They feed in the area around the pit, later exiting and dropping to the ground, where they pupate.

WHAT TO LOOK FOR: Round exit holes are made by the larvae. Infested fruit are small, misshapen, shrivelled on one side, and turn red prior to maturity.

PREVENTION:

Cultural methods:

- Apply fine mesh netting to prevent egg laying.
- Rake up, remove and destroy fallen fruit (not so easy with cherries!). Ensure that the tree is completely stripped of fruit at harvest, as fruit left on the tree can harbour cherry fruit fly.

SOLUTIONS:

Cultural methods:

- Larvae may remain in the fruit up to harvest time. These cherries will float. Destroy any infested fruit.
- In Europe, orchardists use covers, tarps and landscape cloth on the soil to prevent the adults emerging from the soil from finding the fruit. Lay these on the soil in early spring.

Less toxic alternatives:

- Avoid chemical pesticides to encourage natural parasites: braconid wasps.
- Use yellow sticky traps.
- Apply GF-120 NF Naturalyte®.

Currant borer

AFFECTS: currant, gooseberry

More prevalent on black currants than red currants, currant borers (*Synanthedon tipuliformis*) are even less of a problem on gooseberries. The adult is a small, black and yellow,

The larvae of currant borers are yellow-white. They bore into the stems and canes, causing yellowing of foliage and dieback of stems.

clear-winged moth that resembles a wasp or thin housefly. It emerges in June. Females lay eggs in leaf axils. The 12 mm (0.5 in.) yellow-white larvae hatch and bore into the stems or canes, where they feed. They then hibernate and pupate within the stems, emerging in early summer.

WHAT TO LOOK FOR: Infested shoots leaf out late and are stunted, leaves turn yellow, and shoots may die. The tunnelling leaves a dark hole in the pith, visible if the cane is cut open.

PREVENTION:

Cultural methods:

- Remove and destroy damaged canes and branches in spring before the moths emerge in June.
- Prune and thin regularly, removing canes on a rotation based on age.

Currant fruit fly

AFFECTS: currant, gooseberry

The adult currant fruit fly (*Epochra canadensis*) is a small yellow fly that emerges just as currants and gooseberries are blooming. The females lay a single egg in the young berries. The maggots are white, legless and about 6 mm (0.25 in.) in length. After eating the interior of the fruit, they exit and overwinter in the soil.

WHAT TO LOOK FOR: Affected berries are blotched on the side, ripen prematurely and fall to the soil with the resident maggot within. Damage is generally noticed in late July.

PREVENTION:

Cultural methods:

- Rake up and remove fallen fruit.
- Floating row covers prevent the flies from laying eggs on the fruit.

SOLUTIONS:

Cultural methods:

- Place tarps below the fruit to prevent the larvae from entering the soil to pupate.
- Cultivate the soil in late fall to destroy the pupae.

The blotch on the side of the gooseberry indicates that a currant fruit fly is in residence.

Fruit gall midge/ chokecherry midge

AFFECTS: chokecherry

Damage from the fruit gall midge/ chokecherry midge (*Contarinia virginianae*) is seldom severe. The adults are very small flies that emerge in May, laying eggs in the flowers and developing fruit soon after flowering. The yellow-orange larvae tunnel into the fruit, eating out the centre. They feed until late July, then drop to the soil, where they pupate.

WHAT TO LOOK FOR: Infected fruit are at first green then red, swollen and pear-shaped. These generally fall to the ground prior to the unaffected fruit ripening. If cut open, they will be full of reddish-yellow larvae.

SOLUTIONS:

Cultural methods:

- Remove and destroy infested fruit.
- Lay tarps below bushes in early July to interrupt pupation.

Imported currant worm

AFFECTS: red currant

The saving grace of the imported currant worm (*Nematus ribesii*) is that it concentrates on the foliage rather than the fruit, and ignores black currants. The downside is that in large numbers they can quickly defoliate the bushes. The adult sawflies (related to a wasp) are black and emerge in June. The females lay eggs on the undersides of leaves. The larvae, pale green with black spots and a black head and up to 35 mm (1.5 in.) in length, eat their fill, and then pupate in the soil. If disturbed, they lift both the front and rear of their bodies.

WHAT TO LOOK FOR: Bushes become defoliated. Feeding begins on the leaf margins and moves inward.

PREVENTION:

Cultural methods:

- Spray with a strong jet of water from a hose.

Chokecherries infested by the fruit gall midge/chokecherry midge become swollen and pear-shaped and fall prematurely.

In large numbers, imported currant worms can quickly defoliate bushes.

- Prevent the sawfly from laying eggs by using row covers.

SOLUTIONS:

Cultural methods:

- As the currant worms may be crowded together, it is often practical to cut off and destroy the twigs with the worm-infested foliage.

Less toxic alternatives:

- Apply insecticidal soap.
- Apply spinosad.

Saskatoon bud moth

AFFECTS: saskatoon

Often the first insect to attack embryonic fruit in early spring, the saskatoon bud moth (*Epinotia bicordana*) is one of the most damaging insect pests of saskatoon berries. When populations are high, the bud moth is capable of destroying most of the season's fruit.

The small, grey-black and brown moths emerge in early to mid-April, mate and lay their eggs in the creases

Bud moths, such as the striped bud moth shown here, are one of the most damaging insect pests of saskatoon berries, destroying flower buds in early spring.

between stems and developing buds. The larvae hatch from late April to early May, migrate to the developing flower buds, and begin feeding inside them. As the bud moth larvae grow, they web the expanding shoots together. The larvae continue to feed until they mature, about the time flower petals drop. They then tie leaf material or flower petals together, forming a cavity in which to pupate.

Protect saskatoons

Various insects feed on saskatoons. Most of the fruit loss occurs early in the season, during flowering and fruiting, when we're too busy elsewhere in our gardens to notice. Generally, the damage is not observed until we're ready to harvest, and blame is often placed on spring frosts, wind or drought, when in fact the culprits are insects. If you're keen to know who is doing the damage, use an insect sweep net during flowering and early fruit development to see "who's home."

Cultivate in fall to disturb overwintering sites, control weeds to eliminate alternate hosts and provide timely irrigation to prevent drought stress, which makes saskatoons more vulnerable to attack.

Saskatoon bud moth larvae are light yellow to green with a dark head. They web expanding shoots together in early May.

WHAT TO LOOK FOR: Small, grey-brown moths in early to mid-April. Webbing of new shoots and flower buds by larvae occurs in early May.

PREVENTION:

Cultural methods:
- Use fine mesh netting to prevent egg laying, putting it in place by early April.

SOLUTIONS:

Less toxic alternatives:
- Apply Bt *kurstaki*.

Saskatoon sawfly

AFFECTS: saskatoon

The saskatoon sawfly (*Hoplocampa montanicola*) is another insect pest which causes major fruit loss in saskatoons. Inspect your saskatoons for sawflies from shortly before flower buds open until the petals begin to drop.

The saskatoon sawfly is a small (6 mm/0.25 in.) yellow and black insect that takes flight when disturbed. Adults emerge from the leaf litter about the time that saskatoon flowers open, and feed on both pollen and

After eating part of the ovary, saskatoon sawflies emerge through a slit-like scar and begin eating adjacent fruit.

nectar. Eggs are laid in the nectaries of the flowers as petals drop. The eggs hatch, producing legged white larvae. After eating part of the ovary, the larvae emerge from the first berry through a bore hole and begin eating adjacent fruit. Towards the end of June, they drop to the ground, where they pupate until the following spring.

WHAT TO LOOK FOR: A telltale sign of egg laying is a slit-like scar, which remains on the upper part of the berry near the calyx. Affected fruit may drop, or the empty shell may persist. The later the stage at which fruit is attacked, the more likely the fruit is to persist. Infested fruit is held tightly to the stem and not easily picked, or the skin comes off but the flesh remains.

Saskatoon sawflies are small yellow and black insects that take flight when disturbed.

Cultural methods:

* Use fine mesh netting to prevent egg laying.

Strawberry clipper/ strawberry bud weevil

AFFECTS: raspberry, strawberry

A beetle native to North America, the strawberry clipper (*Anthonomus signatus*) uses its long snout to clip off or puncture flower buds. The damaged buds fail to open, resulting in fruit loss.

The adults overwinter in nearby bush and along fence rows, emerging as the strawberries begin to flower. Small (3 mm/0.1 in.) and reddish brown in colour, the clipper has a narrow curved snout about half the length of its body. Adult females deposit a single egg in the flower or bud, and then cut the flower stem so it falls to the ground or hangs by a slender thread.

The strawberry clipper "clips" the flower stems of strawberries, resulting in fruit loss.

The small (1 mm/0.06 in.) larvae, legless white grubs, hatch within a week. They pupate within the bud, emerging as adults in midsummer, and feed on pollen the remainder of the summer. There is one generation per year. Early blooming strawberry cultivars appear to suffer greater damage, and damage is worse in plantings older than three years.

This insect also damages raspberries by severing buds, but is generally not a severe problem.

WHAT TO LOOK FOR: Cut flower stems or flower stems hanging by a slender thread.

PREVENTION:

Cultural methods:

* Control nearby weeds and bush to reduce the habitat of the overwintering adults. Grow strawberries away from wooded areas where adults overwinter.
* Cultivate between the rows and around the patch after harvest to destroy pupae.
* Plant later-blooming cultivars.

Strawberry root weevil

AFFECTS: strawberry

Rarely causing observable damage to strawberries, the strawberry root weevil (*Otiorhynchus ovatus*) is easily recognized with a magnifying glass, as the backs of the adults are black and covered by rows of tiny pits. These are the same weevils that find their way into our homes in late summer and fall, crawling up walls, but otherwise harmless.

The adults are small, 5 to 10 mm (0.2–0.4 in.), brown to black, and feed on the leaf margins of strawberries, giving them a ragged or notched appearance. Both adults and larvae overwinter in debris and trash on the soil surface. Neither adults nor larvae travel far, so their damage is generally restricted rather than wide-ranging.

The soil-dwelling white grubs are legless with brown heads, feeding on the roots or tunnelling into the crowns of strawberries. Once the root system is reduced and weakened by weevils, plants are more vulnerable to disease and winterkill.

WHAT TO LOOK FOR: The foliage turns red and the berries are small. Damage is worse if plants are stressed by drought. If you notice damaged leaves and weak plants, examine the crowns and roots for evidence of weevils.

SOLUTIONS:

Cultural methods:
- If infestations are severe, plant a new strawberry patch as far away from the old one as possible.

Less toxic alternatives:
- Two biological controls have been tried: the parasitic nematode (*Steinernema carpocapsae*) and the carabid beetle (*Pterostichus vulgaris*). Nematodes can be effective for weevil control but the soil must be evenly moist and warm.

Tarnished plant bug/lygus bug

AFFECTS: raspberry, saskatoon, strawberry

A widespread insect pest on strawberries, tarnished plant bug/lygus bug (*Lygus lineolaris*) seems worse on day-neutral and later-maturing cultivars. Adults overwinter in plant debris and leaf litter. The small (0.6 cm/0.25 in.), shield-shaped adults are flat and shiny yellow brown with distinct yellow triangles on their wings. They suck plant juices with their beak-like, piercing mouthparts. In spring, adult females lay eggs on plant stems of strawberries, grasses, dandelion, chickweed, wild mint, creeping charlie and goldenrod. The nymphs are small and green. Adults may move into your garden from nearby alfalfa or sunflower fields.

Saskatoon flower buds are damaged by both the adult and nymph stages of the tarnished plant bug. These sucking insects tend to feed in the early morning or late afternoon, dispersing quickly if disturbed. The

The larvae of strawberry root weevils feed on the roots and crowns of strawberries.

tarnished plant bug also feeds on the buds, blossoms and developing fruit of raspberries.

WHAT TO LOOK FOR:

Raspberries: They pierce the fruit in order to feed, leaving the berries distorted, shrivelled, crumbled and sometimes with an off-colour of violet.

Saskatoons: Pierced flower buds leak amber sap and then die, resulting in fruit loss.

Strawberries: Their feeding results in misshapen "nubbins" or deformed fruit with hollow seeds and a woody texture. These berries are often referred to as "cat-faced." Both adults and nymphs feed on the seeds. This results in an absence of growth hormones, preventing the normal development of nearby tissue, thus the deformed fruit.

PREVENTION:

Cultural methods:

- Use row covers/fine netting to prevent adults from feeding and egg laying.
- Remove weeds that provide egg-laying and overwintering sites.
- Mow nearby lawns or grassy areas in late fall.

SOLUTIONS:

Less toxic alternatives:

- Apply insecticidal soap.
- *Peristenus digoneutis* is a parasite introduced from Europe that has been successfully established in New Jersey and neighbouring states. Releases were made in Ontario in 2007 and 2008, where this parasite also seems to have established itself. It is promising, but not yet commercially available.

Tarnished plant bugs feed on the flowers or developing fruit of raspberries, saskatoons and strawberries resulting in fruit loss.

Tent caterpillar (eastern)

AFFECTS: chokecherry, saskatoon

A defoliator of many species, the eastern tent caterpillar (*Malacosoma disstria*) is only an occasional pest of saskatoons. Neither is it a common problem of chokecherries, but it is quite eye-catching and devastating when it does show up.

WHAT TO LOOK FOR: A silken nest in the crotch of branches filled with hairy, black-and-blue, 2 to 3 cm (1 in.) caterpillars. They feed during the day, returning to the nest at night.

SOLUTIONS:

Cultural methods:

- Cut off and destroy the nest in the late evening when the resident caterpillars are within.

Eastern tent caterpillars leave the nest to feed during the day and return at night.

* Egg cases and pupae can be scraped off branches and burned.

Less toxic alternatives:

* Apply GF-120 or Entrust.
* Apply Bt *kurstaki*.
* For additional information, see Chapter 10, Trees and Shrubs.

Two-spotted spider mite

AFFECTS: raspberry, strawberry

Although other species may be present, two-spotted spider mites (*Tetranychus urticae*) are the most prevalent and damaging mites affecting raspberries on the prairies. They feed mostly on mature leaves and are present during hot, dry weather.

WHAT TO LOOK FOR: Leaves curl up and take on a stippled appearance. Foliage may become grey, later turn bronze, and, in severe infestations, dry up and die.

PREVENTION:

Cultural methods:

* Mites are most active during hot weather. Regular irrigation avoids water stress and reduces damage from mite populations.
* Eliminate weeds that act as alternate hosts in or near raspberry or strawberry plantings. Cultivate in the fall to expose overwintering sites in the soil litter.
* Avoid use of pyrethroids. These are very hard on beneficial insects and can lead to mite outbreaks.
* For additional information, see Chapter 10, Trees and Shrubs.

Leaves of raspberries or strawberries infested with spider mites have a stippled appearance, curl, become grey or brown, and eventually may dry up and die.

Woolly elm aphids

AFFECTS: saskatoon

Woolly elm aphids (*Eriosoma americanum*) damage saskatoon seedlings and young plants, and are found wherever American elms and saskatoons are grown in reasonably close proximity. Established plantings are seldom affected. The aphids migrate

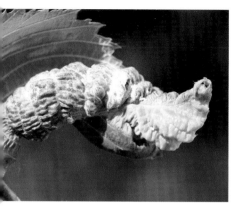

Woolly elm aphids attack the leaves of the elm tree, causing them to fold and curl.

Young saskatoon bushes infested with woolly elm aphids show weak growth and may fail to leaf out.

from elms to saskatoon roots in June, forming large colonies. The aphids continue feeding on the saskatoons until late fall, when they return to the elms.

WHAT TO LOOK FOR: Young saskatoon bushes infested with woolly elm aphids show weak growth, with smaller chlorotic leaves. They may fail to leaf out. Roots infested with woolly elm aphids appear white and fungus-like with a purplish hue.

PREVENTION:

Cultural methods:

- 'Pembina' appears more susceptible to aphids, and 'Smoky' less so.
- See Chapter 10, Trees and Shrubs for additional information.

Diseases

Apple scab

AFFECTS: apple, crabapple

Apple scab (*Venturia inaequalis*) is a fungus whose occurrence is highly weather dependent. Worse during prolonged periods of rain, it spreads slowly if at all when conditions are hot and dry.

Apple scab attacks the foliage, flowers and fruit of apples, crabapples and ornamental flowering crabapples. It overwinters in infected dead or dying leaves on the soil surface. Wind- and water-borne spores are released the following spring as flower buds are opening. Moisture is needed for infection to occur.

WHAT TO LOOK FOR: On leaves, the lesions are at first a velvet-like olive green with irregular margins. They later darken to brown or black. Lesions on the fruit are round, brown or black, and later become corky or "scabby."

PREVENTION:

Cultural methods:

- Use resistant varieties such as 'Honeycrisp.' The University of Saskatchewan apple breeding program is currently selecting for apple scab resistance.

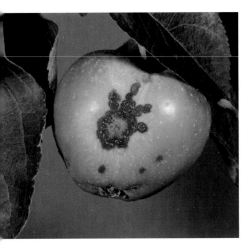

Apple scab lesions on fruit are at first round, brown or black, later becoming corky or "scabby."

Black knot on chokecherry is easily identified by the black growths that encircle the branches.

- Prune to encourage open canopies and good air circulation so that the fruit and foliage dry quickly.

SOLUTIONS:

Cultural methods:

- Clean up infected dead or dying leaves below the trees to reduce overwintering sites. Alternatively, cultivate to turn the fallen leaves under the soil to speed up their decay.

Less toxic alternatives:

- Spray with sulphur or lime sulphur, following directions carefully to avoid foliage burn.

Black knot

AFFECTS: chokecherry

The fungal disease black knot (*Dibotryon morbosum*) is present wherever native chokecherries are found. While a few clones appear more resistant, particularly those with yellow fruit, to date none have been marketed as black knot resistant.

WHAT TO LOOK FOR: Black knot is easily identified by the black knots (somewhat resembling dry dog droppings) that encircle the branches.

Lime sulphur caution

Lime sulphur is very hard on beneficial insects and mites. It can also spot some fruit if applied after fruit set. Timing is important. If there is a history of scab infection in trees, you need to treat them beginning in the early spring, and maintain control if the summer is wet. The disease organisms are ready and waiting, present before symptoms appear. The severity of the disease will depend on how wet the spring and summer are.

SOLUTIONS:

Cultural methods:

- Pruning of infected parts is the only control.
- For additional information, see Chapter 10, Trees and Shrubs.

Black leaf/witches' broom

AFFECTS: saskatoon

Black leaf (*Apiosporina collinsii*) is a fungal disease that can infect saskatoons at any stage of growth. It becomes systemic in new growth, but does not seem to go back into the previous older growth. The fungus may invade the crown of young bushes, in which case the whole plant must be removed. Spores overwinter in twigs and branches as well as in infected debris on the ground. These may be a source of infection the following spring.

WHAT TO LOOK FOR: The first symptom is the downward rolling of not-quite-mature leaves, together with the appearance of a grey, felt-like, spore-producing fungal growth on the undersides of these leaves. The leaves die, and the felt becomes black (hence the common name, black leaf). Spores released the next spring from these blackened leaves spread the infection to healthy plants. Infected stems swell slightly and show a proliferation of branches, creating the typical witches' broom effect from which the second common name is derived. Fruit on infected branches dries up or ripens prematurely. Moisture stress eventually causes the death of infected branches.

Black felt-like foliage that persists into fall is a telltale symptom of black leaf on saskatoon berry bushes.

SOLUTIONS:

Cultural methods:

- Remove infected seedlings and suckers.
- Prune and burn all plant parts showing signs of infection (both the black felty leaves and the branches showing witches' broom), cutting 10 cm (4 in.) below the visible signs of infection. Prune either in early spring prior to bud break, or after autumn leaf fall (when the felty persistent leaves will signal infected areas). Disinfect pruning tools after each cut.

Crown gall

AFFECTS: raspberry

Crown gall (*Agrobacterium tumefaciens*) is a bacterial disease that infects the roots and crowns of red raspberries. It lives in the roots of many plants and is capable of surviving in the soil for a number of years.

Infection takes place through wounds to the plant tissue caused by cultivation, pruning, insects, rodents or winter injury. The bacteria stimulate abnormal galls that block the upward flow of water and nutrients.

WHAT TO LOOK FOR: Galls are found on the roots, crown and lower portion of the canes. At first cream to brown in colour, they later become black, hard and warty. Eventually, the galls decay.

PREVENTION:

Cultural methods:

- Plant gall-free stock.
- Control aphids, which may spread the disease, and avoid injury to plants during cultivation.

Less toxic alternatives:

- A non-pathogenic bacterium, *Agrobacterium radiobacter,* strain K-84, is used as a biological control of crown gall. Registered

Crown gall of raspberry is a bacteria that stimulates abnormal growth on the roots, crown and lower portion of the canes that blocks the upward flow of water and nutrients.

commercially as Dygall, it is applied to the roots of healthy plants when they are first set out. It prevents crown gall from entering a plant but cannot cure an infected one.

SOLUTIONS:

Cultural methods:

- Pull out and burn any infected plants.
- For additional information, see Chapter 10, Trees and Shrubs.

Cytospora dieback and canker disease

AFFECTS: saskatoon

Cytospora (*Cytospora leucostoma*) can be an extremely damaging disease. Without control, dieback and canker can destroy a saskatoon planting in as little as five years. The fungus is thought to damage plants by excreting oxalic acid, which depletes calcium, lowering the pH and weakening the plant tissue. This makes the plant tissue more vulnerable to cell-wall-degrading enzyme activity by other harmful fungal organisms.

The spores are wind- or insect-borne and generally enter the tissue through a wound. Frost damage, pruning and root injury caused by cultivation can produce sites of potential infection. Cool, moist conditions in spring encourage the spread of Cytospora, as do waterlogged soil conditions. Too much nitrogen fertilizer causes lush, succulent growth that is more vulnerable to Cytospora infection.

Once the fungus has entered the stem, it spreads internally, killing the plant. In some cases, infection may spread into the crown and reappear on other stems and root suckers.

WHAT TO LOOK FOR: Shoots and branches of infected plants begin dying from the top, with the dieback progressing downward to the crown. Buds and leaves shrivel and die. Young bark contracts, wrinkles and collapses, resulting in vertical splitting and folding back (exfoliation). Affected bark appears darker and water-soaked at first, later turning dry and grey. There is an abrupt transition from healthy to infected bark. Dieback is usually evident from bud break to petal fall. "Flagging," the development of fall colouration during the growing season, is also symptomatic of infection. In the season following the death of a branch, small pimples appear on the dead bark that release spores under humid conditions.

PREVENTION:

Cultural methods:

- Do not irrigate or fertilize saskatoons in the fall as these practices tend to delay hardening.
- Do not plant saskatoons in low-lying areas or where soil drainage or air circulation is poor. Avoid locations with a high water table that would maintain high shoot succulence in fall, making plants more vulnerable to frost damage.

SOLUTIONS:

Cultural methods:

- Prune out and burn all dead and dying twigs and branches 30 cm (12 in.) below external signs of

Cytospora dieback in saskatoons begins at the top of the bush. Young bark contracts, wrinkles and collapses, resulting in vertical splitting and folding back (exfoliation).

infection. Disinfect pruning tools after each cut.

- For more information, see Chapter 10, Trees and Shrubs.

Entomosporium leaf and berry spot

AFFECTS: saskatoon

Entomosporium leaf and berry spot (*Entomosporium mespili*) disease occurs throughout the natural range of saskatoons. Fungal spores are produced in blisters beneath the epidermis of infected leaves. In rainy, humid conditions, spores are carried by rain splash, wind and insects to other leaves and fruit. Low humidity and temperatures higher than 25°C (77°F) inhibit the development of the disease. Warm, wet weather produces the most severe outbreaks.

WHAT TO LOOK FOR: The first symptoms are small, angular, brown leaf spots, often with a yellow halo or margin, on succulent new growth at the base of the plants. These may expand and coalesce. Under humid or rainy conditions, infection may occur on the entire plant. Fruit will abort or develop blight-like infections.

PREVENTION:

Cultural methods:

- Good weed control, combined with pruning out excess suckers, improves air circulation.

SOLUTIONS:

Cultural methods:

- The use of trickle irrigation (rather than overhead irrigation, which wets the foliage) slows the spread of the disease.
- Mulching can cover the fallen infected leaves that harbour spores, reducing spore release the following spring.

Entomosporium leaf and berry spot on saskatoons begins as small, angular, brown leaf spots, often with a yellow halo or margin, on succulent new growth at the base of plants.

Fireblight

AFFECTS: apple, pear, saskatoon

Fireblight (*Erwinia amylovora*) is probably the most destructive disease of apples on the prairies, but much of the apple breeding in the last few decades has been directed towards fireblight resistance. So select your cultivars with fireblight resistance in mind.

Fireblight can also be a serious disease of saskatoons when there are periods of prolonged wet weather in spring and early summer. Ensure there are no sources of fireblight (such as an infected apple tree) close to saskatoon berry bushes. This can be very devastating, leading to multiple shoot infections.

Anecdotal evidence suggests that there may be two strains of fireblight in Saskatchewan, one in the south and one in the north.

WHAT TO LOOK FOR: Blossoms wilt and turn brown. Twigs and leaves turn brown as though scorched by fire. Fruit is first watery or oily, later leathery and black. Both leaves and fruit remain attached into fall and early winter. The tips of young shoots bend to form a "shepherd's crook."

SOLUTIONS:

Cultural methods:

- Prune and destroy diseased branches, suckers and cankers, remembering to disinfect tools after each cut. Cut at least 15 to 23 cm (6–9 in.) below infected wood.
- Select resistant varieties.

Less toxic alternatives:

- BlightBan C9-1 is a commercially registered microbial product that

Twigs and leaves affected by fireblight turn brown as though scorched by fire and remain attached into fall and early winter. The tips of young shoots bend to form a "shepherd's crook."

is registered for control of fireblight in saskatoon berries. It is a bacteria that inhabits the same host sites as the fireblight bacteria and prevents fireblight from infecting plants. Bloomtime™ is also registered commercially. It contains a naturally occurring strain of beneficial bacterium (*Pantoea agglomerans* E325), which competes to exclude the fireblight bacterium. It is applied to the open flowers.

- For additional information, see Chapter 10, Trees and Shrubs.

Grey mould

AFFECTS: raspberry, saskatoon, strawberry

Grey mould (*Botrytis cinerea*) is a fungus that overwinters in decaying plant debris on the soil surface and in infected plants. Spores produced during wet periods are windblown, infecting healthy plants. Initial infection occurs through the flower and develops quickly when the moisture content of the fruit increases just prior to harvest. Infection is worse during periods of wet weather in dense plantings.

Grey mould is probably the most common and destructive disease of strawberries, less so with raspberries. During periods of cool, wet weather, or with too much overhead irrigation, insufficient light or poor air circulation, it can cause substantial fruit loss. Strawberries are especially vulnerable during flowering and fruit ripening.

Although not a major problem in saskatoon berries, grey mould causes ripening and overripe saskatoon berries to rot. It enters the fruit through wounds caused by wind abrasion, hail and insects, and is favoured by cool, damp weather conditions. Overripe berries are most susceptible.

Infection, which begins in the blossom end, is wind and rain splashed, and is easily spread to adjacent healthy ber-ries. Spores overwinter on infected plant debris.

WHAT TO LOOK FOR:

Raspberry: Shoots and fruit become covered with a soft grey fungal growth. This powder-like growth on the flowers and fruit soon becomes a soft, light brown fruit rot. Infected fruit has an "off" taste.

Saskatoon: Berries, especially those that are overripe, rot.

Strawberry: Felty grey growth covers the fruit. Ripe and overripe berries rot.

PREVENTION:

Cultural methods:

- Avoid over-fertilization with nitrogen, which produces excessive leaf growth, thus reducing air circulation, and stimulates soft, succulent growth that is more susceptible to fungal infection.
- Plant in full sun, provide good air circulation through cane thinning and recommended row widths.
- Avoid bruising or wounding the fruit while working in the garden.
- With saskatoons, harvest only healthy fruit and cool it as soon as

Strawberry fruit infected with grey mould is covered with a grey felty growth causing ripe and overripe berries to rot.

possible after picking. Allowing overripe fruit to remain on the plant encourages the spread of the disease.

- Prune out and destroy infected canes.

SOLUTIONS:

Less toxic alternatives:

- Apply Serenade® (*Bacillus subtilis*), a biological product registered for the control of grey mould.
- For additional information, see Chapter 8, Vegetables, Chapter 9, Flowers, Bulbs and Vines and Chapter 10, Trees and Shrubs.

Mosaic virus

AFFECTS: raspberry

Transmitted by feeding aphids, mosaic virus has no treatment or cure. It is spread from plant to plant during the summer months almost entirely by one vector, the large raspberry aphid (*Amphorophora agathonica*).

WHAT TO LOOK FOR: Symptoms are more pronounced during cool weather early in the growing season, and less evident in summer. Leaves are mottled with yellowish tissue along the veins, puckering and curling downward towards the edges. These symptoms appear mainly on the lower leaves. Infected plants produce short, weak canes. Yield declines, and the fruit is dry, seedy, crumbly and of poor flavour.

PREVENTION:

Cultural methods:

- Plant virus-free stock.
- Cultivars with hairy leaves and stems seem to present a physical

Mosaic virus, transmitted by the large raspberry aphid, is characterized by mottled leaves with yellow tissue along the veins, puckering and curling downward.

barrier to aphids, discouraging feeding and decreasing the spread of the virus.
- Remove any wild brambles nearby that could be a source of infection.
- Remove and burn old fruiting canes after harvest.

SOLUTIONS:

Cultural methods:
- Infected plants should be dug up and burned.

Less toxic alternatives:
- Aphid control is critical. Use insecticidal soap.

Plum pocket
AFFECTS: plum

Plum pocket (*Taphrina communis*) is a fungal disease that is worse under cool, wet conditions, when it can cause extensive fruit loss. The spores are wind-borne in late spring, but remain in a dormant state until buds break the following spring.

WHAT TO LOOK FOR: Easily recognized, infection of the fruit begins with small, white, blister-like lesions. The fruit is later covered with a greyish powder, or may become dark and velvety. The fruits enlarge, but are hollow and bladder-like. Shoots become enlarged and somewhat deformed, and the leaves may curl.

SOLUTIONS:

Less toxic alternatives:
- Apply a dormant spray of lime sulphur after leaf fall in the autumn when temperatures are above freezing, or in early spring before leaves emerge. Timing is critical as this spray burns foliage.

Plums infected with plum pocket are either hollow and bladder-like – eventually covered with a greyish powder – or turn dark and velvety.

Powdery mildew
AFFECTS: currant, raspberry, saskatoon, strawberry

Powdery mildew (*Sphaerotheca macularis* and other species) appears as a white powdery coating on fruit, foliage and young shoots. It is generally not

Powdery mildew appears as a white powdery growth on fruit, foliage and young shoots of currants, raspberries, saskatoons and strawberries.

Powdery mildew is not a serious problem unless it affects the fruit, as seen on these saskatoon berries.

a serious problem in strawberries unless it affects the fruit. Infection can begin in early spring.

WHAT TO LOOK FOR: Powdery white coating; poor fruit set; fruit may be either hard, or soft and pulpy.

PREVENTION:

Cultural methods:
- Maintain adequate air circulation.
- Avoid wetting foliage.
- Plant saskatoons that show resistance to powdery mildew such as 'Moonlake', 'Honeywood', 'Thiessen', 'Smoky' and 'Pembina'.

SOLUTIONS:

Cultural methods:
- Remove and destroy infected plant tissue to remove a source of infection, as the disease organism can survive only on living host tissue.
- Apply sulphur at the first sign of mildew.
- Apply Serenade®.
- For additional information, see Chapter 8, Vegetables, Chapter 9, Flowers, Bulbs and Vines and Chapter 10, Trees and Shrubs.

Root rot

AFFECTS: raspberry

Root rot (*Phytophthora* and *Pythium* species) is a disease caused by several related species of fungi. It is favoured by excessive moisture, heavy soils and poor drainage. It can become a problem in long-established raspberry plantings. Sources of infection include infected roots and dormant resting spores within the soil. These spores become active and mobile when the soil is saturated with water, moving to infect healthy roots. Raspberries in standing water are deprived of oxygen and more prone to infection.

WHAT TO LOOK FOR: Infected fruiting canes are stunted, with weak lateral shoots and yellowed or scorched leaves. They may die prior to fruiting. Fewer first-year canes emerge. Root tissue just under the epidermis of infected plants shows a characteristic red-brown colour that becomes darker as the root decays. A distinct line, delineating healthy and infected tissue, is often visible, especially on the crown.

PREVENTION:

Cultural methods:

- The most important factor in controlling root rot is adequate soil drainage. In heavy wet soils, use raised beds to which generous amounts of organic matter have been added.
- Plant disease-free stock.

Raspberries in heavy soil with poor drainage are vulnerable to root rot. A distinct line, delineating healthy and infected tissue, is often visible on the crown.

Saskatoon-juniper rust

AFFECTS: saskatoon

Both berries and leaves of saskatoons can become infected with saskatoon-juniper rust (*Gymnosporangium nelsonii*). To survive, this rust disease requires both saskatoons and junipers. The disease organism overwinters on junipers, infecting saskatoons in spring. Spores are wind-borne and reinfect junipers in the fall.

WHAT TO LOOK FOR: Berries and leaves show typical raised yellow-orange spots. Later in the season, the undersides of the leaves and the spots on the berries are covered with tiny, spiny projections that release spores.

Saskatoon fruit infected with saskatoon-juniper rust shows raised, yellow-orange spots. Later in the season, tiny, spiny projections will release spores from the fruit.

Cultural methods:

- Use resistant varieties of junipers, such as 'Arcadia', 'Broadmoor', 'Buffalo', 'Calgary Carpet™', 'Moor-dense', 'Skandia'. 'Nelson' saskatoon shows some resistance.

SOLUTIONS:

Cultural methods:

- This disease cannot overwinter on the leaves, fruit or leaf litter of saskatoons. Try to locate your saskatoons as far as possible from junipers, at least 0.5 km (0.3 mi), as spores are easily spread under windy conditions.
- See Chapter 10, Trees and Shrubs for additional information.

Silverleaf

AFFECTS: apple, cotoneaster, other trees and shrubs

A fungal disease that attacks many trees and shrubs, silverleaf (*Chondrostereum purpureum*) is most commonly seen on apple and cotoneaster on the prairies. It generally enters through pruning wounds (a good reason, labour aside, for allowing cotoneaster to grow in its natural form rather than hedging it). The bracket-like fruiting bodies are found on dead wood and produce wind-borne spores that enter susceptible plants through wounds. Release and infection are worse under cloudy or rainy conditions.

WHAT TO LOOK FOR: The foliage of infected plants takes on a silvery or leaden sheen. The silvery effect is caused by toxins and/or enzymes released by

the fungus that damage the cells, allowing the reflection of light. Depending on the location of the wound, the silvering may appear on a single branch or the entire plant. The extent of silvering is also influenced by the species, age and general health and vigour of the host. Apples can show characteristic symptoms and then recover.

PREVENTION:

Cultural methods:

- Follow pruning guidelines, being especially careful to disinfect tools and destroy infected prunings.

The foliage of plants infected with silverleaf takes on a silvery or leaden sheen. Prune off infected foliage and branches, being especially careful to disinfect tools after every cut and to destroy infected prunings.

Less toxic alternatives:

- *Trichoderma*, a mycoparasitic fungus is available in Canada as Rootshield® HC Biological Fungicide.

Spur blight

AFFECTS: raspberry

Spur blight (*Didymella applanata*) is a common disease, involving several fungi, that infects plants through healthy or wounded tissue, resulting in fruit loss. It overwinters on diseased canes. Spore-containing bodies, which are seen as black spots, release spores during wet periods. These are carried by insects, wind or rain to nearby healthy plants.

Leaves of raspberries infected with spur blight may appear chlorotic and fall prematurely. Look for purple or chocolate-brown spots on the canes just below the leaf attachment or "spurs."

WHAT TO LOOK FOR: Purple or chocolate-brown spots appear on the canes just below the leaf attachments or "spurs." These lesions enlarge and spread to the buds and leaf stems. Infected fruiting canes may die back between flowering and fruit set, or become brittle and break off. Leaves, especially on the lower part of the plant, may appear chlorotic and fall prematurely. Infected bark dries out and cracks by late summer. Yields are reduced, and plants become more susceptible to winter injury.

PREVENTION:

Cultural methods:

- Plant disease-free stock.
- Prune, remove and destroy old fruiting canes after harvest.
- Encourage good air circulation through cane thinning, following recommended row width and spacing.
- Control weeds.
- Avoid excessive nitrogen fertilizer, which promotes succulent growth that is more vulnerable to fungal entry.
- Resistant cultivars include 'Chief', 'Boyne' and 'Festival'.

Disorders

These are caused by adverse environmental factors rather than disease organisms.

Lime-induced chlorosis

AFFECTS: apple, raspberry, strawberry

Lime-induced chlorosis is an iron deficiency that appears on plants growing in heavy soils with a high pH, generally over 7.5. Other plants susceptible to lime-induced chlorosis include roses, Amur maple and mountain ash. Although iron may be present in these soils, it is tied up in a non-soluble form and is therefore unavailable for plant use.

WHAT TO LOOK FOR: Chlorosis is easily recognized. New foliage shows yellow-green leaf blades, while the leaf veins remain a dark green. Plants are generally stunted and have decreased yields.

PREVENTION:

Cultural methods:

- Plant in well-drained soils with a pH below 7.5. Changing the pH of our soils is not easy, but it is helpful to incorporate generous amounts of organic material and peat moss before planting.

SOLUTIONS:

Less toxic alternatives:

- If chlorosis is present, apply iron chelates according to label directions. Foliar applications are less expensive and more effective than soil applications in the short term.
- See Chapter 3, Growing Healthier Plants and Chapter 10, Trees and Shrubs for additional information.

Chlorosis is easily recognized by the yellow-green leaf blades and the contrasting dark green veins. Plants may be stunted with decreased yields.

Bibliography

Bailey, L.H., *The Standard Cyclopedia of Horticulture,* second edition, New York, NY: The Macmillan Company, 1917.

Bors, Bob and Linda Matthews, *Dwarf Sour Cherries, A Guide for Commercial Production,* Saskatoon, SK: University of Saskatchewan Extension Press, 2004.

Bowers, Warner and Lucile, *Common Sense Organic Gardening,* Harrisburg, PA: Stockpole Books, 1974.

Bradley, Fern Marshall, Barbara W. Ellis, and Deborah L. Martin, editors, *The Organic Gardener's Handbook of Natural Pest and Disease Control,* New York, NY: Rodale Inc., 2009.

Brady, Nyle C., *The Nature and Properties of Soil,* New York, NY: Macmillan Publishing Co. Inc., 1974.

Brandenburg, Rick L. and Michael G. Villani, editors, *Handbook of Turfgrass Insect Pests,* Lanham, MD: The Entomological Society of America, 1995.

Brickell, Christopher and David Joyce, *Pruning and Training,* New York, NY: DK Publishing , Inc., 1996.

Bryan, Nora and Ruth Staal, *The Prairie Gardener's Book of Bugs,* Calgary, AB: Fifth House Ltd., 2003.

Budd, Archibald C. and Keith F. Best, *Wild Plants of the Canadian Prairies,* Ottawa, ON: Research Branch, Canada Department of Agriculture, 1969.

Carr, Anna, *Good Neighbors: Companion Planting for Gardeners,* Emmaus, PA: Rodale Press, 1985.

Carr, Anna, *Rodale's Color Handbook of Garden Insects,* Emmaus, PA: Rodale Press, 1979.

Carroll, Steven B. and Steven D. Salt, *Ecology for Gardeners,* Portland, OR: Timber Press Inc., 2004.

Cavanaugh, Christopher, editor in chief, *The Reader's Digest Garden Problem Solver,* Pleasantville, NY: U.S. General Books, Reader's Digest, 1999.

Crete, René, *Diseases of Carrots in Canada,* Ottawa, ON: Agriculture Canada, 1980

Crete, René, Leon Tartier, and Alain Devaux, *Diseases of Onions in Canada,* Quebec, QC: Agriculture Canada, 1981.

Dodge, Bernard O. and Harold W. Rickett, *Diseases and Pests of Ornamental Plants,* revised edition, New York, NY: The Ronald Press Company, 1948.

Flanagan, June, *Native Plants for Prairie Gardens,* Markham, ON: Fifth House Ltd., 2005.

Fromartz, Samuel, *Organic, Inc.: Natural Foods and How They Grew,* Orlando, FL: Harcourt, Inc., 2006.

Gillman, Jeff, *The Truth About Garden Remedies,* Portland, OR: Timber Press Inc., 2008.

Gillman, Jeff, *The Truth About Organic Gardening,* Portland, OR: Timber Press Inc., 2008.

Grissell, Eric, *Insects and Gardens: In Pursuit of a Garden Ecology,* Portland, OR: Timber Press Inc., 2001.

Helyer, Neil, Kevin Brown, and Nigel D. Cattlin, *A Color Handbook of Biological Control in Plant Protection,* Portland, OR: Timber Press Inc., 2003.

Hiratsuka, Y., *Forest Tree Diseases of the Prairie Provinces,* Edmonton, AB: Northern Forestry Centre, Canadian Forestry Service, 1987.

Hodgson, W. A., D. D. Pond, and J. Munro, *Diseases and Pests of Potatoes,* Ottawa, ON: Department of Agriculture, 1977.

Howard, Ronald J., Garland, J. Allan, and W. Lloyd Seaman, *Diseases and Pests of Vegetable Crops in Canada,* Ottawa, ON: The Canadian Phytopathological Society and the Entomological Society of Canada, 1994.

Jarvis, W. R. and V. W. Nuttal, *Cucumber Diseases,* Ottawa, ON: Agriculture Canada, 1979.

Jarvis, W. R. and C. D. McKeen, *Tomato Diseases,* Ottawa, ON: Agriculture Canada, 1984.

Lamp'l, Joe, *The Green Gardener's Guide,* Franklin, TN: Cool Springs Press, 2007.

Lowenfels, Jeff and Wayne Lewis, *Teaming with Microbes, The Organic Gardener's Guide to the Soil Food Web,* revised edition, Portland, OR: Timber Press Inc., 2009.

Maas, J. L. (editor), *Compendium of Strawberry Diseases,* St. Paul, MN: American Phytopathological Society, 1984.

Mulligan, Gerald A., *Common Weeds of Canada,* Toronto, ON: NC Press Limited, 1987.

Nancarrow, Loren and Janet Hogan Taylor, *Dead Daisies Make Me Crazy,* Berkeley, CA: Ten Speed Press, 2000.

Philip, Hugh and Ernest Mengersen, *Insect Pests of the Prairies,* Edmonton, AB: Universtiy of Alberta, 1989.

Pirone, P. P., *Tree Maintenance* (Fourth Edition), New York, NY: Oxford University Press, 1972.

Pirone, Pascal, *Diseases and Pests of Ornamental Plants,* New York, NY: John Wiley & Sons, Inc., 1978.

Pleasant, Barbara and Deborah L. Martin, *The Complete Compost Gardening Guide,* North Adams, MA: Storey Publishing, 2008.

Royer, France and Richard Dickinson, *Weeds of Canada and the Northern United States,* Edmonton, AB: Lone Pine Publishing & University of Alberta Press, 1999.

Shosteck, Robert, *Flowers and Plants,* New York, NY: Times Book Co., 1974.

Sinclair, Wayne A., Lyon, Howard H., and Warren T. Johnson, *Diseases of Trees and Shrubs,* Ithaca, NY: Cornell University Press, 1987.

Skinner, Hugh and Sara Williams, *Best Groundcovers and Vines for the Prairies,* Calgary, AB: Fifth House Ltd., 2007.

Skinner, Hugh and Sara Williams, *Best Trees and Shrubs for the Prairies,* Calgary, AB: Fifth House Ltd., 2004.

Smith, Miranda and Anna Carr, *Rodale's Garden Insect, Disease and Weed Identification Guide,* Emmaus, PA: Rodale Press, 1988.

St. Pierre, Richard G., *The Chokecherry: A Guide for Growers,* Saskatoon, SK: University of Saskatchewan, 1993.

Stout, Ruth, *How to Have a Green Thumb Without an Aching Back,* New York, NY: Exposition Press, 1955.

Tukey, Paul, *The Organic Lawn Care Manual,* North Adams, MA: Storey Publishing, 2007.

Westcott, Cynthia, *The Gardener's Bug Book,* New York, NY: Doubleday & Company, 1973.

Williams, Sara, *Commercial Raspberry Production on the Prairies, A Growers' Guide,* Saskatoon, SK: University of Saskatchewan Extension Press, 1993.

Williams, Sara, *Commercial Saskatoon Berry Production on the Prairies, A Growers' Guide,* Saskatoon, SK: University of Saskatchewan Extension Press, 1994.

Williams, Sara, *Creating the Prairie Xeriscape,* Saskatoon, SK: University of Saskatchewan Extension Press, University of Saskatchewan, 1997.

Yepsen, Roger B. Jr., editor, *The Encyclopedia of Natural Insect and Disease Control,* Emmaus, PA: Rodale Press, 1984.

Internet Resources:

Agriculture and Agri-food Canada, Agroforestry Development Centre; *Publications,* [Online] Available http://www4.agr.gc.ca/AAFC-AAC/display-afficher.do?id=1186590611493&eng, December 15, 2009.

Biocontrol Network, Agriculture and Agri-food Canada, and World Wildlife Fund, *Biocontrol Files* [Online] Available http://www.biocontrol.ca/bcf/main.html, November 19, 2008.

California Environmental Protection Agency, Department of Pesticide Regulation, Environmental Monitoring and Pest Management Branch, Charles D. Hunter; *Suppliers of Beneficial Organisms in North America,* [Online] Available http://www.cdpr.ca.gov/docs/pestmgt/ipminov/bensup.pdf, December 22, 2008.

Colorado State University, Extension, Publications, *Yard and Garden Publications,* [Online], Available http://www.ext.colostate.edu/pubs/pubs.html#garden April 10, 2010.

Cornell University, College of Agriculture and Life Sciences, Department of Entomology, Shelton, Anthony; *Biological Control, A Guide to Natural Enemies in North America,* [Online] Available http://www.nysaes.cornell.edu/ent/biocontrol/index.php , June 17, 2010.

Government of Saskatchewan, Agriculture, *Vegetables*, [Online], Available http://www.agriculture.gov.sk.ca/vegetables, December 4, 2009.

Health Canada, Pest Management Regulatory Agency; *Pesticides and Pest Management*, [Online] Available http://www.hc-sc.gc.ca/cps-spc/pest/index-eng.php ́, June 18, 2010.

Natural Resources Canada; *Canada's Forests, Insects*, [Online] Available http://canadaforests.nrcan.gc.ca/article/insects, April 7, 2010.

North Dakota State University, Extension; *Lawns, Gardens and Trees*, [Online] Available http://www.ag.ndsu.edu/horticulture/, June 15, 2010.

Ohio State University, College of Food, Agricultural and Environmental Sciences, Ohioline; *Yard and Garden*, [Online] Available http://ohioline.osu.edu/lines/hygs.html, April 1, 2010.

Ontario College of Family Physicians; *Pesticide Literature Review*, Sanborn, Margaret, David Cole, Kathleen Kerr, Cathy Vakil, Luz Helena Sanin and Kate Bassil, [Online] Available http://www.ocfp.on.ca/local/files/communications/current% 20issues/pesticides/final%20paper%2023apr2004.pdf, January 6, 2010.

University of Georgia, Center for Invasive Species and Ecosystem Health; *Entomology*, [Online] Available http://www.bugwood.org/entomology.html, April 7, 2010.

University of Manitoba, Agricultural and Food Sciences, Department of Plant Science; *Horticultural Inquiries*, [Online] Available http://www.umanitoba.ca/afs/hort_inquiries/, April 7, 2010.

University of Minnesota, Extension; *Yard and Garden*, [Online] Available http://www.extension.umn.edu/ConsumerHort/, December 15, 2009.

University of Saskatchewan Department of Plant Sciences, Vegetable Program; *Recommended varieties for Saskatchewan producers*, [Online] Available http://www.usask.ca/agriculture/plantsci/vegetable/vegetable/vrecommendvar.htm, April 7, 2010.

University of Saskatchewan Extension Division, GardenLine; *Common Saskatchewan Pests*, [Online] Available http://gardenline.usask.ca/pests/ , May 28, 2010.

Index

Page numbers in **bold** = major entry

Page numbers in *italics* = photograph

Author Acknowledgements

To the kind and competent folks at Coteau who made this possible: Barbara, Geoffrey, Bobbi, Susan, Tania, Nik and Amber.

To Erl Svendsen, for guiding Sara gently through her Mac and Cyberspace, and leading her to Bugwood.org

For technical review of various parts of the manuscript:

Forrest Scharf, fruit specialist, Saskatchewan Agriculture

Jeff Boone, entomologist, City of Saskatoon

Cedric Gillott, Professor Emeritus, Biology Department, University of Saskatchewan

Jackie Bantle

Jill R. Thomson, Plant Science Department, University of Saskatchewan

Allyson Brady, Saskatchewan Environmental Society

Greg Rooke, Saskatchewan Environmental Society

Tom Yates, Department of Soil Science, University of Saskatchewan

Anne Lindsay, Manitoba Eco Network

To Bugwood.org for their generosity of spirit and competence in sharing images.

To Laura Poppy, Agriculture and Agri-food Canada, Agroforestry Development Centre for going the extra mile to provide images.

Photo Credits

Photographs for this book have been provided courtesy of the following people and organizations.

Agriculture and Agri-Food Canada (AAFC) Agroforestry Development Centre: Pages 184, 185, 186, 192, 195, 216

All-America Selections: Page 93, 98

American Phytopathological Society: Page 208, 222

Anderson, Robert L., USDA Forest Service, Bugwood.org: Page 50

Asmundson, Karen, City of Winnipeg: Page 197

Averre, Charles, North Carolina State University, Bugwood.org: Page 118

Bantle, Jackie: Pages 2, 9, 51, 91, 115, 123, 130, 135, 199

Bauer, Scott, USDA Agricultural Research Service, Bugwood.org: Pages 61, 217

Berger, Joseph, Bugwood.org: Pages 59, 60, 209

Brown, William M. Jr., Bugwood.org: Pages 121, 125, 177

Bryan, Nora: Page 142

Bush, Elizabeth, Virginia Polytechnic Institute and State University, Bugwood.org: Page 118

Ciesia, William M., Forest Health Management International, Bugwood.org: Page 49

Clemson University, USDA Cooperative Extension Slide Series, Bugwood.org: Pages 104, 107, 109, 113, 126, 135, 220

Cranshaw, Whitney, Colorado State University, Bugwood.org: Pages 89, 103, 104, 106, 111, 112, 114, 116, 119, 140, 148, 149, 172, 173, 179, 186, 211, 212, 219

Daily O'Brien, Dawn: Page 154

Day, Eric. R., Virginia Polytechnic Institute and State University, Bugwood.org: Page 176

Dewey, Steve, Utah State University, Bugwood.org; Page 41

Dickens, Lester E., Bugwood.org: Page 83

Elliott, B., Government of Manitoba: Pages 213, 214, 223

Elsinger, Mae: Page 150

Florida Division of Plant Industry Archive, Bugwood.org: Page 124

Foulston, Joan: Page 141

Fry, Ken, Olds College: Pages 80, 82

Gonthier, Giles: Page 143

Greb, Peggy, USDA Agricultural Resources Service, Bugwood.org: Page 58

Hansen, Mary Ann, Virginia Polytechnic Institute and State University, Bugwood.org: Page 134

Hanson, James B., USDA Forest Service, Bugwood.org: Page 174

Herms, Daniel, The Ohio State University, Bugwood.org: Page 176

Heutte, Tom, USDA Forest Service, Bugwood.org: page 44

Higbee, Bradley, Paramount Farming, Bugwood.org: Page 60

Jones, R. K., North Carolina State University, Bugwood.org: Page 151

Katovich, Steven, USDA Forest Service, Bugwood.org: Pages 171, 219

Kelley, Ronald S., Vermont Department of Forests, Parks and Recreation, Bugwood.org: Pages: 183, 186

Koike, S. T., University of California Cooperative Extension: Page 135

Lamb, Bob: Page 143

Langston, David B., University of Georgia, Bugwood.org: Page 132

Lee Valley Tools: Pages 52, 65

Lenhard, Gerald J., Louisiana State University, Bugwood.org: Page 177

Lutz, Tim: Page 4

Manitoba Agriculture, Food and Rural Initiatives: Pages 221, 227, 228, 229

Old, Richard, XID Services, Inc., Bugwood.org: Page 42

Olsen, Charles, USDA APHIS PPQ, Bugwood.org: Page 107

Olsson, Christer, Swedish Board of Agriculture, Bugwood.org: Page 229

Ottens, Russ, University of Georgia, Bugwood.org: Pages 7, 62

Pataky, Nancy: Page 150

Peairs, Frank, Colorado State University, Bugwood.org: Pages 79, 109, 110, 117, 182

Pennsylvania Department of Conservation and Natural Resources - Forestry Archive, Bugwood.org: Page 60

Pest and Diseases Image Library, Bugwood.org: Page 107

Pest Management, City of Saskatoon: Page 174

Peters, Clarence, Saskatchewan Ministry of Agriculture: Pages 209, 210, 218, 228

Philip, Hugh G.: Page 210

R.J. Reynolds Tobacco Company Slide Set, R. J. Reynolds Tobacco Company, Bugwood.org: Pages 61, 130

Schwartz, Howard F., Colorado State University, Bugwood.org: Pages 105, 106, 121, 122, 126, 127

Shen, Yuan-Min, Taichung District Agricultural Research and Extension Station, Bugwood.org: Page 127

Skinner, Hugh: Pages 1, 3, , 8, 10, 13, 35, 38, 41, 42, 43, 44, 45, 46, 47,48, 57, 59, 63, 64, 71, 72, 77, 139, 151, 156, 159, 160, 162, 163, 164, 170, 175, 177, 178, 180, 181, 182, 184, 187, 188, 189, 191, 193, 194, 196, 200, 201, 227, 230, 232

Solomon, James, USDA Forest Service, Bugwood.org: Page 179

Sparks, Alton N., Jr., University of Georgia, Bugwood.org: Page 108

Spencer, Robert, Alberta Agriculture & Rural Development: Pages 218, 229

Starr, Forest & Kim, U.S. Geological Survey, Bugwood.org: Page 116

St-Pierre, Richard: Page 214

Tigner, Tim, Virginia Department of Forestry, Bugwood.org: Page 174

Thomson, Jill R., University of Saskatchewan: Page 158

Troesch, Maureen: Pages 113, 146, 147

University of Georgia Plant Pathology Archive, University of Georgia, Bugwood.org: Page 215

Vangool, Bernadette: Pages 36, 132

Wallen: V. K., Agriculture and Agri-Food Canada, Bugwood.org: Page 123

Warkentin, Tom, Crop Development Centre, University of Saskatchewan: Page 119

Weidhass, John A., Virginia Polytechnic Institute and State University, Bugwood.org: Pages 142, 149

Weller, Keith, USDA Agricultural Research Service, Bugwood.org: Page 62

Williams, Sara: Pages 2, 4, 8, 9, 11, 12, 14, 15, 16, 17, 18, 19, 20, 23, 26, 27, 30, 33, 39, 53,56, 58, 61, 63, 64, 65, 66, 68, 84, 85, 86, 88, 92, 94, 95, 97, 98, 99, 100, 102, 107, 110, 113, 114, 120, 128, 129, 131, 133, 134, 136, 137, 139, 140, 141, 143, 144, 145, 152, 153, 154, 155, 156, 157, 158, 170, 171, 172, 190, 202, 203, 204, 211, 220, 224, 225, 226, 230, 231

HUGH SKINNER received a B.S.A. (Horticulture) from the University of Manitoba prior to returning to manage the family nursery where he grew up. In 2002, he received the Prairie Garden Award for Excellence, and he is currently the President of the Manitoba Horticultural Association. He has developed course materials for Assiniboine Community College, including an Integrated Pest Management course for the nursery, greenhouse and golf course industry.

In addition to the books he has co-written with Sara Williams, he is a regular contributor to *Manitoba Gardener* and *The Prairie Garden* magazines.

Both Sara and Hugh have been a well-respected part of the prairie horticulture workshop and lecture circuit for many years.

PHOTOGRAPH: Darlene Polachic

SARA WILLIAMS'S previous books include *Perennials for the Prairies, In a Cold Land: Saskatchewan's Horticultural Pioneers,* and, with co-author Hugh Skinner, *Best Trees and Shrubs for the Prairies* and *Best Groundcovers and Vines for the Prairies.* She was the founder and first editor of *The Saskatchewan Gardener,* now called *Gardener for the Prairies* and currently contributes to a weekly gardening column that appears in many prairie newspapers.

Creating the Prairie Xeriscape, originally published in 1997 and winner of two Saskatchewan Book Awards, is currently being revised and expanded.

Sara Williams has a B.Sc. (with great distinction) and a M.Sc. in Horticultural Extension from the University of Saskatchewan, as well as a B.A. in English and History from the University of Michigan. She served as the horticultural specialist with the Extension Division of the University of Saskatchewan for 12 years, retiring in 2001.

In memory of Brian Baldwin

Like many of his colleagues, Brian did his stint at the University of Saskatchewan's Garden Line phone-in service, from which came the inspiration for his song.

> Black spots on roses with fungal conditions,
> Trees struck by lightning in need of physicians,
> Lawns full of mushrooms all growing in rings!
> These are a few of my favourite things.
>
> Vascular blockages, spores by the oodles,
> Slime flux and slime mould and shits left by poodles,
> Virus-gorged aphids that finally sprout wings!
> These are a few of my favourite things.
>
> Borers in birches and frost cracks in ashes,
> Winter-burned cedars and pesticide splashes,
> Silver-leafed apple trees dying in springs!
> These are a few of my favourite things.
>
> Irish late blights,
> Frosty June nights,
> Leave you feeling sad.
> Just phone me and ask for some garden advice,
> And soon you won't feel so bad!

Sung to the tune of *"My Favorite Things"*
Original music by Rodgers and Hammerstein for *The Sound of Music*.
Revised lyrics by Brian Baldwin.

Mixed Sources
Cert no. SW-COC-001271
© 1996 FSC

FSC

ENVIRONMENTAL BENEFITS STATEMENT

Coteau Books saved the following resources by printing the pages of this book on chlorine free paper made with 10% post-consumer waste.

TREES	WATER	SOLID WASTE	GREENHOUSE GASES
3	**1,306**	**79**	**271**
FULLY GROWN	GALLONS	POUNDS	POUNDS

 Calculations based on research by Environmental Defense and the Paper Task Force. Manufactured at Friesens Corporation